WHITMAN

WHITMAN

BY

NEWTON

ARVIN

NEW YORK / RUSSELL & RUSSELL

TO

M. G. A.

PREFACE

I WISH TO ACKNOWLEDGE my indebtedness to Doubleday, Doran and Company for permission to quote from the *Complete Writings of Walt Whitman* and from *With Walt Whitman in Camden,* by Horace Traubel;

To the same publishers and to Mr. Emory Holloway for permission to quote from the Inclusive Edition of *Leaves of Grass* and *The Uncollected Poetry and Prose of Walt Whitman;*

To G. P. Putnam's Sons and to Mr. Cleveland Rodgers for permission to quote from *The Gathering of the Forces;*

To the Harvard University Press and to Mr. Clifton J. Furness for permission to quote from *Walt Whitman's Workshop;*

To the Columbia University Press and to Mr. Emory Holloway for permission to quote from *I Sit and Look Out;*

To Mr. Rufus Rockwell Wilson, Mr. Emory Holloway, and Mr. Ralph Adimari for permission to quote from *New York Dissected;*

To the publishers of the *American Mercury,* Mr. Clifton J. Furness, and Mr. Mark Van Doren for permission to quote from articles on "Whitman on His Contemporaries," "Walt Whitman's Politics," and "Walt Whitman, Stranger";

To Mr. Fremont C. Peck for permission to examine the files of the Brooklyn *Daily Times* and to quote from them;

To the Long Island Historical Society, the J. Pierpont Morgan Library, the American Antiquarian Society (Worcester, Mass.), the Walt Whitman Foundation (Camden, N. J.), and the Division of Manuscripts at the Library of Congress for many helpful courtesies;

To the John Simon Guggenheim Memorial Foundation for making much of the work on this book possible;

To Mr. and Mrs. Ralph Wescott, Mr. M. A. DeWolfe Howe, Mr. Emory Holloway, Mr. Alfred F. Goldsmith, and certain other acquaintances and friends for generous assistance of many kinds.

N. A.

Northampton, Massachusetts
July, 1938.

CONTENTS

WHITMAN

THE MAIN CONCERN

ONE EVENING IN THE SUMMER of his seventieth year, Walt Whitman remarked to his young friend Horace Traubel that he had just been reading, in an English magazine called *To-day,* an article on himself as a socialist poet. "Of course," he went on to say, "I find I'm a good deal more of a Socialist than I thought I was: maybe not technically, politically, so, but intrinsically, in my meanings." Certainly Reginald Beckett, the author of the article, had neither made out nor tried to make out a case for Whitman as a socialist poet in any rigorous sense; he had hardly discussed with any concreteness the political or social bearings of *Leaves of Grass;* idealistic and generous as the spirit of his article was, he had confined himself mainly to the larger ethical and philosophic aspects of the book. Yet he had been one of the earliest writers to raise a question that was to be asked more and more frequently and insistently as time went on, and eventually to seem, on a certain level, the most urgent question that can be asked about Walt Whitman. It is a question, too, that has somehow never received a detailed and searching answer.

It is easy to see why it should be asked so repeatedly as it has been. For one thing, it is the kind of question that is bound to be asked increasingly about all the writers,

especially the great writers, of the last century or two: the
clearer it becomes that the next inevitable step in human
history is the establishment and construction of a socialist
order, the more interested every thoughtful man becomes
in scanning the work of writers and artists in the recent
past for whatever resources there may be in it on which a
socialist culture may draw. Everyone feels more and more
consciously how much of that work was the expression of
circumstances that have passed once and for all; how much
of it can no longer have the intimate and lively meaning
for us that it naturally had for contemporaries. What remains beyond this is likely to seem even more important to
us than it seemed to them: at any rate, we are bound to
feel an anxious concern, which the men of earlier generations could hardly have felt, for the preservation and the
active use in cultural life of everything enlightened, positive, hopeful, and humane in our recent heritage. We
should feel this if only because the ugly menace of de-
civilization presses upon us as it never pressed upon them.
In this sense our feeling about Whitman is very much what
our feeling is about a good many other writers of his
century.

Everyone, however, is conscious of there being something more special than this in the question whether or not
Walt Whitman is a "socialist poet." Not that "technically"
or "politically," as he said, the question is a very real or
difficult one. On that level it is obvious enough that Whitman was a Jacksonian Democrat whose life was mostly
spent in the midst of a culture still prevailingly individualistic and not even on the verge of a transition to socialism. Far from being a thoroughgoing socialist poet, he was
the highly affirmative poet of American middle-class cul-

2

ture in the era of Emerson, of Vanderbilt, of Lincoln. Yet perhaps no one ever opened *Leaves of Grass* without feeling that its author is "something more" than just this. One would feel it no doubt if only because Whitman himself claimed so much more for his book—if only because, for example, he appealed so frankly to the future. Not many poets are content with writing simply for their own day: most of them either believe or wish that their powerful rhyme will outlive marble and the gilded monuments of princes. But not many poets have so boldly rested their case on the meaning of their work to posterity. "My volume," Whitman once characteristically said, "is a candidate for the future." Notoriously he claimed for himself the role of prophet, and that not merely in the mystical but almost in the popular sense:

> *Chanter of Personality, outlining what is yet to be,*
> *I project the history of the future.*

A poet who makes such claims as this will suffer more than most writers if the future belies his view of it: he will also profit more than most writers if the future confirms him. Whitman's fate is certain to be the one or the other. And he not only appealed to posterity in this daring way: he appealed on grounds that set him off from most of the other American writers of his time—set him off, in fact, from all but a few writers in Europe too. Like certain other deliberately prophetic poets of the age, Whitman insisted that he was no mere spokesman for a single locality or class any more than for a single generation: he was the spokesman of the modern world and of modern man in general, and his book was to be regarded not merely as *belles lettres* but as a New Bible, the expression of a fresh

3

and revolutionary religion intended for no small sect but, universally, for the democratic masses of a new age stretching indefinitely into the future, a religion in perfect harmony with modern science and radically progressive in its whole spirit. He might feel, at least at the beginning, that all this was only what was to be demanded of the bard who would really be "commensurate" with the achieved American democracy of his day, but inescapably, in an age that saw the appearance of mature socialist theory and the beginnings of socialist struggle, Whitman was bound to be regarded as having raised expectations beyond those suggested by Jefferson and Emerson. Without yielding an inch, he said late in life, the working-man and working-woman were to be in his pages from first to last. What wonder if, like Heine, like Shelley, like Tolstoy—and more than any of them—he should seem to have taken a long step toward the literature of socialism?

So natural is this impression of Whitman and of *Leaves of Grass* that many socialist writers from Reginald Beckett on—and including Maxim Gorky—have claimed the man and the book, with little qualification, for socialist culture. Inevitably the claim has been repudiated, directly or in effect, by more than one individualistic middle-class writer, especially in recent years. The late Stuart Sherman, for example, once observed that "if Whitman had lived at the right place in these years of the Proletarian Millennium, he would have been hanged as a reactionary member of the *bourgeoisie*"; and Mr. H. S. Canby has declared that, since Whitman never wrote for classes but always for individuals, "the idea of a world proletariat based on economic grounds would have been repugnant to him." These may not strike us as very well-rounded judgments, but Sher-

4

man's and Mr. Canby's dicta have at any rate enough co-
gency to have been anticipated or echoed by socialist or
quasi-socialist writers too. Some years ago Mr. Floyd Dell
remarked that Whitman is "the most complete and thoroughgoing anti-Socialist in all literature." More recently
Mr. V. F. Calverton has found that the author of *Leaves
of Grass* "was just as much a petty bourgeois individualist
in social philosophy, just as much a believer in private
property, as were most of his contemporaries." When the
jarring sects agree to this extent, it would seem as if the
debate were closed for good and all.

Actually it has been hardly more than opened by these
pronouncements: they suggest that the question is a many-
sided one, but beyond this they say rather little. On a moment's reflection it is clear that they are simple and rigid
formulas and not flexible interpretations that have been
arrived at by taking everything relevant into account. The
work of lesser writers can sometimes be disposed of in
these monochromatic terms, but the larger the writer the
more certain it is that the unity of his work will be an intricate unity, the result of bringing many contradictory or
apparently contradictory thoughts, feelings, and perceptions somehow into creative focus. A criticism that makes
no reckoning of such vital contradictions is a criticism that
is still green and raw. It is a criticism that would give as
simple an account of Dante as of Cino da Pistoia, of Shakespeare as of Dekker, of Goethe as of Tieck. It would also
give as simple an account of Walt Whitman as of Joaquin
Miller. The feat can be performed, but only with a comic
effect. We need not elevate Whitman to some fantastic
height as transcendently the greatest writer of his time in
order to hold that his nature was too interestingly complex

and his work too comprehensive to be ticketed, either of them, as one-sidedly "individualistic," "petty bourgeois," or "anti-Socialist."

His nature itself, as I say, was too complex for this, and these tickets are false psychologically if in no other way. Not even a man like Joaquin Miller, it is truistic enough to observe, was a man all of one piece, and certainly there was nothing easefully simple about Walt Whitman the solitary and the lover of crowds, the pacifist and the angry rebel, the egoist and the wound-dresser, the yea-sayer and the iconoclast, the commonplace journalist and the man of genius. He himself recognized all this better than many of his critics have done: he himself proposed to "sing"

The vehement struggle so fierce for unity in one's-self.

Of course he achieved a genuine unity as a person, but it was only at the cost of a struggle, and it was no one-dimensional unity that resulted. Moreover, Whitman lived at a time and in a society that were themselves full of the most startling contradictions, and more inclusively perhaps than any other American writer—certainly more deliberately— he gathered these to him, "embraced" them, and gave them their several stations in his book. He intended to take in everything, representatively and impartially, and though he naturally failed to do so much as this, he took in more than anyone else even attempted to do. Is it remarkable if *Leaves of Grass* should have to be described in language of the most elastic dialectical fullness?

To describe it so is what, without arrogance, one must at least aim at doing. The possible senses in which Whitman is a "socialist poet" will be really clear only when this

6

is done. And this means, in the first place, going behind the book itself to the personal and historical circumstances that produced it and gave it its special color. The book itself, needless to say, is the important thing: its real value, to us and to the future, is of course contained wholly within its own two covers, and no account of its setting will enhance or diminish in the slightest its essential meaning. But it was not written in the dry and gasless spaces of a perfect vacuum: it was written by a sharply characterized individual who lived on Long Island and elsewhere between the beginning of the third and the beginning of the last decade of the nineteenth century, and without superhuman insight we shall get at its essential meaning only after we have seen it, as dynamically as may be, issuing from the form and pressure of those seventy teeming years.

It was a period of time that witnessed the development of American social life from the condition of a largely agrarian society, dominated by landed and commercial wealth, to that of a largely industrial society, dominated by monopoly capital; it witnessed, during that development, the constant and complicated interplay of political groupings that stretches from the Democratic Republicanism of James Monroe to the Republicanism of Benjamin Harrison; it witnessed the ebb of Calvinism and other fundamentalisms, the rise of liberal Christianity, the domestication of Kantian idealism, the progress of American geology, astronomy, zoölogy, and other sciences, the expansion of technology, the triumph and the decline of a native romanticism in the arts, the emergence of a school of realist writers and painters. Where did Walt Whitman stand in relation to this many-sided process? How was he affected by the conflicts between Whig and Jacksonian? What were his

7

feelings amid the sectional struggles of the forties, fifties, and sixties? How conscious was he, and to what effect, of the economic transformations that were going on about him? Was he at all aware of what the geological historians and the physicists of electromagnetism and the biologists who led up to and followed Darwin were accomplishing? If so, did his awareness of it decide the whole tenor of his thought, or was this also controlled, perhaps even more powerfully, by the romantic idealism that moved so largely toward the opposite pole? How, finally, did he feel about the emerging trade-unionism and the socialist movement itself of his time?

These are the sorts of questions that ought to be answered before one can say, critically and responsibly, whether or not Whitman was "more of a Socialist" than he had thought he was, "intrinsically" and "in his meanings." Not that the answers to such questions, however full they may be, will of themselves decide the issue. Without setting up any mystical dualism between "the man" and "the poet," we have always to remember how far the creative artist is from being entirely absorbed and limited by the profane individual of biography. Goethe the privy councillor will never explain the whole of *Faust*, no matter how much we may know of him; Tolstoy the arbiter of the peace will never explain the whole of *War and Peace;* and Walt Whitman the editor or the government clerk is something less than Walt Whitman the author of *Leaves of Grass:* the two are not mechanically identical. What the salaried citizen may think on the topmost layers of his conscious mind is often, and familiarly, at war with what he may see or feel in his moments of deepest excitement and truest insight. It is partly because the opinions of Whit-

man the mere resident are so likely to be cited unimagina-
tively as decisive for his book that we wish to know everything about him and about them, and to estimate both at
their real worth. It is still more, however, because Whitman the man and the poet, if not mechanically identical,
are vitally one: together, not separately, they are of incalculable importance to us; and we need urgently to see
them—to see *him*—in the fullest and clearest setting we can
reconstruct.

Chapter Two

THE TENOR OF POLITICS

THE PARK IN FRONT of the City Hall in New York was
filled, late one afternoon in midsummer of the year 1841,
with what the *Evening Post* the next day called a "vast
multitude" of aroused and angry Democrats; Democrats
not only from the city itself but from Staten Island and
Brooklyn and the Long Island villages; between eight and
twelve thousand of them, said the *Post*. They had been
summoned to this mass-meeting by the leaders of the New
York Democracy in order to make their voices unmistakably heard in a national crisis of the moment. Two or
three months earlier, General William Henry Harrison,
who had been sent to the White House by the great Whig
victory in the preceding fall, had succumbed to old age
and the bombardment of office-seekers, and died within a
month after his inauguration. Now the Vice-President,
John Tyler of Virginia, had become President, and so ambiguous had his career been hitherto that neither Whigs
nor Democrats knew just what was in store for them. He
had been a bitter enemy of "this terrible old man," as the
Whig merchant Philip Hone called Andrew Jackson; but
he was far from being consistently and reliably Whiggish
in his record, and no one on either side could now be sure
whether he would work with the party that had elected

10

him, in its attempts to revive the hateful United States Bank, or would confess himself the unrepentant Jeffersonian that many men suspected him to be beneath the skin.

It was chiefly to protest against the Fiscal Bank Bill which Henry Clay had introduced in the Senate, and to strengthen the hand of John Tyler against the forces of financial monopoly, that the mass-meeting in the Park had been called. It was also to serve as a general show of Democratic strength, however, and the speeches cut a wide swath. A rising young attorney named S. J. Tilden made one of them, and the last, as it appears, was made by a young newspaper-man and political worker from Long Island. He was hardly more than a college student in years, but the young men of the party were evidently being encouraged to speak out, and he seems not to have been abashed by the thousands of faces turned toward him; no doubt they were mainly the faces of small shopkeepers, mechanics, even farmers, and if so he was in his element. At any rate, he did not shrink from speaking his mind, and the *Post* the next day, perhaps in Bryant's person, summarized his remarks approvingly. There was much agitation already—he appears to have said—of the question of a candidate to lead them in the next presidential campaign, but he begged his listeners to entertain a nobler idea of their aims as a party than to suppose that they strove merely to elevate this man or that to power. It was great principles for which in fact they were fighting, and the young Long Islander said boldly that he would not work for the best Democratic candidate ever nominated if he were merely the right individual. What good Democrats should seek to do was to raise up not a man or a set of

11

men but a creed, a doctrine; and now was the time to discuss not candidates but measures and policy. If his fellow-partisans would do this, he declared in closing, he assured them that, despite the catastrophe of 1840, he foresaw a certain and glorious victory for them three years hence.

The young Long Islander was of course Walt Whitman, and the events of 1844, whether historically happy or not, were to justify his sanguine prophecy. However that may be, our glimpse of him in these early months of John Tyler's administration is an invaluable one. At a time when Henry Thoreau, his senior by only two years, was planting apple-trees for Waldo Emerson and writing essays for the *Dial,* and when Herman Melville, who was just his age—having fled in bitterness from his school-room at Pittsfield—was standing mastheads on the whaler *Acushnet,* the future author of *Leaves of Grass* was up to his ears in the popular political turmoil of his day. He was to have something in common with both Thoreau and Melville, but for the moment he was not holding himself scornfully aside, like the young Yankee surveyor, from the noisy struggles of Whig and Democrat and invoking a plague on both their houses; and he was not convinced, like the disappointed grandson of the great General Gansevoort, that his hand was against every man and every man's hand against him. On the contrary, the times seemed to him to be the best of times and the life about him to be an excellent life. He had no quarrel with this world of mass-meetings and parades, of caucuses and rallies, of stormy conventions and boisterous election-days. To young Walt Whitman the turbulence of democracy in action—the vulgar turbulence, as fine gentlemen called it—was a sublime spectacle, and he threw himself into the fray with a whole heart. To him the difference between the friends of General Jackson and the partisans of Daniel Webster was not a mere difference between publicans and sinners on the one hand, scribes and Pharisees on the other; it was a difference between light and darkness, and he wished to be counted among the cohorts of the light.

What this meant in practice was that he wished to be counted among the majority of good Americans in the forties. The young man who spoke at the anti-Bank meeting was not leading a lost cause or fighting for some distant goal which he himself might never see attained; and he certainly did not think of himself in that guise. In his opinion, at this stage, the goal had already been won—the goal, that is, of political emancipation; and, though he foresaw an endless series of changes for the better in the future, he thought that the problem of the time was mainly to defend the conquests of democracy against its enemies. He was far from being in passionate rebellion against the system of things as he found it; on the contrary, he embraced with all the zeal of which he was capable the principles, the convictions, the loyalties of the huge class to which he belonged. It was a class that was highly articulate, if not far-sightedly critical, in Whitman's youth. His forebears had been country people of the old breed: plain but prosperous Long Island farmers, stock-raisers, and sailors; decliningly prosperous in his father's generation, they had taken to tavern-keeping and the trades, and his father himself, Walter Whitman, joining in the drift to the cities, had become a "mechanic," a skilled workman, a carpenter; Walt himself had been trained, like Howells and Mark Twain a little later, as a printer. These were the people who had looked with suspicion and anger upon the machi-

13

nations of the Hamiltonian bond-holders, merchants, and land-speculators—in short, of the Federalists; they were the people who had rushed to the support of Jefferson in the 1790's and furnished the great popular basis for the agrarian party Jefferson had built up; they later came close to the unpropertied city masses whom Aaron Burr and the founders of Tammany had gathered into the same generous fold. They had seemed to triumph, in 1800, over the rich and well-born Federalists; and in 1828, again, they had apparently frustrated the newer generation of "aristocrats" by rising in their vigor and trooping into Washington with Andrew Jackson almost literally on their shoulders.

In such an atmosphere of republican enthusiasms Walt Whitman had spent his Brooklyn childhood, and he was not of the least mind to react against it. The names of Jefferson and Jackson he had heard all his life spoken with affectionate reverence: two of his younger brothers, in fact, had been loyally named Thomas Jefferson Whitman and Andrew Jackson Whitman, and Walt may well have envied both Andrew and Jeff the happy auspices under which, in this respect, they started life. Certainly his imagination had been early touched and kindled by the personalities of the two great agrarian leaders: to him they were what the Gracchi must have been to many a young Roman of the later Republic; and it was as "the sainted Jefferson and Jackson" that he naturally thought of them. Among the books he owned as a young man was some copy or set of the works of Jefferson, and the impression these writings made upon him was never to be effaced. In his youth he could of course speak of the founder of his party as "the Columbus of our political faith": in his old

14

age too, however, he could still think of Thomas Jefferson as "among the greatest of the great."

He could never have seen Jefferson in person, though he would certainly have remembered that famous Fourth of July, when he himself was seven, on which both the Virginian and John Adams had died. Jackson, however, he did once see as a small boy; President Jackson, riding in a fine carriage up Fulton Street from the ferry, bowing affably to left and right at the cheering crowds, and doffing to them his big-brimmed white-beaver hat. It was during the General's grand tour through the North, of course, in the lowering summer of 1833; that tour which took him also to New England, and gave Nathaniel Hawthorne an excuse to steal out of his solitary chamber and catch a glimpse, on the outskirts of Salem, of the Hero of New Orleans. Neither the reserved New Englander nor the expansive little Brooklyn boy ever forgot the sight: in their different ways, and of course for plenty of other reasons too, they were good Jacksonians ever after. To Hawthorne, Andrew Jackson was "surely a great man"; to Walt Whitman he was "the Hero and Sage," a "noble, yet simple-souled old man," a "massive, yet most sweet and plain character." In his old age, the curious illusion possessed him that he had seen Jackson many times and "often talked with him": so, at least, he maintained in conversation. A youthful editorial, on the contrary, makes it evident that he had seen the General only once, and any other possibility is most unlikely. But this tangling of the fine wires of memory is itself a tribute to the strength of the early image. To his dying day, at all events, Whitman continued to venerate the terrible old man whom the Whig merchants had hated so passionately; to venerate him for

15

the "true gold," as he said, of his character; to believe that
that gold was "unmined, unforged, unanything, in fact—
anything wholly done, completed—just the genuine ore in
the rough."

As for the great Federalists and Whigs, on the other
hand—well, the case here was by no means so splendidly
simple. Of George Washington, Federalist though he had
certainly been, Whitman never thought or spoke as if he
had been involved in any way in the distinction of parties:
elevated to a plane high above faction, he was simply "a
pure and august being," "the Beloved One," "the match-
less WASHINGTON." Alexander Hamilton, however, was
another matter: of course he had played a considerable
role in the Revolution and deserved to be honored for
that by all patriots, as well as for the intellectual powers
which, as Whitman thought, no one could deny him.
Yet was he not, after all, the enemy of Jefferson? was he
not a man who, though perhaps he had sowed the seeds of
some good, had certainly sowed the seeds of much evil?
had he not been more or less frankly a monarchist, moreover, and in general was there anything in his character
seriously to appeal to the democratic instincts of good
Americans? The case with the mighty Daniel Webster was,
to Whitman's mind, little better. Here was a personage
still to be seen in the flesh on the balconies of New York
hotels and heard as he spoke from banner-draped stands at
places like Jamaica: Whitman had listened to the great
spell-binder more than once and had been genuinely impressed by the grandeur of his manner. Nevertheless he felt
that Webster was a cynical and corrupt man who dis-
trusted the people at heart and was rightly, therefore, dis-
trusted by them. Everyone knew that he was indebted to

the brandy bottle for his "indignant eloquence," and for
the supplies of his pocket-book to the "ill-got funds of
Whig brokers," and how could he be deeply respected? In
the personality of his great rival, Henry Clay, there was of
course an undeniable magnetism; barring his politics, he
was "a noble souled fellow," "the truest, heartiest man the
Whigs ever had"; but Clay's political principles too were
against him, and in short the Whigs had no leaders who
could be compared for a moment with the heroes of the
Democracy.

In such sentiments as these Whitman was at one with
the majority of plain people and certainly of good Loco-
focos—as the Whigs called the Democrats—in the forties.
Like them he believed that the Democratic Party embodied the true purposes of the republican experiment, and
like them he had little disposition—as an individual he had
only a latent capacity—to scrutinize closely and critically
the realities of partisan prose, or coolly to compare profes-
sion with performance. Analysis and destructive criticism
were not very congenial to his nature, at least in early
youth; and the fact that Jefferson had been singularly slow
to commit himself to a full democratic suffrage, that he
had looked upon "the mobs of great cities" as fearfully as
any Hamiltonian, that as president he had aimed to ap-
pease the financial classes he had formerly castigated—these
unromantic facts were never to become rancors in the ves-
sel of Whitman's peace. Just as little was he ever to be
troubled by the shadier side of Jacksonianism in its initial
phase. The friends of General Jackson may have manipu-
lated the evolving electoral machinery with a cheerful
cynicism; they may have exploited the executive patronage
grossly and defiantly; they may have condoned every spec-

17

ulative insanity and connived at the pilfering of the public domain by unscrupulous crooks; they may have worked in the interests of great planters and importing merchants and wild-cat bankers while practising, some of them, a conscienceless demagogy; they may have harried the Cherokees and plotted the extension of slavery and turned a deaf ear to the demands of city artisans and industrial workers; they may have been guilty in all these ways of treason to the democratic ideal, but if so they covered their tracks from the eyes of men like Whitman.

He was not disposed by temperament, as I have said, to cool and exacting criticism: he had none of the instincts of a Thoreau in this direction; and he was little inclined to resentment and bitter doubt: he was no Poe, no Melville. His temper was intensely sanguine; he came to maturity in decades which, whatever sufferings and whatever disasters they may have witnessed, were decades of lush material growth and jubilant expansion; he belonged to a social order that was still in its hopeful youth, and all his associations were with men and women who, "little" as they were, felt that the world was all before them and that, with the party of Jefferson and Jackson to lead them, they would inevitably prosper and grow fat. There was something illusory in this, as we can now see: nevertheless, it was not all a mere illusion; compared with what had preceded it, the world of these plain people—Whitman's world —was a free and promising one; the party of Jefferson and Jackson stood, practically speaking, for whatever was effectually progressive in it, and both Whitman and his people obeyed a sound instinct in giving that party their loyalty. What was more natural than that, in his cheerful youth, Whitman should accept as his political creed the liberal principles of the Democracy and, as a young editor in the middle years of James K. Polk's presidency, give expression to them, in the Brooklyn *Eagle,* in one editorial article after another? Those principles were as valid to him as to his carpenter father and his whole class.

We know well enough what they were, but Whitman as an editor once summarized them in terms to which, for their simplicity, we might for a moment recur. It was essential to this doctrine, of course, that the true principles of government were simple, clear, and easy to understand; that there were no mysteries in it to which the average mind could not penetrate. The people, the whole people, it held, were the only source of legitimate power; election should therefore be free and suffrage universal. Hereditary offices and titles were banned, nor could democracy endure any favored classes or monopolies of whatever sort. The civil was to be paramount to the military power, and church and state were to be absolutely severed. The administration of government should be thrifty, homely, and severely circumscribed; if possible, there should be no national debt, and public funds should be expended only on warrants and specific appropriations. Costly internal improvements were a device of monopolists and self-seeking profit-makers. The Union of the States was sacred and to challenge it was treason, but it was a Union of States that, beyond the powers they expressly granted to the federal arm, were sovereign and independent. Political government in general, indeed, could be more easily described in negative than in positive language: the necessity for it was a sad and not a happy one, and the ideal was to pare it down to a minimum. Government might do the people, as Whitman wrote, "an immense deal of harm," but it

19

could do little positive good, and no political principle was more fundamental than that according to which the best government is the one that governs least.

Such was the political philosophy that dominated American life during Whitman's impressionable years and that sank deep into the fabric of his thought. It was a philosophy which he had no curiosity to trace to its origins in the social apologetics of an emerging middle class, and he never inquired closely into its possibilities for evil as well as for good. Like many of the writers of his time—like Bryant, like Hawthorne, like Mark Twain later—he accepted this philosophy in good faith and in the most natural way, and whatever uncertainties may later have plagued him, he never consciously and completely abandoned it. Only for a few years in his teens and twenties, however, did Whitman think or act as if all hope of realizing such political ideals depended on the fortunes of a particular faction. Only for eight or ten years was he a willing instrument of organized Jacksonianism, but that phase he did pass through, and it left its mark upon him.

He had been printer's devil, as a small boy, on a Democratic-Republican newspaper in Brooklyn during the great days of Andrew Jackson's first term; for nearly a year, in Van Buren's presidency, he had edited a Locofoco paper of his own at Huntington, and had then worked as typesetter on the *Long Island Democrat* at Jamaica; and all this had brought him close to the practical workings of the Democracy. The late thirties, when Whitman was approaching his majority, could hardly have been piping times for loyal Van Burenites. The terrible depression that followed the panic of 1837 could plausibly be laid at the door of the ruling dynasty in Washington, and the apparently vindi-

20

cated Whigs, with the aid of disgruntled Democrats, conducted a bitter and unflagging war on the much-tried Van
Buren. In this uneasy atmosphere, young Whitman, who
was about to cast his first vote, bore witness to the faith
that was in him: to all the sensational appeals of that feverish Whig campaign of 1840—to the log-cabins borne
through the streets on floats and the barrels of hard cider
gushing abundantly on street-corners and the high-pitched
songs about the Eagle of Tippecanoe—he remained blind
and deaf; and when the Democrats obediently re-nomi-
nated Van Buren, despite his handicaps, Whitman took
the stump and made speeches for Little Van throughout
Queens County. He even entered into an acrimonious controversy with a certain Whig leader—the son, in fact, of
Rufus King—a gentleman whom he described publicly as
a "liar and blackguard" for an attack he had made upon
the Democratic Party at the great Webster meeting at Jamaica. The town, as it happened, went for Van Buren at
the election that followed.

Young Whitman must have seemed a useful recruit to
the party managers, for we have seen how they made a
place for him on the speaker's platform, the next summer,
at an important mass-meeting; and the following spring,
after Tyler's veto of the Bank Bill—and other actions—had
turned the Whigs fiercely against him, Whitman appears
as the editor, in New York, of a pro-Tyler paper called the
Aurora—a sheet, we are told, "that made itself greatly
hated by the more respectable citizens." It is not easy to
keep Whitman in sight during these very early years, but
he must have been a good party worker during the campaign of 1844: he was editing another Locofoco paper in
the city that summer, and there can be little doubt that he

21

threw himself wholeheartedly into the support of Young
Hickory, as the astute Jacksonian managers had nicknamed
the worthy Polk. A few years later Whitman was secretary,
for a time, to the General Committee of the party in Kings
County, but even earlier, twelve months after Polk's inauguration indeed, his services to the cause had been still
more signally recognized by his being made editor—at the
age of twenty-seven—of a recently-established organ of the
Democrats in Brooklyn, the already influential *Daily Eagle*.

Events were to show that the days of Whitman's uncritical partisanship were numbered even when, early in the
spring of 1846, he took up his new job; but for many
months the young editor continued to use the language
and maintain the spirit of party regularity. For the last
time in his life, during those crowded months of the war
on Mexico, the party of Jefferson and Jackson was to Whitman the party of democracy herself. Whenever local or
state elections began to draw near, the *Eagle* would re-
sound with urgent appeals to good Democrats to close up
their ranks, draw in and discipline the laggards, and move
forward as a compact body upon the strongholds of the
enemy. Everyone among us, it would cry, *"who through
discontent or any other motive, would mar the union of
our ranks,"* is little better than an ally of Whiggery. "Nothing but the Whole Ticket," it would thunder at those
weaker vessels who might be seduced into "scratching";
and to those who might dally with compromise it shouted
that the Democratic Party should *"stick to its own identity,"* and enter into no flirtation with any other faction
whatever. The party of Democracy, declared the *Eagle* on
one occasion, can never become "essentially corrupt"; and
so, if only "THE TRUE MEN OF THE PARTY" remain faithful

in the coming trial at the polls, there will be no need to
fear for the result.

How much violence, in this devotion to general party
discipline, Whitman may have done to his own wayward
nature, we can guess from later tokens; and even in the
face of concrete issues, he must sometimes have had to
stifle his truest impulses painfully. His conscience, as a
child of the old colonial yeomanry, can hardly have borne
it easily when partisan journalism forced him to support
a Democratic governor, Silas Wright, by denouncing the
Anti-Rent rioters of up-state New York; to speak of farmers who were revolting desperately against the obstinate
feudalism of the great patroons, as "the most violent faction which has disgraced the State since laws were heard
of in this hemisphere." Self-injury such as this was one of
the prices Whitman paid for his political conformism, but
it was seldom that he was required to inflict it. With most
of the established policies of Silas Wright's and James K.
Polk's party he was of course, as he then understood them,
in spontaneous sympathy; and nothing could have come
easier to him than to compose those vehement editorials of
his on "the poisonous influence of the United States bank,"
or on the wisdom of the Sub-Treasury law, or on the "Case
of People, *vs.* Paper," or on "the antiquated bandages of
the tariff system" and the blessings of free trade.

The rich planters of the cotton kingdom may have been
quite as enthusiastic as the editor of the *Eagle* over decen-
tralized banking and a tariff for revenue only, but it was
not their cause that Whitman was consciously pleading: it
was the cause, as he saw it, of the small shopkeepers and
artisans and farmers. And it was through no conscious or
cynical adherence to the ambitious designs of the slave-

23

holders that he raised his voice in behalf of the great salient adventure of the Polk administration, the Mexican
War. Yet raise his voice in its behalf he did. He was to
speak of Mexico, many years later, as "the only [nation] to
whom we have ever really done wrong," but in the days
when Zachary Taylor was winning Buena Vista and Scott
and his men were scrambling up the rocks at Cerro Gordo,
Whitman was visited by no such disloyal qualms. A fever
of imperialist emotion, worked up by the interested groups,
had seized upon the whole nation in the days before and
after Polk's election, and Whitman, caught on his most
exposed side, inevitably succumbed to it. In those months
when Theodore Parker was crying out, in Faneuil Hall
and elsewhere, against this "mean and infamous war"—
which he said was as bad as the war for the partition of
Poland—and when Lowell was jeering at "the overreachin'
o' them nigger-drivin' States," and not long after Henry
Thoreau had refused to pay taxes to a government capable
of so base a crime as even the annexation of Texas—in
those months Walt Whitman was calling out like any jingo
for "prompt and effectual demonstrations of force," and
declaring with editorial boldness that "Yes: Mexico must
be thoroughly chastised!" He never went so far as to suppose, with Lowell's Birdofredom Sawin, "thet Mexicans
worn't human beans," but he did believe for the moment,
or made himself believe, that they were "an ignorant,
prejudiced, and perfectly faithless people"—"a nation of
bravos" who had long enough tried the patience of a for-
bearing America. So gross, indeed, were the sins of Mexico,
he protested, that she richly deserved to be "a severed and
cut up nation"; and if, in the process of dismemberment,
the United States should acquire a vast domain of new ter-

24

ritory—if, in fact, it should annex "even the main bulk of that republic"—the cause of progress, he argued, could only be advanced by the result.

It was a popular conviction to entertain at just that moment, but Whitman was no more content than the real agrarian expansionists with a program of aggression confined to the Rio Grande: directing his gaze toward a still remoter distance, he watched with excited anticipation the progress of Polk's conquests in the farther Southwest and on the Coast. A year or two earlier, when Britain and the United States had clashed in Oregon, he had joined in the cry of "Fifty-four-Forty or fight," but he saw nothing suspicious in the willingness of the plantation-owners' government at Washington to compromise on that score—to confine their expansion to potential slave territory, however the Northwestern farmers might fare—and when word of the treaty with England, which in the first summer of the Mexican War settled the dispute in Oregon, came clicking over the new Magnetic Telegraph, he greeted it in capital letters as "VERY excellent news." The "Fifty-four-Forty" line had not been achieved, but the British government had been conveniently placated. New Mexico and California were another matter, and Whitman seems to have kept an eager eye on every development in those quarters. In the very month when Kearny set out from Fort Leavenworth for the conquest of New Mexico, Whitman was speculating in the *Eagle* on the possibility that Santa Fe would soon be shining as a star "in our mighty firmament"; and a month later, turning toward California, he observed that "even at this moment, the Star Spangled Banner may be floating" over San Francisco and Monterey. For once at least his guess was so inspired that, on the very

25

day his remarks appeared, Commodore Sloat was taking possession of Monterey and, two days later, Montgomery was raising the American flag over the little cluster of houses at San Francisco.

To men like Lowell these moves of the intoxicated empire-builders were visible in a cold realistic light:

> *They jest want this Californy*
> *So's to lug new slave-states in*
> *To abuse ye, an' to scorn ye,*
> *An' to plunder ye like sin.*

Lowell too may have over-simplified: the imperial dreams of Yankee merchants may have had much to do with the seizure of Monterey, and the war to defend the annexation of Texas may have been easily "sold" to the thousands of men in northern states who held great quantities of Texas land-scrip and Texas state bonds. To Whitman, in any case, none of these pragmatic motives were disturbingly apparent: there were almost oceanic depths of ingenuous affirmation in his nature, and certainly he accepted the official version of the Mexican War—until it was nearly over—in simple good faith. No one could have had his tongue in his cheek less than the editor of the *Eagle* when he spoke of "our good President Polk," or when he defended that gentleman spiritedly against the aspersions of Horace Greeley in the *Tribune*. It has to be remembered, too, that there was a certain plausibility in the case against the corrupt Mexican governments and the Mexican military adventurers of the thirties and forties. Such incidents as the massacre by Mexican troops of the Texan leader Fannin and his men at Goliad in 1836 had left a bitter scar

in Whitman's imagination: was he not still to commemo-
rate, in a passage of the "Song of Myself," "the murder in
cold blood of four hundred and twelve young men"?

He was less troubled, if he knew of them, by the wrongs
done to the Mexicans, but in any case his nationalism at
this stage was of the headiest sort, and he can have had no
difficulty whatever in believing that the extension of American territory, since it presumably meant the extension of
democratic institutions, was simply a new conquest for liberty and equality. It was not the "lust of power and territory," he could say sincerely, however naïvely, that made
Americans support the war so heartily: that might be the
motive for expanding "a less liberal form of government"
—but not ours. "It is for the interest of mankind that its
power and territory should be extended—the farther the
better." No doubt the readers of Dickens might have de-
tected the peculiar touch of Mr. Jefferson Brick, or something like it, in these sonorous phrases; no doubt the conviction behind them had its uses to the sagacious men in
Washington. The fact remains that the young Whitman's
imperialism was subjectively quite as idealistic a faith as
his democracy. It had not kept him from expressing, six
months before the final defeat of Santa Anna, and repeat-
ing more than once in the interval, his "devout wish for
the very *earliest possible honorable PEACE.*" And it did
not continue indefinitely to blind him—any more than it
continued to blind the plain people of the North—to the
real aims of the plantation imperialists. When, a few
months after war had been declared, David Wilmot of
Pennsylvania introduced a famous anti-slavery resolution
in the House of Representatives, the political effects that
followed gradually opened Whitman's eyes to the actuali-

ties, and ended by driving him, the best of young Jacksonians, into the wilds outside the party.

II

"When I was eighteen," said Goethe to Eckermann, "all
my country was eighteen too." Walt Whitman in old age
might have used a similar metaphor of a comparable period in his life. The dozen years that intervened between
the Treaty of Guadalupe Hidalgo and the firing on Fort
Sumter were tense and ominous yet expansive and strangely
contradictory years in American life, and in Whitman's
career, too, they were years of crowded development for
which it is not easy to find a simple principle of unity. We
shall understand his relations to American politics in those
years only if we do justice to the intensity of his personal
life and the curious complexity of his nature. He was ex-
periencing in those days the growing excitement of arriv-
ing at creative maturity; he was learning month by month
what his great powers as a writer really were, and testing
his wings in bolder and bolder flights; and this happy sense
of flowering energies was in no easy harmony with the dismal seismic premonitions of a national calamity to come.
It *was* in harmony with the new prosperity that, following
on the lean years of the forties, and in spite of the darkness
in one quarter of the skies, had begun to flow genially over
the land; and the cataract of gold that, soon after the word
had gone out from Sutter's Fort, had poured in increasing
torrents into the economic life of the country, was an emblem of the enrichment that Walt Whitman, a spiritual
Forty-Niner, was simultaneously enjoying. The time had

come for him to write the "Poem of Walt Whitman, an American"; the time had come for him to "celebrate" himself; and this, more even than the bitterly sharpening conflicts in his political and social world, was what absorbed his deepest life in the fifties.

Nor was this all that kept him, belligerent democrat that he was, from throwing himself into the very thick of the struggles of the decade. Among the contradictions in a far from simple nature was a real ambiguity on this plane. He was the sworn poet, he said, of every dauntless rebel the world over; however much others might hold up peace, it was his intention to hold up agitation and conflict. "As for me," he once wrote, "I love screaming, wrestling, boiling-hot days." It was quite true that part of his nature loved them, and he could say with perfect sincerity that he dreaded "the rage and disputes of hell" less than he dreaded a death-like lethargy. But there was a stratum in him that overlay all this, and in practice it kept him pretty well aloof from the Garrisons and the Parkers and even the Emersons. It was not simply a caprice that led him as a young man to consider becoming a real Quaker: something within him moved powerfully toward the quietism, the pacifism, the uncontentiousness of the Friends as well as toward their moral independence. A trifling illustration of this has a certain quaint significance. Swimming, as everyone knows, was Whitman's favorite exercise, but his forte in the water, he once said to Traubel, was really floating. "I possessed almost unlimited capacity," he remarked, "for floating on my back—for however long." The picture has a psychological truthfulness of its own. To think of Whitman as he was in his most "native moments"

29

is not to think of a man striking out defiantly against great oncoming waves, but of a man lying naked and secure on his back, afloat in a friendly and sustaining medium.

The poet of dauntless rebels was anything but an impostor: the strain of revolt was a powerful strain in Whitman's blood, and when he spoke of "myself and this contentious soul of mine," it was not without true self-knowledge. There are many kinds of belligerency, however, and it was not in the smoke and din of unintermittent warfare that Whitman's individual temper made him most at home. Acceptance was inherently easier to him than denial: his gait, as he said, was no fault-finder's or rejecter's gait; and no one who has become familiar with his personal habit—as distinguished from his insight and reach as a poet—can easily imagine Whitman joining Garrison in the burning of the Constitution on Framingham Common, or plotting secretly with Parker and Sanborn to render aid to John Brown, or even confronting a hooting audience with Emerson to denounce the Fugitive Slave Law. For such undertakings he lacked something, the right acrimony, the right concentration, the right passion; and he knew it. "I like to see the scuffle," he said to Traubel—"I feel the necessity of hearing the last word of challenge—but am not to be lured into the fight." It was not quite true that he had never been lured into it in any way, and certainly he liked much of the time to be *near* the scuffle; but he was not at his best in the role of partisan fighter. "Apart from the pulling and hauling," as he put it, "stands what I am"; and we do best when we visualize him, in his own words, "both in and out of the game and watching and wondering at it."

There was a great fund of conservatism in this radical,

30

personally, and unexpected practical conformities in this non-conformist; and we are brought face to face with them when we confront the record of his vacillations and inconsistencies on the slavery question. It would be exhilarating if we could know that, throughout the struggle, Whitman thought and felt, not with the apathetic Hawthorne or the pro-slavery Poe, but with the men and women of letters who never wavered in their anti-slavery convictions. Unhappily the truth about him is by no means so clear-cut. For all his determination to break with routine and convention, he could yield whole areas of his mind to a tyrannous prevailing opinion, and he was not a New York Democrat for nothing. The institution of slavery had survived in his state longer than elsewhere in the North: it was not until Whitman was a child of eight that the last slave in New York was finally manumitted; in the eighteenth century his own grandparents had been slave-holders in Suffolk County, and he himself could well remember some of the aged freedmen—Old Mose, for example—who had survived at West Hills into his own boyhood. The plain people whose way of life had so powerfully shaped Whitman's temper were good democrats, to be sure, but they were white men to whom slavery was a near memory, and they indulged in no "visionary" thought, most of them, about freedom and equality for the blacks. The fertile passiveness which was so real an aspect of Whitman's nature came near to disarming him completely in his resistance to such crass influences, and he did not overstate the fact when he remarked to Traubel: "After all I may have been tainted a bit, just a little bit, with the New York feeling with regard to anti-slavery."

An extreme candor was not one of Whitman's vices, and

31

the taint he spoke of was more than the trifle he made of it. As a prophet-poet he could find "equals and lovers" ready for him in all lands; he could preach, with a special order of sincerity, the universal equality of mankind; as a mere unredeemed natural man he could not always transcend certain heavy limitations of sympathy. Toward the Negro as a human being, his emotions were by no means so expansive or so tenderly inclusive as the language of his verse would imply. The poet of "Salut au Monde!" could feel and speak elsewhere like a commonplace reporter or government clerk. The testimony of his friend Eldridge was that he had a poor opinion of Negroes, and had no friends among them while he lived in Washington. "He never seemed to care for them," said Eldridge, "or they for him, although he never manifested any particular aversion to them." "Aversion" would have been a strange attitude indeed for this lover of all men, and yet in fact the word is hardly too strong for what is expressed in some of his casual allusions. There is a letter to his mother, written in the summer of 1868, in which he speaks of a large parade of Negroes in Washington to celebrate their success in electing to the mayoralty of the city a friend of the colored man. It was a tumultuous scene, not unnaturally, and to Whitman "very disgusting & alarming in some respects": the colored men and women, he added, "looked like so many wild brutes let loose." A people cruelly degraded for generations may well have had an air of barbaric abandon in their rejoicings, but is it easy to endure this language from Whitman? Or the language he used to the Englishman Wallace years later in Camden? He was speaking of the ease with which unscrupulous politicians corrupted the Negroes. "Poor wretches!" he continued. "They are invariably—invariably—almost without exception—a superstitious, ignorant and thievish race."

Such was the great humanitarian's harsh estimate of an "inferior" people. We shall find no other dose so acrid or so hard to swallow in our attempt to get at Whitman's true measure as man and poet, but if we swallow it we shall understand all the better his rather inglorious record in the days of the Abolitionists. A knowledge of *Leaves of Grass* alone might lead one to imagine that, even in earliest youth, its author would have been drawn by irresistible fellow-feeling into the orbit of Phillips and Garrison. Nothing of the sort, in fact, took place. The youth who stumped for Van Buren and probably worked for the election of Polk was too loyal to his party to have a moment's sympathy, in his official capacity, with those "extremists" who proposed the immediate confiscation of slave property and the emancipation of the slaves. To him, on this unideal side, those men and women were what they seemed to the vast majority of worldly northerners. "A few foolish and red-hot fanatics" is what the journalist Whitman called the associates of Whittier and Lydia Maria Child—"this angry-voiced and silly set." "The mad fanaticism or ranting of ultra 'Abolitionists,' " he declared in the *Eagle*, "has done far more harm than good to the very cause it professed to aid." Ten years later, Whitman's animus had softened a good deal, but even then—in the months following the Dred Scott decision, for example—he would not have said with Emerson that "every sane human being" was an Abolitionist. He was editing the Brooklyn *Times* in the summer of 1857 when an Abolitionist convention was being held in New York, but a visit to one of its sessions failed to disturb his phlegm appreciably. "While the ideas

33

of abolition . . . are great ideas," he remarked feebly in an editorial, "there is no particular need of running them into the ground."

There was certainly no danger of Whitman's doing so, or of his losing his head when, two years later, John Brown struck the blow at Harper's Ferry which, leading to his execution in Virginia, stirred the quiet Longfellow to say in his diary that this was "the date of a new Revolution— quite as much needed as the old one." Whitman's feeling about the grim terrorist of Osawatomie was a very mixed feeling, as we shall see, but his own testimony in old age was that his emotions at the time of John Brown's execution, though not without strength, were "not enough to take away my appetite—to spoil my supper." Something in the grand but narrow vehemence of just such a character as this evoked a vague antagonism in Whitman, and he revealed much, in his easygoing way, when he remarked to Traubel—not quite truly—that he had "never enthused greatly" over John Brown: for his part, he said, he "could never see in Brown himself, merely of himself, the evidence of great human quality." His range of appreciation was far wider than most men's, but it had its frontiers.

To John Brown, as to thousands of far less zealous men, there had never been a moment's question whether slavery was or was not a tragic evil: to Whitman, of all men, the case had not always been so clear. He had never, it is true, imagined slavery to be what Calhoun had called it —"the most safe and stable basis for free institutions in the world"; but the almost independent being within him who shrank from ugly facts and leaned indolently on the workings of Providence, had sometimes persuaded him that even slavery was not an unmitigated wrong. In *Franklin*

34

Evans, the wretched temperance novel he had written at about the time he was editing the *Aurora,* Whitman had apologized, with evident discomfort, for the peculiar institution of the South. There is a character in that little tract, a French émigré, who in spite of the most advanced political sentiments, has become a plantation-owner and slave-holder in Virginia, and who compares in his own mind the tangible miseries of the European proletariat with the "merely nominal oppression" of the American Negroes! "He beheld, it is true, a large number of men and women in bondage," wrote the young libertarian blandly; "but he could not shut his eyes to the fact that they would be far more unhappy if possessed of freedom."

It was not for long that Walt Whitman was induced to believe that *any* oppression was "merely nominal," and he never again committed himself to the view that bondage could sometimes be preferable to freedom. But at no time, before or after the emancipation of American slaves, did he wholly abandon the genial fatalism that affected his feelings, as a mere citizen, on this as on so many subjects. Even in the days of the Kansas struggle he could speak of slavery in the Brooklyn *Times* as "not at all without its redeeming points," and say that "on politico-economic grounds" the use of slave labor in Brazil, in Cuba, and possibly in the Southern states, was not objectionable. "Slaves are there," he could say resignedly, "because they must be—when the time arrives for them not to be proper there, they will leave." That happy date, he estimated, within five years of Lincoln's Proclamation, would certainly arrive "before a hundred years have rolled on"! Moderation, meanwhile, was moderation.

Whitman the mere citizen, however, was not always at

one with Whitman the poet, the imaginative man, the artist. Consider, for example, a passage in one of his private notebooks that, written probably in the early fifties, has only recently found its way into print. "Everyone that speaks his word for slavery," it runs, "is himself the worst slave—the spirit of a freeman is not light enough in him to show that all the fatness of the earth were bitter to a bondaged neck." Is it the author of *Franklin Evans,* is it the editor of the Brooklyn *Times,* who thus expresses himself? The hands are Esau's, of course, but the voice is the voice of Jacob. Walt Whitman might put the skins of the kids of goats upon his hands and upon the smooth of his neck, but he could not, for all his constitutional quietism, consistently disguise his instinctive sympathies. The good philistine that he was during so many hours in his life, could pick no quarrel with social arrangements as he found them; the turbulent poet who lived in the same body was not so easily silenced. Whatever the householder Whitman might say, his daimon, his unconscious, was a real Abolitionist, and it insisted on being heard no matter how obliquely.

"The horror of slavery," said Whitman in his old age, "always had a strong hold on me." It is a reminiscence which, considering the whole record, we have a right to take with a certain reservation, but it cannot be left out of the whole picture. The editor of the *Eagle* might jeer at the anti-slavery fanatics, but he was not so infatuated an opportunist or so timid a party-man that he could be kept from calling slavery in his paper a "plague-spot," or from asking there whether the institution was not an evil and one that demanded the "anxious consideration" of every Democrat. The editor of the *Times* might deprecate the running into the ground of Abolitionist ideas, but he could not be kept from asserting, with magnificent inconsistency, that "the recorded theory of America denies slavery any existence in justice, law, or as a moral fact." This editor might temporize with a legal injustice, but when it was a question of the *illegal* slave trade, his natural emotions came out unmistakably in the language he used of it: "that most abominable of all man's schemes for making money" is what he called the slave trade in the *Eagle:* in the *Times,* it became "the horrible traffic." Whitman might fold his hands, in 1857, and trust that the courses of the stars would abolish slavery within a century: this was not his posture in the dithyrambic preface he had published, two years earlier, in the first issue of *Leaves of Grass.* There he had announced that, among the "real things" which must enter into the vision of the true American bard, were "slavery and the tremulous spreading of hands to protect it, and the stern opposition to it which shall never cease until it ceases or the speaking of tongues and the moving of lips cease."

How much freer the poet was than the man from the littleness of locality, of class, and of time, that first edition of his book, and the edition that followed it within a year, had testified in other ways. Walt Whitman the government clerk of the late sixties was to have no friends among the Negroes of Washington, and even in his experiments as a poet he had once written, in the sketch of a poem to be called "Pictures," this phrase describing a slave-gang at work on a road in the South:

> . . . *see, how clumsy, hideous, black, panting, grinning, sly, besotted, sensual, shameless.*

37

It cannot be wholly meaningless, however, that he had never put this poem into print, and that on the contrary, in the long poem that was eventually to be called the "Song of Myself," he *had* published the fine passage about the Negro driving a dray in a stone-yard—the Negro with his "calm and commanding glance" and the sun falling on "the black of his polish'd and perfect limbs":

> *I behold the picturesque giant and love him.*

In such lines, perhaps, it was the poet's eye and not his philosophy that was at work, but no such second thought need qualify the passage in "Salut au Monde!"—a poem of 1856, though it was then called "Poem of Salutation"— in which the son of Manhattan issued his fraternal greetings to all the peoples of the earth without forgetting the drudges of the plantation:

> *You dim-descended, black, divine-soul'd African, large, fine-headed, nobly-form'd, superbly destin'd, on equal terms with me!*

Here at least there was no concession to the Southern oligarchs or the dough-faces of the North.

Even toward the "angry-voiced" Abolitionists Whitman's attitude had not always been well-defined and sustained. Their extremism might repel him, and he might shrink from the agitation of their lives, but he was drawn to them and their whereabouts in spite of himself. He was drawn, for example, again and again, to the tumultuous Abolitionist conventions in the big turtle-shaped hall of the Tabernacle on Broadway where the great fire-eaters held forth and where the Tammany gangsters under Captain Isaiah Rynders did what they could to break up the meetings and preserve the Union. He liked to remember, late in life, that the gangsters met their match; that the Abolitionists were "tough, tough," and always maintained their ground. He went to these meetings year after year, he recollected, and "learn'd much from them—was sure to be on hand when J. P. Hale or Cash Clay made speeches." He had heard the celebrated orators of the time—Webster, Henry Clay, Edward Everett, and their like; yet he recalled the "minor but life-eloquence" of one or two of the old Abolitionist "fanatics" "ahead of all those stereotyped fames." Hale, Phillips, Cassius Clay—here were men from whom this praiser of unrestraint could hardly withhold his homage; and he paid them the subtlest tribute, years later, when he prefaced a reprinted group of his youthful magazine tales with the splendidly inaccurate statement: "I was then quite an 'abolitionist.'"

He had practically no literal claim whatever to the honorable title: still, the man who could say in old age that he ranked W. L. Garrison "way up" and regarded him as "of the noblest race of revolutionaries" did not wholly fail to redress the balance. His imagination had been with the Abolitionists all along. He may not have "enthused" over John Brown, but it was of Brown nevertheless that he spoke to Traubel on another occasion as "a great and precious memory," and added that such devotion, such superb courage as his would never be forgotten. In saying such things Whitman might only have been yielding grudgingly to the verdict of time, yet the fact is that, even in the days when the shots fired at Harper's Ferry were still echoing, he had not been wholly immune to the swift emotion that had torn from Emerson his famous dictum about the gallows and the cross. Preoccupied with the

39

fine rush of productivity that was about to bear fruit in the third great edition of his book, Whitman may have eaten his supper with appetite unimpaired while John Brown was lying in jail or undergoing trial, but it may have been not many months later that, as a scrap of manuscript tells us, he planned to write a poem which he thus described: "Sing the death of Kepler—Columbus—Cervantes—John Brown—Burns." That context of venerable names is hardly indicative of mere indifference on the poet's part, and certainly the execution of John Brown had not seemed to him one of the least fateful events of the "brooding year," 1859–60: the poem called "Year of Meteors" records several other facts, but it records at the very outset the scene that took place at Charlestown in Virginia on the second of December:

> I would sing how an old man, tall, with white hair,
>   mounted the scaffold in Virginia,
> (I was at hand, silent I stood with teeth shut close,
>   I watch'd,
> I stood very near you old man when cool and indiffer-
>   ent, but trembling with age and your unheal'd
>   wounds, you mounted the scaffold).

One April morning during the following spring—the spring of 1860—in the old Court House in Boston, Frank Sanborn, the Concord schoolmaster, was on trial for complicity in John Brown's conspiracy. As he stood at the bar before Chief Justice Shaw, the prisoner noticed "a distinguished-looking man, in peculiar dress," near the door. This individual, Sanborn later learned, was Walt Whitman; and Whitman, who was seeing the new edition of his book through the press in Boston, had come to the court-room, he afterwards said, to make sure that, if the court's decision should go against Sanborn, he himself might take part in the attempt to free the prisoner from his captors.

If so, this was probably as near as Whitman ever came to participating personally in the "scuffle" as carried on by anti-slavery extremists. At an early stage and on a less advanced line, however, he had himself been "lured into the fight." If he had never been in any active or practical sense an Abolitionist, Whitman had been in both senses a good Free Soiler. The difference is indicative of the real matrix of Whitman's anti-slavery sentiment. Inconsistent as he was on a certain level, there was a hard substratum beneath Whitman's hatred of slavery, and it determined both his thought and his conduct in the whole connection. The abstract wrong of property in human beings cannot have been the obsession with him that it was with the Quakers and the Transcendentalists: certainly it is not often discernible in what he said, even between the lines; and the lot of the Negro as a human being seems rarely to have preoccupied him. No more than Lincoln did he believe that social equality among black men and white would ever or should ever prevail, and he rejoiced when, in 1858, the new state of Oregon prohibited, in its constitution, the entrance of any Negro, free or slave, within its borders. In all this Whitman was less close to the humanitarian idealists than he was to thousands of ordinary Americans with whom his fellow-feeling was more instinctive: less close to Parker and Thoreau than to many a Northern farmer, shopkeeper, or workman of those decades. His opposition to slavery was essentially—on the practical level—the opposition felt to it in the North (and in the South, too, for that matter) by the men who raised corn and hogs, by the workers in mill and mine, by the skilled artisans and the trade unionists.

41

On such men's lives the effects of slavery were direct and tangible: it was a chronic menace to their essential status in society, and their increasingly passionate opposition to it took, quite understandably, a realistic, a hard-headed, and sometimes a narrow form. At any rate, it was the heavy bass of their half-articulate resentment that Whitman's hearing caught; and to this still largely unorganized feeling, even while he was editing the *Eagle,* he gave expression. "The voice of the North," he announced, at the end of his first year on the paper, "proclaims that *labor must not be degraded";* and the next fall he gave full rein to his sentiments on the subject in one of the longest and most eloquent editorials he was ever to write. It was an editorial entitled "American Workingmen, versus Slavery," and it raised in bold and explicit form the question whether or not there should be slavery in the new territories that were certain to be acquired by the war on Mexico. This, he wrote, was "a question between *the grand body of white workingmen, the millions of mechanics, farmers, and operatives of our country,* with their interests on the one side —and the interests of the few thousand rich, 'polished,' and aristocratic owners of slaves at the South, on the other side." The real case against slavery, he here came close to saying, is not that it is unjust to the slave, but that it is "destructive to the dignity and independence of all who work, and to labor itself." This being true, he called upon "every mechanic of the North, East, and West"—upon carpenters and masons, stone-cutters and blacksmiths, cartmen and shoemakers and machinists—to proclaim to the world in massive tones that their calling was not to be sunk to a brutish level and that they would not under any circumstances endure the further extension of slavery.

For it was only against this further extension of the peculiar institution that Whitman, like Lincoln, ever took (except as a bard) an outspoken stand. The Union of the States was to him a kind of absolute, and there was never a moment in his life when, with Garrison and Phillips, he would gladly have seen it shattered for the sake of emancipation. To him the Constitution was not at all "an agreement with hell"; it was not even a merely ingenious political instrument for the attainment of certain practical ends; it was "a perfect and entire thing," "the grandest piece of moral building ever constructed," and its framers he described, with a touch of deliberate poetry, as "some mighty prophets and gods." Feeling this, he could only recognize that slavery was protected by the Constitution in the states where it existed; that in those states it could not be touched by outsiders; and what Lincoln called its "ultimate extinction" there, Whitman was willing to leave to Providence. Its extension into new territories or states was another matter, and toward that Whitman never had more than one attitude. His discovery that the official Democracy would take no position against the spread of slavery, that in fact it was waging the Mexican War mainly in the interests of the plantation system, was what finally aroused his reluctant distrust of the party, and led in the end to his break with it. In the August after war was declared, Polk's appeal to Congress for funds to prosecute it was countered by David Wilmot with his famous Proviso against admitting slavery into any of the probable new territories. Walt Whitman seems to have become a Proviso man almost at once. "Set Down Your Feet, Democrats!" he cried in the *Eagle* four months later. If any states, he continued, are to be formed out of the new territory, let

43

the Democratic members of Congress support Wilmot and "plant themselves quietly, without bluster, but fixedly and without compromise, on the requirement that *Slavery be prohibited in them forever.*"

The majority of Democrats planted themselves on no such rigid position; and Whitman, after attempting for another year to reconcile his Jacksonian loyalties with his devotion to free labor, broke with the right-wing or Hunker owners of the *Eagle,* resigned from his editorial connection, and six months later emerged as a full-fledged Free Soiler. The party of Polk and Cass had left him no other choice. In the summer of 1847 the New York state machine, at a convention of the Democrats at Syracuse, had ridden rough-shod over the Proviso men or Barnburners in its own ranks and refused to commit the party to free soil. In spite of this warning, Whitman had swallowed his disappointment for the moment and supported the Democrats in the state elections that fall; but when General Cass, the leading candidate for the presidential nomination in 1848, came out against the Proviso, and was nevertheless made the party's standard-bearer in the national campaign, Whitman was forced to recognize at last that the Southern oligarchs and their Northern allies had successfully captured and made their own the party of freedom and democracy.

The summer and fall of 1848 found him therefore, as they found that other ex-Democrat, Bryant, working enthusiastically for the building up of a new party dedicated to Free Soil, Free Speech, Free Labor, and Free Men. Early in August a meeting of Barnburners and "Conscience Whigs" was held in Brooklyn to elect delegates from that city to the national Free Soil convention about to assemble

44

in Buffalo. Of the fifteen men chosen, Whitman was one; moreover, he introduced at the Brooklyn meeting a resolution instructing the Kings County delegates to go unconditionally for his old hero, Martin Van Buren. At the request of others present he withdrew the "unconditionally," but the Buffalo meeting went for Van Buren after all; and thus confirmed in his loyalty to the movement, Whitman threw himself zealously into the work of running a new paper, the *Freeman,* just launched in Brooklyn by the supporters of Van Buren and Adams.

III

There had been something anomalous from the beginning in the spectacle of Walt Whitman as a good sectarian, and now that he had reached his early thirties he was passing out of that phase once and for all. Intense partisanship, to be sure, came more naturally to him than to many men: the need to be intimately associated with his fellows was a powerful need of his nature, and whatever forms it was later to take, it was never to give way to mere estrangement. Freedom from certain sorts of connections, however, was another strong need, no less real for being contradictory: the Emersonian preachings were just now reënforcing it vigorously in Whitman's mind; and besides, even if the growing awareness of his own triumphant "identity" had not by this time drawn a kind of circle round him, Whitman could hardly have applied his energies much longer to the swirl of practical politics. As he knew, his task lay elsewhere. "What I really had to give out," he later said, "was something more serious, more off from politics and towards the general life." The year of Van

Buren's last candidacy was the deciding year. In the fall of
1848 Whitman was not only willingly but eagerly serving
the Free Soil Party in Kings County by acting on its general committee and editing the *Freeman;* meanwhile, however, the home-made notebooks he had taken to carrying
round with him were slowly being filled with experimental passages of a new and extraordinary sort of verse which
neither Judge Johnson nor Mr. Alden Spooner—both Free
Soil leaders in Brooklyn and both honorable men—knew
anything of; and this meant, among other things, that
Walt Whitman was acting in his last routine capacity as a
politician.

At this crisis in his personal life, moreover, the murky
dynamics of American political history would themselves
certainly have worked a great change in Whitman's conduct. The new party he had fought for on the *Freeman,*
it is true, was encouragingly successful at the polls: thousands of Northerners cast their votes for Van Buren and
Adams, and by throwing the state of New York away from
Cass and the Democrats, they had at least the satisfaction of
punishing the Hunkers and giving the presidency to Zachary
Taylor and the Whigs. Just as the new lines, however,
began to be sharply drawn, the whole situation was confused anew by the controversy over California and New
Mexico, and by the time the country could draw its breath,
as it seemed, over the Compromise of 1850 which "settled"
that controversy, the Free Soil Party had passed its premature zenith. It was a short period of unwholesome and portentous calm that followed; hour by hour the political
humidity was increasing, and a few men with barometric
minds did not fail to foresee the electric storm that was
sooner or later to break. But the people in general were

46

relatively untroubled. Whitman was one of the dwindling number of loyal Free Soilers who voted for John P. Hale of New Hampshire in the dull campaign of 1852; a Democratic Party that could cynically put forward Franklin Pierce, the Yankee friend of the great planters, had no power to draw him back into the fold—and he was not likely, at this late hour, to vote Whig. When, in 1855, the new Republican Party, which had appeared in the West a year earlier, was becoming a force in New York politics, Whitman was publishing the first edition of *Leaves of Grass* and viewing the whole struggle of political groups with a detachment he had meanwhile achieved.

This detachment was by no means a mere indifference to public issues: on the contrary, Whitman was to feel more strongly about such matters than he had ever felt in the days of the Bank or of Annexation. But the democrat who had once believed that the "fierce struggle" of popular politics was a spectacle "full of the most august and sublime attributes," had at last been profoundly disenchanted with the workings of the electoral machinery and the party system. Exactly what experiences produced this state of mind it is neither possible nor important to say. The chances are good that Whitman learned one unforgettable lesson from that rascally Democratic convention of 1848 at which the New York left-wingers or Barnburners were so unceremoniously shown the door. In any case the revulsion of feeling was so strong that, in an essay written after the Civil War, Whitman could say that in accounting for the great conflict "the most significant general fact" was the corruption of the party system in the preceding decades. For twenty-five years, he declared, the Democratic conventions had come to represent and be

47

made up of "more and more putrid and dangerous materials"; and in a passage lifted from an earlier unpublished
broadside of his own, he proceeded to describe the typical members of such conventions in language of singular
violence for a "caresser of life": "pimps," "malignants,"
"murderers," "kept-editors," "spaniels," "slave-catchers,"
"sponges," "crawling, serpentine men, the lousy combings
and born freedom-sellers of the earth"—such were Whitman's Old Testament epithets for the men who had made
Pierce and then Buchanan president.

The broadside from which this passage was lifted had
been called *The Eighteenth Presidency;* it had been written in 1856 for the sake of giving support to the candidacy
of the Republican, Frémont; but even if Whitman had
published it—as he was kept from doing by some unknown
consideration—the piece could have given little real comfort to Thurlow Weed or Simon Cameron or any of the
other astute managers of the Republican Party—or even to
its idealistic supporters. If Whitman was a partisan of Frémont it was in a dubious and undependable style. "Are
not political parties about played out?" asked the disillu-
sioned iconoclast who composed *The Eighteenth Presidency.* "I say they are, all round," he answered. "America
has outgrown parties; henceforth it is too large, and they
too small." "I place no reliance upon any old party," he
insisted, "nor upon any new party." Even if a new movement were to be launched under the noblest auspices, let
it only succeed politically, let it only find itself in power,
and the day of its decline will have dawned: at once the
corruptionists will flee from the old parties and rush toward it—"and it ripens and rots with the rest." How much
intuitive truth there was in all this is now evident enough;

48

and it might have meant that Whitman was beginning to understand the real function of parties in a merely political democracy; to see, with men like Theodore Parker and Albert Brisbane, that in a society divided among economic classes, partisan electoral factions will necessarily serve the compelling and dominating interests. Intimations of such realities Whitman may indeed have had, but at this middle stage they were faint and fugitive at the best: he was not yet inclined to push his disenchantment to so fundamental a point; and he was content to draw the Emersonian conclusion that was even then a classic. "Platforms," he decided, "are of no account. The right man is everything."

The pronouncement pays no tribute to Whitman's acumen in this phase, but a certain cynicism about party platforms was far from unnatural in the middle fifties, and the right men, it is certainly true, were hardly dominating American politics in the years of the great surrender called the Compromise. To suppress the discussion of agitating questions was as much the aim of Northern politicians who lived off the two big parties as it was of the Southern oligarchs. Lowell had satirized these "Northern men with Southern principles"—these "dough-faces"—in his crackling stanzas on John P. Robinson and on the Pious Editor, and Whittier was to lampoon them with an even deeper indignation in his lines about "the mean traitor, breathing northern air"—

> *With nasal speech and puritanic hair,*
> *Whose cant the loss of principle survives,*
> *As the mud-turtle e'en its head outlives;*
> *Who, caught, chin-buried in some foul offence,*
> *Puts on a look of injured innocence,*
> *And consecrates his baseness to the cause*
> *Of constitution, union, and the laws.*

49

To these gentry Whitman too devoted his by no means negligible powers of invective. The compromise measures were under debate in the Senate when the late editor of the *Freeman* sent his "Song for Certain Congressmen" to Bryant's *Evening Post*. The piece—which was later to be called "Dough-Face Song"—is in this vein:

> *Principle—freedom!—fiddlesticks!*
>   *We know not where they're found.*
> *Rights of the masses—progress!—bah!*
>   *Words that tickle and sound;*
> *But claiming to rule o'er "practical men"*
>   *Is very different ground.*
>
> *Beyond all such we know a term*
>   *Charming to ears and eyes,*
> *With it we'll stab young Freedom,*
>   *And do it in disguise;*
> *Speak soft, ye wily dough-faces—*
>   *That term is "compromise."*

A few days after these rather crudely Biglovian stanzas appeared—for Bryant had welcomed and printed them—Daniel Webster arose ponderously in the Senate and, with his hand held out amicably and reassuringly to the delegation from Dixie, delivered his Seventh of March speech. The spokesman for the Cotton Whigs had now said his say, and the fugitive slave might know what was in store for him. Everyone remembers the manner in which Whittier expressed his throe of disappointment on hearing of the "great refusal," but almost no one remembers the magniloquent lines entitled "Blood Money"—his first published free verse—which Whitman dedicated (in the *Tribune*) to the incident that inspired "Ichabod"; or the bitter poem called "The House of Friends" with which, again in

the *Tribune,* he returned a few months later to the attack
on the

Doughfaces, Crawlers, Lice of Humanity. . . .
Muck-worms, creeping flat to the ground. . . .
All loves, all hopes, less than the thought of gain.

These were his sentiments at the beginning of the fifties:
before the decade was over, Whitman was to extend his
contempt for the politics of manipulation and evasion to
even higher dignitaries than Congressmen. The presidency
itself, under Fillmore, Pierce, and Buchanan, had now become so unmistakably a tool in the hands of slave-holders
and their Northern allies—Cotton Whigs or Democratic
spoilsmen—that Whitman could later speak of those three
administrations as "so far our topmost warning and shame."
"Never," he said, "were publicly display'd more deform'd,
mediocre, snivelling, unreliable, false-hearted men." One
of these men was the worthy whom Emerson had called
"that paltry Franklin Pierce," and in the open letter to
Emerson which Whitman printed in the 1856 edition of
his poems, the younger man spoke of Pierce in even stronger
terms: "I think," he said, "there can never be again upon
the festive earth more bad-disordered persons deliberately
taking seats, as of late in These States, at the heads of the
public tables—such corpses' eyes for judges—such a rascal
and thief in the Presidency." Bad as Pierce's administration was, however, the following was the administration of
which Bryant said that it was "the most extravagant and
the most corrupt the country has ever known"; and it was
of Buchanan chiefly that Whitman was probably thinking
when he wrote, in the little poem "To the States, To Identify the 16th, 17th, or 18th Presidentiad":

51

Who are they as bats and night-dogs askant in the
*   capitol?*
What a filthy Presidentiad! . . .
Are those really Congressmen? are those the great
*   Judges? is that the President?*

By the time this poem appeared the Republicans were
about to gather for their second national convention at
Chicago and there to nominate Abraham Lincoln for the
presidency: the "brooding year" was about to hatch its
violent offspring of insurrection and civil strife. In spite of
the Finality Men who, like Hawthorne, had persuaded
themselves that the Compromise had quieted all sectional
agitations forever, the conflict of interests had proved to
be deeper and harsher than they had wished to believe;
and it was now unappeasable. The Southern oligarchs had
not only challenged the Northern farmers and workers who
were determined to keep the territories open to Free Soil
and Free Labor; they had not only flouted the hopes of
these classes by defeating one Homestead Bill after another; they had also declared war on Northern capital by
continuing to resist its demand for a protective tariff, for
centralized banking, for "sound money," for generous im-
migration laws, and for government subsidies to shippers
and railroaders; and by threatening secession they had
threatened to tear away from the national sovereignty the
great Southern market for Northern goods. In these ways,
as modern historians have shown, they had aroused and
antagonized a class that was to be more than their match
in a final show-down, and when the Republican Party,
between Frémont's and Lincoln's candidacies, succeeded
in bringing farmers, workers, industrialists, merchants, and

bankers together on a single platform, the hour of the plantation system's doom was about to strike.

To Whitman, who habitually mingled in almost un-analyzable fusion a sense of the economic needs of the plain people with an ingenuous political idealism, the out-lines of this essential struggle between agrarian and indus-trial plutocrats were never to be evident—as indeed they were not to be for any of his literary contemporaries. Cer-tainly he had no conscious or unconscious fellow-feeling with the industrialists. The banking system that had tri-umphed under Tyler he had always supposed to be an un-mitigated good, and though he seems never to have spoken on the subject, we can be sure that the defiantly low tariff of 1857 would have seemed to this life-long free trader a triumph of true principles. It was not through the motives that animated Jay Cooke or John Murray Forbes or A. T. Stewart that Whitman and the common men and women he felt with became passionate supporters of Lincoln and the Union cause. For him the great events of the fifties meant an almost continuous conflict between two power-ful feelings increasingly hard to reconcile—his hatred of a more and more aggressive slave system and his religious sentiment for the integrity of the national Union. It was probably not until the spring days when Lincoln was issu-ing his call for volunteers—not until the days when, as George Ticknor put it, the heather was on fire—that these two emotions were finally fused into one.

The outcome of the Mexican War had demonstrated to Whitman, as to thousands of people in his class, that the slave power was now on the aggressive; and we have seen how he acted in consequence. The adoption of the Fugi-

53

tive Slave Law and the attempts to enforce it, under Fillmore and Pierce, had fanned this new indignation to a
leaping flame. The "filthy enactment," as Emerson called
it—the enactment which, as he said, "was made in the nineteenth century by people who could read and write"—enraged Whitman as it did the man he called master, and he
might certainly have said with Emerson, "I will not obey
it, by God." We know of no overt action Whitman may
have taken in expression of that feeling, but *The Eighteenth Presidency,* among other things, tells us what his
feeling was. "As to what is called the Fugitive Slave Law,"
he there wrote, "insolently put over the people by their
Congress and President, it contravenes the whole of the
organic compacts, and is at all times to be defied in all
parts of These States, South or North, by speech, by men,
and, if need be, by the bullet and sword."

Not chiefly, moreover, because the law meant injustice
to the fugitive Negro himself: that question, wrote Whitman in certain manuscript notes, he would defer for the
present. The real odiousness of the law was its ruthless in-
vasion of the rights of Northern white men—its empower-
ing of officers from the slave states to enter free communities
in the North and there to "decide at their pleasure, or the
pleasure of a petty commissioner, which man among us
has right to his liberty and which has not." This was a very
different matter, he felt, from asking Northern Unionists
to put up with slavery in states where the Constitution had
recognized its existence; it was asking and indeed coercing
Northern citizens to degrade themselves into slave-hunters
and informers. "Is this a small matter?" asked Whitman.
"The matter of tea and writing paper was smaller." Yet
the hated law, under Franklin Pierce of New Hampshire,

54

was to be rigorously enforced. In 1854 the escaped slave, Anthony Burns, was arrested by federal officers in Boston, tried at the Court House, and ordered back to slavery by a Yankee federal commissioner. When this shameful news came to him, said Henry Thoreau at Framingham a few weeks later, the remembrance of his country spoiled his walk. The same event stirred Whittier to write "The Rendition":

> And, as I thought of Liberty
> Marched handcuffed down that sworded street,
> The solid earth beneath my feet
> Reeled fluid as the sea.

On Whitman, too, as on those passionate New Englanders, the incident had the effect of a personal outrage: his version of it, printed the following year in *Leaves of Grass*, was "A Boston Ballad"—a poem which evoked the spectral re-appearance in Boston streets, while Anthony Burns was being led along in handcuffs, of the Revolutionary heroes of the old city who had fought against comparable wrongs. To those "Yankee phantoms" the poet represented himself as crying out sardonically:

> If you blind your eyes with tears you will not see
> the President's marshal,
> If you groan such groans you might balk the gov-
> ernment cannon.

The Fugitive Slave Law was monstrous enough, and it had been followed, a few days after the arrest of Anthony Burns, by the repeal of the Missouri Compromise—by the adoption, that is, of the Kansas-Nebraska Bill and the opening up of territories hitherto presumably free, to the militant expansion of slavery. It was probably of this Bill that Whitman was thinking when he charged the Pierce ad-

ministration with "the basest outrage of our times": the
Southern leaders were now bent not only on suppressing
the Homestead Bill—"that important and every way com-
mendable project," as Whitman was later to call it—they
were bent on resisting the attempts of middle-class and
working-class Northerners and Westerners to make homes
for themselves in the national territories free from the competition of slave labor. The "national tendency," as Whitman called it, toward populating the territories with "free
work-peoples"—"a tendency vital to the life and thrift of
the masses of the citizens"—was being "violently put back
under the feet of slavery." Yet a Democratic administration was conniving with the plantation leaders through
every resource at its command, and the Democratic administration that succeeded it was to prove, if possible,
even more supine in its surrender to the Southern extremists. The sense of this, of course, was what had led thousands of Northern workers, farmers, and small business-
men to flock to the Republican Party in 1856; and it was
his fellow-feeling with them that led Whitman to support
and to vote for Frémont. Less than a year later, however,
the Kansas question was still unsettled; Buchanan was tem-
porizing, just as Pierce had done, with the "arrogant Slave-
ocracy"; and in this situation Whitman declared editorially
in the Brooklyn *Times* that, if Kansas should even now
become a slave state, "the 'national democracy' will be
thenceforth a worse wreck than any that lies buried in the
sands along Barnegat."

Such were his emotions in the presence of civil war in
the territories: to him, apparently, the whole course of the
Free State men in Kansas, though not John Brown's ter-
rorism, was what it should have been. Meanwhile, how-

ever, he was far from being unaware of the catastrophic potentialities in this whole conflict, and far from being phlegmatic in his attitude toward them. If any political feeling was stronger in Whitman than his devotion to political and social freedom, it was his profound devotion to the idea of the Union. The depth and the fervor of this sentiment it may not be easy for us now to recapture: it has ceased to be a powerful imaginative conviction with Americans because the fact it stands for has ceased to be challenged and the achievement it represents is no longer in the process of being realized. Whitman had been born at a time when the achievement was a fresh memory and by no means even then uninterestingly secure: he was only a year old when the Missouri Compromise averted for a time the menace of disruption, and he was a small boy working on the *Long Island Star* when South Carolina, rebelling against the "tariff of abominations," took the first, and of course abortive, steps toward secession. These were among the reasons why the Union seemed so great a good to the men and women among whom he grew up: on it the status of America among the nations of the world seemed almost wholly to depend, and they could hardly imagine a social or political hope for the future that would not have been crushed by dismemberment. Beneath this feeling lay a solid bed of economic truth: it was a fact that the middle-class democratic order on which their well-being rested, would certainly have been terribly shaken and perhaps compromised for generations by the breakdown of federalism. In their imaginations, however, as in Whitman's, the Union was no mere pragmatic expedient; it was a high political ideal, and since history was at work on that side, it deserved to be.

57

There had been no time, since he had been conscious of such matters at all, when Whitman would not have shared the sentiment that, in the face of South Carolina's threat of nullification, Andrew Jackson had expressed in words that were to become so text-bookishly familiar: "The UNION! it must and shall be preserved!" The foolish violence of Whitman's thrusts at the Abolitionists was largely inspired by an honest belief that their agitation, if undiscouraged, might eventually lead to disunion; and when, during his editorship of the *Eagle,* the debates in Congress over the Wilmot Proviso elicited new threats of secession, he could scarcely express the horror this outlook aroused in him. "This Union dissolved?" he cried. "Why the very words are murky with their own most monstrous portent!" His fingers, he said, almost revolted from tracing the words that were being flippantly turned over in the mouths of some men as involving a contingency that might come to pass. In Whitman's mind there was a real sacrilege in this mere discussion of the rights and wrongs of disunion: for him there was simply no question at all about "the sacredness of the *bond of union of these States.*" On that bond, it seemed axiomatic to him, depended "quite all the happiness that we enjoy, which springs from the political institutions of our country." Far from dying down as time went on, this sentiment became, if anything, more vehement: in the gloomy days of Buchananism, Whitman could speak of "devilish disunion"; and years later, attempting to express his reverent sense of Abraham Lincoln's personality, he could say that among the virtues which formed "the hard-pan of his character" was a new virtue, "unknown to other lands," namely "UNIONISM, in its truest and amplest sense."

58

With these feelings, Whitman could only look on with anxiety, during the fifties, at the growing virulence of sectional controversy; and as menacing talk of secession became more and more the order of the day, undoubtedly he shrank from the prospect of pushing even the fight for free soil to the last ditch. He could hardly have been more profoundly dedicated to the Union than Lincoln was, yet his dread of disunion was so intense that he would probably have considered paying a price to forestall it that Lincoln would not have paid. He had supported Frémont in 1856 despite the noisy threats in the South of what would happen if the Black Republicans were victorious at the polls; yet two years later, in an atmosphere still more heavily charged, he seems to have wavered in his already gingerly and tentative loyalty to the new party. Seward, at Rochester, had spoken bluntly of the irrepressible conflict; Lincoln had spoken at Springfield of what would befall a house divided against itself; Douglas and Lincoln had conducted their debates in the Illinois campaign, and Douglas had been reëlected Senator, when Whitman expressed in the Brooklyn *Times* a curiously symptomatic hope that the Little Giant would yet save the country from disaster. He knew that Douglas had voted for the Fugitive Slave Law; that he had engineered the repeal of the Missouri Compromise; that he had taken his stand even on the odious Dred Scott decision. Yet so strong were Whitman's old Unionist emotions that he could even now persuade himself that Douglas might organize "a great middle conservative party, neither proscribing slavery, like Seward, nor fostering it, like Buchanan." And he could hint that such a freakishly "neutral" party would have his support.

It says little for Whitman's acuteness as an observer that,

59

in 1858, he should have imagined so evasive a program to be feasible, but of course he would have considered it not as evasion but as a desperate measure to be taken in the face of possible catastrophe. Just how far he was really willing to push neutrality the events of the next few years were abundantly to show. He ceased to write for the *Times* in the summer of 1859, and we cannot trace as closely as we could wish the movement of his sentiments through the lowering months that ensued. In any case, the outcome of events in the next two years was to indicate unmistakably the general direction in which they had moved. In his view of slavery Whitman may have been guilty of the most startling inconsistencies, but one subject, as we have seen, never appeared to him to be open to debate: it was the subject of Union; and nothing could be easier to imagine than his emotions on that April night when, after listening to an opera at the Academy on Fourteenth Street, Whitman wandered down Broadway on his way to the Brooklyn ferry, heard the loud shouts of the newsboys, and saw them, as they came up the street, rushing from side to side with even more energy than usual. The great news that occasioned all this, as he learned after he had bought an "extra" and stepped into the blazing light of the lamps at Niblo's to read it with the rest of the crowd, was the news of the firing on Fort Sumter; and Whitman was never to forget the silence with which the group of thirty or forty men received it and, after standing a minute or two under the lamps at midnight, dispersed. The rebel troops of South Carolina had fired on the "thick-sprinkled bunting," and Whitman had all the sensations of a man who has just heard of a peculiarly atrocious matricide.

Toward many of the clear and many of the clouded is-

sues of his age Whitman had had, and was to have, the
most contradictory attitudes; but the single great revolutionary situation he was ever to be involved in, found him
wholly at one with himself and the dominant purposes of
his social world. For no other Northern writer was the
crisis of what he called the Secession War to be so profound an experience: no other was to identify himself so
absorbingly and so personally as he with the whole life and
ordeal of his people. Beside Whitman, of course, an older
man like Hawthorne and a younger man like Mark Twain
seem lifelessly apathetic; but even Emerson and Lowell,
Whittier and Bryant seem cool and a little detached beside
the author of *Drum-Taps*. A shade or two more responsive
than any of them, despite his "phlegm," to the specific appeal of public and historic crises of this sort, Whitman felt
that the Civil War was, for him, far from being merely a
political issue; it was a life-and-death struggle on the outcome of which the prosperity of his personal life and his
mission as a poet somehow hinged; and he was to look
back upon it as the culminating event not only of the century in America but of his own career: "the most profound
lesson," as he said, "of my life." His whole book, he was
later to declare strangely—for the bulk of it had been written by 1860—"revolves around that Four Years' War,
which, as I was in the midst of it, becomes, in *Drum-Taps*,
pivotal to the rest entire." It is not a very objective de-
scription of the real unity of *Leaves of Grass*, but it says
volumes for Whitman's feeling both then and later. So
strong as this was his loathing of the idea of separatism; so
strong his conviction that, as he said years afterward, the
Negro was not the chief thing: "the chief thing was to stick
together."

61

Without bewilderment like Hawthorne's, or pacifist reservations like Whittier's, or indifference like young Clemens's; without regret for the means to be used, or awareness of the pragmatic and even sordid accompaniments, Whitman gave himself emotionally to the Union cause as he had never given himself to any other. Rancor was not for him a natural quality of feeling, and his occasional lapses into it were mostly transitory; but, though he never fell into the Northern habit of vilifying the great mass of the Southern people, his hatred of the men who had planned and carried through secession, the political leaders of the Confederacy, did certainly amount to a settled rancor. Whitman had much earlier pointed out how small a class it was that really profited by slavery, even in the South, and of this small class he knew very well that the extremists were not the whole. To him, however, these few men were simply "villains"; a "banditti [*sic*] of scoundrels that have stuck themselves up there [at Richmond] as a 'government' "; and long afterward he was to say that he knew of no parallels in history for the "dark, low, mean, damnable methods they pursued to break up the country." Speaking of Jefferson Davis, for example, Whitman once observed to Traubel that he did not begrudge the man his eventual freedom from imprisonment or execution, but he added that he did not forget, either, that the rattlesnake and the asp could not help being the rattlesnake and the asp. Against the disloyal men of the North, the successors of the dough-faces, the Copperheads, he naturally felt almost as strongly: in a war-time letter to one of his soldier friends, in fact, he declared that he could have more personal good will for Lee and his fighting men than for the Copperheads; he rejoiced too when, in the New York elections of 1863, the Copperheads, as he said, "got flaxed out handsomely"; and for all his belief in civil liberties, Whitman probably acquiesced without much reluctance in their suppression by Lincoln's government.

His emotions during the great contest could be thus unified, thus unmixed, because, as we have seen, he had ignored the prosaic play of economic interests that, working below the ideal impulsions, had brought the contest on. For him it was as if a tariff on iron or hemp or cotton-goods, or a sound currency, or immigrant contract labor, or land-grants for railroad-building did not exist. That realistic considerations such as these could influence a Republican Congress or a Secretary of the Treasury, even in the "arm'd year—year of the struggle," was of less than no significance to Whitman. For him it was a war, as he wrote in later years, "for a bare idea and abstraction—a mere, at bottom, heroic dream and reminiscence"; and far from imagining that pragmatic motives could be decisively at work, had he not, in such poems as "Beat! Beat! Drums!" and the "Song of the Banner at Daybreak," specifically welcomed the outbreak of hostilities because it would demonstrate to all men how little the "flapping pennant" stood for mere chaffering, mere thrift and revenue, and how truly for "an idea only"? "Are beds prepared," he cried,

> Are beds prepared for sleepers at night in the houses?
> no sleepers must sleep in those beds,
> No bargainers' bargains by day—no brokers or specu-
> lators—would they continue? . . .
> Then rattle quicker, heavier drums—you bugles wilder
> blow.

As it happened, the bugles and the drums not only did not discomfit or distract the bargainers and the speculators

63

but, on the contrary, provided a martial accompaniment for such a lively dance of unscrupulous profiteering as the land had never known before. The years of the war, once the slump of the first few months was superseded, were to be years of intense prosperity in the North, and, as a conservative historian has said, it was a "class-prosperity," absorbed by "parasites who fattened upon the necessities of the Government and the sacrifices of the people."

While Whitman's young artisan friends and his own brother, George Whitman, were enlisting in the Fifty-First or some other New York regiment, and going into camp along the James or the Rappahannock, the shoddy-contractors and the meat-packers and the arms-dealers were driving their excellent bargains with the War Department; the speculators in gold were gambling on every set-back to the Union arms; and the iron industry, the wool trade, and the stock market were heaping up fortunes in the hands of a few unwarlike citizens. Wages were rising, it is true, but prices were soaring steadily and unapproachably beyond them, and in this sense the classes that mainly fought the war were also the classes that were paying for it. There was some justice in the bitter scoff that it was "a rich man's war and a poor man's fight," and when, in the dark months after Fredericksburg, the government sought to replenish the thinning ranks of the armies by means of a Conscription Act, it drew the class lines frankly and even cynically by providing for a large exemption fee from the draft. By this time Whitman was himself living in Washington, but somehow all these sordid contradictions were mercifully hidden from him, and he wrote to his brother Jeff that he hoped and prayed from the bottom of his heart that the government would carry out the Conscription Act and enroll every man in the land. He seems not to have observed the ugly gap between mere enrollment and actual conscription.

There were thousands of men in the Northern states, however, who could not find three hundred dollars each to pay a substitute, and who therefore did see that gap: their resentment soon began to make itself ominously heard, and the following summer it came to a terrible climax in the draft riots in Whitman's own Manhattan. When news of these insurrectionary and blood-stained riots first reached him in Washington, his deep democratic instincts revealed themselves in a quiet suspension of judgment; and in the midst of unmeasured denunciations of the rioters, he remained silent, as he wrote his mother, "partly amused, partly scornful": he could not, he said, feel it in his heart "to abuse the poor people, or call for a rope or bullets for them." Yet there was another side to the case, and it is true that self-seeking and treasonable men—ruthless saboteurs of the federal government's program—had exploited an honest indignation for their own obstructive ends; and that what began as a justifiable demonstration had quickly fallen into reckless, even criminal hands and degenerated into a wanton and bloody *émeute*. Inevitably Whitman came to know of this, and a month later he wrote that, when he found out what it had really been, he felt that it was the devil's own work all through. "I guess," he added, "the strong arm will be exhibited this time up to the shoulder." His guess was well-founded: on the day after he wrote this letter, there were said to be thirty thousand troops in New York to police the resumption of the draft. A government engaged in a mortal struggle, and hard pressed on every front, could hardly be expected not to

65

resort to desperate measures; and Whitman's hatred of the pro-Southern Vallandighams and Fernando Woods, the Copperheads who in their way had helped to bring on the riots, was both a natural and a warrantable emotion. But the rankly unjust provision for exemption from the draft was not repealed, and the whole series of events had no influence, at the time or later, on Whitman's understanding of the Civil War.

He neither saw nor, given all the circumstances, could have seen the "second American revolution" in fine historical perspective. Imaginatively speaking, who can wholly regret it? The interlocking of "real" and "ideal" in human history is an intricate one at best, and if Whitman might conceivably have written greater poems for having seen the dreadful struggle in a somewhat sharper and truer light, it is far more likely that Walt Whitman of Brooklyn, in the early eighteen-sixties, would in that event have written no poems at all. He would have had neither the impetus nor the audience that are indispensable. His role at the moment had to be the role of Tyrtaeus or Taillefer: it could not possibly be that of Amos or Juvenal, even if Whitman's gifts had lain in that quarter. Otherwise he might of course have discerned all the forces, humane and self-interested both, that were implementing the leadership of Abraham Lincoln: if so, it is barely imaginable that he might have written a more durable poem than any he did write. What is quite certain is that he would not have written *Drum-Taps*, would not have written "When Lilacs Last"; and after historical analysis has said its legitimate say, such pieces as these remain ultimate facts. American literature is almost certainly the richer and not the poorer because Lincoln was for Walt Whitman simply the

66

"large sweet soul" that he venerated—and because the other elements were in accordance.

He had earned the right, so far as it could be earned, to ignore all the less ideal aspects of the Civil War; to believe it a war, as to many men it was, for a bare idea and abstraction. He had earned it during those excruciating years in Washington when, week after week, and especially on the days that followed the great slaughters in Maryland and Virginia, the streets that led up from the wharves on the river and on to the hospitals, became somber pathways for the long processions of ambulance-wagons filled with wounded and dying men. What the stock-market reports or the *Congressional Globe* said on those days it is unlikely that Whitman knew. He was occupied and in fact engrossed in other ways. He would do his journalist's stint or his clerical jobs at a government bureau in the morning; and then, after bathing and putting on clean clothes and having a meal, he would fill his pockets with sweet crackers, oranges, writing-paper, packages of tobacco, or what not, and with "as cheerful an appearance as possible" set out for Armory Square or elsewhere on his round of visits to the hospital-wards. Our thought of Whitman in this whole connection, after moving among various realities, may well come back in the end to the picture of him as, passing from cot to cot, he distributes his homely gifts to dying or convalescent soldiers, or sitting among them gives declamatory recitations or plays with them "an amusing game called the game of twenty questions." The last image of all, however, ought to show him engaged, not in these genial activities, but in some grimmer office at the bedside of a desperately sick or wounded man, or even in those final attentions through which he becomes wholly

67

and solemnly identified, as he wanted to be, with the people who were his people.

IV

For the two decades or so that immediately followed Appomattox, three men may be taken as representative, in their feelings about the American political scene, of three half-generations of American writers. The aged skalds, the men whose boyhood memories reached back to the War of 1812, had their true spokesman in Emerson; in the Emerson whose fatalistic optimism had become so inflexible a posture as to lead his disciple, Charles Eliot Norton, to say that "if by mistake he were to visit Hell he would deny its existence, or find it what he believes it, still the abode of good and the realm of order." The surface of an optimism such as this was not likely to be ruffled or broken by nasty ephemerids like the Tweed Ring or Crédit Mobilier, and the true quality of Emerson's set smile, among the obscenities and the stenches of the Gilded Age, can only be touched off by some such image as Norton's. Henry Adams, on the other hand, a whole generation younger, could by no means accept the march of events so blandly. For him the evil aspect of politics on the Potomac or the Hudson was a far more serious matter, and even in the late sixties he knew, as he was later to say, that Grantism had "cut short" the life he had laid out for himself in the future: "the country might outlive it," he realized, "but not he."

Halfway between these generations stood Whitman, who could neither enjoy nor suffer quite the clear-cut emotions of either. The younger writers—Henry Adams, Mark Twain, Henry James—could take refuge in defeatism, ribaldry, or exile. The older men—Emerson, Whittier, Longfellow, Bryant—could sit in the sunlight along the wall, confiding in that happy future toward which the Flood of Years, as they had little doubt, was moving. For the men who were still in their prime—for Lowell, for Melville, for Whitman—the spectacle of Grantism and what followed it could be neither so fatal as it was to their juniors nor so indifferent as to their elders. To Melville, it is true, the worst had already happened, and few things could have been less important to him than the fact that Chester A. Arthur or any other spoilsman was his chief at the New York Customhouse; yet the Civil War had roused in Melville a new interest in the fate of his countrymen, and this can only have been blasted by the sequel. For Lowell the seventies and eighties meant a mild vacillation between the official complacencies of a diplomat and occasional twinges of the ostensibly healed radicalism of his youth. Closer than either of them to the hubbub of the Gilded Age, Walt Whitman was divided, more strikingly than ever before in his career, between genial acceptance and troubled repudiation.

It was not quite an anguished conflict that went on in his spirit as he sat at his desk in the Attorney General's office looking out at the hills of Arlington or, later, sat patiently in his invalid's arm-chair at Camden. That kind of conflict had never been a habit with him, and it was no time now for him to succumb to it. The great fund of placidity in his nature fortified him against such sharp internal strife, at least over questions of that order; and the large, loose, shadowy Transcendentalism that more and more possessed his mind, was an almost—but never quite —inexhaustible opiate. The War itself, moreover, had been for Whitman one of those prolonged and absorbing emotional experiences that a whole lifetime is not too long to digest: it would have been extraordinary if he had come out of it with enough resilience for a series of renewed and violent emotions. Ill health, moreover, descended upon him within less than a decade; and for all these reasons his conflicts of political feeling and opinion were mainly of a low-pitched and bearable sort. A real battle, nevertheless, did go on in his mind, and there was intellectual drama in its ebb and flow.

The War had proved triumphantly, he felt, that the country could weather the most terrible of political storms; and the good burgher in Whitman, collaborating with the good Emersonian in him, was willing now to let his muscles relax and believe that all serious dangers were past. The facile affirmations that lay so near the surface of his mind had hardly before been exercised so incongruously as in the midst of the post-war grossnesses. Late in the winter before Grant's first election he wrote to Moncure Conway from Washington that American politics were in an unusually effervescent condition, and that at a distance they might seem to offer certain alarming and portentous signals: "yet we old stagers," he went on to say, "take things very coolly, & count on coming out all right in due time." The next eight years—with their long list of knaveries, scandals, and exposures—might have drenched the optimism of many an old stager as well as that of Henry Adams, and in fact they did not pass over Whitman's head, as we shall see, without effect. Yet at the end of those two raffish terms of President Grant's he could still say, in a new preface to his book, that the United States was henceforth to enter upon its real history, "the way being now . . . clear'd of death-threatening impedimenta, and the free areas around and ahead of us assured and certain, which were not so before." The way ahead was certainly cleared for someone, in that year of the centennial of our freedom, but what could be more ironic than Whitman's thinking it was for him and his like?

He had early imbibed a Jacksonian regard for the office and even the person of the president, and this, after suffering complete suspension under Pierce and Buchanan, had come to life again with new emotional overtones at the touch of Abraham Lincoln. It was now to take forms of which the innocence is not easy to overstate. He could certainly have no great respect for Andrew Johnson as a person—Johnson who, he told Traubel, was "without brains, without conscience"—but of course he had never been biased toward Radical Republicanism at any point: he had been a Jacksonian too long to sympathize now with the wavers of the bloody flag; and once the War was over, his old moderatism began to reassert itself in his hostility toward Stevens, Wade, Sumner, and the other Radicals, and toward their attempts to concentrate all power in Congress. He was never to be a rigorous Reconstructionist. He "went," as he said in a newspaper interview, "for general amnesty and oblivion to secessionists"; he opposed, too, the extension of the suffrage to Negroes; and all this made him, oddly enough, a partisan of Andrew Johnson's in the famous impeachment proceedings. The real drive behind Radical Republicanism—the determination to crush the plantation power once and for all, and to consolidate, at any cost, the political and economic gains of the War for Northern business—was no more apparent to Whitman, quite naturally, than the essential drive that brought on the War had ever been.

71

As for Grant himself, it was neither as a friend of the Radicals and Stalwarts nor in any other political light, but only as a democratic hero that Whitman would allow himself to think of Johnson's successor. Disagreeable facts affected Whitman's reverence for the victor of Appomattox as little as they affected Mark Twain's. "The good, worthy, non-demonstrative, average-representing Grant"—such he thought him, not unnaturally, in the days when Johnson was still in the White House; but even two or three years later, when Grant had occupied the presidency long enough to reveal his feet of clay, Whitman could write to his mother, with amusing unction, of the mutual salutes with which Grant and he habitually greeted each other—though without personal acquaintance—as they passed in the streets of Washington. An interchange of courtesies between Shelley and Castlereagh would be only somewhat more incongruous on a merely political level, but Castlereagh, of course, was a Tory aristocrat *tout pur;* to Whitman, the plebeian Grant might easily seem to "justify," as he said, those "prairie sovereigns of the West"—the farmers of Indiana, Ohio, Illinois, and so forth—whose invisible presences he conjured up as companions for the inexpressive General as, with his term of office behind him, he set out to "promenade" round the world and to talk with kings and kaisers. With every allowance made, however, could anything but a kindly and almost willful blindness have concealed from Whitman the appalling littleness of Grant as a statesman, or have allowed him to write, after Grant's death, that astonishing line of tribute:

Man of the mighty days—and equal to the days!

72

He was of course thinking of the War when he wrote this, but with all that had intervened, might he not have struck a less strident note?

His gift, in any case, for keeping the right lobe of his brain from knowing what his left lobe was thinking, had become, with age and practice, a kind of genius; and all that was incurably childlike in his nature had always encouraged in him a guileless deference to the established fact. With his long background of practical experience, Whitman might have been expected to see that the incorruptible "reform" president who followed Grant, Rutherford B. Hayes, was simply the highly respectable representative of the protectionist and "sound money" classes; and it is hard to believe that he did not know how Hayes, for the first time in the history of the presidency, had called out federal troops, during the great railroad strikes of 1877, to put down a revolt of American workers. Howells, who was half a generation younger than Whitman, and still at this stage wholly unpolitical in his thinking, had, it is true, written Hayes's campaign biography, and had even praised in it the "promptness" with which, as governor of Ohio, Hayes had put down a strike of coal-miners. In this there is nothing in the least astonishing, but it adds to the piquancy of our whole conception of Whitman that he could have found it in his heart to praise so conservative a mediocrity as Hayes for the speeches he delivered throughout the West during the Congressional campaign of 1879. "They are shrewd, good-natur'd, face-to-face speeches," wrote Whitman ingenuously, and added that, though he had heard them criticized for a want of dignity, "to me they are just what they should be."

73

Meanwhile, our picture of the benignant Whitman among the moral ambiguities of the Gilded Age acquires a vivid touch or two more from our glimpse of him—which we owe to his conductor friend Pete Doyle—riding up and down Pennsylvania Avenue on a horse-car in lively conversation with "an M. C. from Ohio," James A. Garfield, with whom he had struck up a friendship during the War; or from another glimpse which shows us Garfield—the president-to-be—approaching Whitman along the Avenue, raising his right arm in salute, and greeting the poet humorously with his own line of verse: "After all not to create only." If Whitman ever knew of Garfield's dubious associations, before his presidency, with Oakes Ames and Crédit Mobilier, or of his connection with those embarrassing paving-contracts in Washington, no hint of it remains in anything he said or wrote; on the other side, there is the little poem called "The Sobbing of the Bells" which he wrote after Garfield's assassination. The bells might well have sobbed inconsolably, a cynic could have remarked, at the prospect of "Chet" Arthur's now entering the White House; but on every personal ground nothing is easier to understand and respect than Whitman's genuine grief. Nevertheless, the last echo of his warm association with Garfield is surely an ironic one.

Ironic, too, considering what was to happen in the Pullman strike and the free-silver agitation after Whitman's death, was his attempt to work up in himself, now that he was a really old man, a kind of rebirth of his ancient Democratic ardors in the form of an enthusiasm for Grover Cleveland. It was not a very successful attempt, and he probably confessed his truest feeling when he observed to Horace Traubel that for Cleveland personally he cared

THE TENOR OF POLITICS

nothing; that he found him "rather beefy, elephantine."
He did care, however, he went on to say, for some of the
things Cleveland represented; and no doubt an "old stager"
who had never been a very good Republican at any time,
could not fail to be beguiled by Cleveland's gingerly movements away from a protective tariff. The free trader in
Whitman had never budged, and late in Cleveland's third
year as president he wrote a note to the New York *Herald*
to say that he wished "to heartily thank President Cleveland for his free trade message and," he added, "for his
jubilee gift to the Pope." "Thousands of America's quiet
thinkers everywhere," he declared, "will be well satisfied"
with both; and if Whitman had a regret, it seems only to
have been that Queen Victoria—for whom he more and
more professed a regard—could not also have been sent
some gift. The Queen, to tell the truth, may have been
quite content with the tariff message; but if this touch of
Whitman's seems to border on the grotesque, we can recall
—to reënforce it—a dinner of planked shad at a village
near Camden, two or three months later, at which we are
told Whitman's cronies begged him to give them a toast to
"three eminent good fellows," and he obliged them by giving them "President Cleveland, Gladstone and the Em-
peror of Germany." It was in such company that the poet
of democracy had taken, in these late years, to toasting the
American presidents; perhaps, though wholly without conscious irony, he could not have chosen a happier way of
betraying his instinctive judgment of them.

As it happens, all these quaint manifestations of Whitman's surface conformity do not really mean that he had
thrown away all his old critical weapons on the day on
which Lee had surrendered. Despite his inclination to

affirm as much and deny as little as might be, Whitman
had by no means simply shut his eyes to that political
spectacle which Henry Adams later described as "one dirty
cesspool of vulgar corruption." He might say a good word
for queens and emperors and Tory presidents, but he never
quite forgot his purpose to hold up agitation and conflict.
In one of the last poems·of *Drum-Taps,* a poem called
"Adieu to a Soldier," probably written some time after
the War was over, he had even declared that, though hïs
comrade's mission was now fulfilled by military victory, he
himself, "more warlike," and that "contentious soul" of
his were still bound on their own campaigning, and that
they, in the midst of dangers and defeats,

> *Here marching, ever marching on, a war fight out—*
> *   aye here,*
> *To fiercer, weightier battles give expression.*

Needless to say, Whitman was thinking of contests on
levels not mainly political when he wrote these lines: he
is not to be seen, moreover, in the thick of any struggle
whatever in the decades that followed; still, he thought
and spoke too much, during those years, in a drastically
critical vein to be open, like Emerson, to the charge of
finding Hell the realm of order. The War, indeed, had
hardly begun to take on the reminiscent aspect of legend,
and Grantism had only begun to reveal its unlovely fea-
tures, when Whitman's first real qualms at some of the
fruits of Northern victory expressed themselves openly and
pointedly in the strong pages of *Democratic Vistas.* The
drift of that essay, as everyone knows, is mainly ethical and
cultural; and almost its leading thought is the relative in-
significance of political mechanisms in the building up of
a full democratic life. Nevertheless, it does not pass over

in complacent silence the problems posed by the Washington of Roscoe Conkling and Schuyler Colfax or the New York of W. M. Tweed and Oakey Hall. The unprecedented shamelessness of the new corruptionism had shocked Whitman more profoundly than he usually let it be known. "I will not gloss over," he wrote in *Democratic Vistas* late in the sixties, "the appaling dangers of universal suffrage in the United States." If the phrasing of this remark betrays a lamentable confusion in the mind of so radical a democrat, only obtuseness could fail to make out what, aside from his language, the bearing of the sentence is. A later passage in the essay makes it clear enough for the most casual reader. Whitman, it appears, had had certain talks in Washington with an officer in the revenue department whose duties had taken him from city to city throughout the country for the specific sake of investigating frauds. These talks had taught Whitman a great deal. "The official services of America," he wrote, "national, state, and municipal, in all their branches and departments, except the judiciary, are saturated in corruption, bribery, falsehood, mal-administration; and the judiciary is tainted."

The "democratic" vistas opened up by such facts as these were vistas down which Whitman preferred, on the whole, not to look too curiously, but he neither could nor would wholly shut his eyes to them. A few years later, at a time when the sordid story of the Union Pacific and Crédit Mobilier was coming out chapter by chapter in Congress and incriminating one eminent statesman after another, Whitman could not conceal his dismay at

> *The merciless reports still branding forehead after*
> *forehead,*
> *The guilty column following guilty column.*

77

He called the poem that contains these lines "Nay, Tell Me Not To-day the Publish'd Shame," and characteristically he listened as little as he could to the voice of political scandal; but it is impossible to miss the note of indignant grief in his utterance here—or in another short poem belonging to the days of the Salary Grab Acts and the unsavory Sanborn Contracts. In this poem Whitman represents himself "wandering at morn" after a night of gloomy thoughts about his country:

> *Thee coil'd in evil times my country, with craft and*
> *black dismay, with every meanness, treason thrust*
> *upon thee.*

It was at about this time that Whitman's health broke down completely and that, shaken by both his illness and the intense grief of his mother's death, he found himself forced to relinquish his government post and to move in with his brother George's family at Camden. The next two or three years were the most difficult period of his life and they put the severest strain on his temperamental as well as his systematic optimism. No doubt it was partly of his own trials but it was also certainly of the discouraging omens in the public skies—for the days of the Whisky Ring exposures had intervened and the stench of corruption had come as close as it well could come to the White House itself—it was of both these things that Whitman was probably thinking when he described himself, in lines that are among the few melancholy verses he ever wrote, as

> *sitting in dark days,*
> *Lone, sulky, through the time's thick murk looking*
> *in vain for light, for hope.*

The full historical meaning of all this political squalor —in Congress, in the Cabinet, in the legislatures, in the

78

city halls—was not then and was never to be perfectly evident to Whitman; he was a man in his fifties when Grant was president, and the decisive political victory of industrial capital on the national scene had come too late for him to begin thinking in quite new terms about these questions. The terms he had long thought in were those of the old agrarian and mercantile world of his youth; he could hardly have been expected to see how inevitably the conquest of power by the industrialists would be accompanied by moral friction of just this sort. He came closer to seeing it than all but a few men of his generation, but we can understand easily enough the attempt he made to minimize, for himself and for others, the seriousness of these evils for the future; we can understand his profound reluctance to regard them as genuine portents. What could be more natural, given all the circumstances, than Whitman's remark, in a magazine article during Grant's second term (later reprinted in the 1876 preface), to the effect that the "morbid facts" of American politics and society were only "passing incidents and flanges of our unbounded impetus of growth—weeds, annuals of the rank, rich soil, —not central, enduring, perennial things"? What could be more natural than his desire to believe that, just as "worms, snakes, loathsome grubs" could be transformed to "sweet spiritual songs" by a singing thrush, so (as he speculated in a poem of the time) his country could transform, by some mysterious metabolism, the noisome facts of the present into future blessings? "Who knows," he asked,

Who knows but these may be the lessons fit for you?

Lessons of a sort they certainly were, and unwilling as Whitman was to put his mind to such questions continu-

79

ously and analytically, he by no means wholly failed to make out, in his indolent intuitive way, the real burden of those lessons. It is true that he showed a curious lack of interest, so far as we can tell, in the groping attempts of third parties, during the seventies and eighties, to give expression to popular interests and class demands which the Republicans and Democrats were either ignoring or betraying: and we look in vain for any acknowledgment by Whitman of even the existence of Liberal Republicans or Greenbackers or Greenback Laborites, to say nothing of the smaller groups on the farther left, the Working-men's Party, the Union Labor Party, or the Socialist Labor Party itself. If nothing else, he was too remote from the struggle personally to take in the real importance of these apparently negligible movements.

Negatively, however, for all he might say so genially about Grant and Hayes and Cleveland, Whitman the political malcontent was quite capable of lashing out at a Republican Party dominated by Blaines and Conklings and a Democratic Party dominated by Tildens and Lamars. "These savage, wolfish parties," he had declared in *Democratic Vistas*, "alarm me." Twenty years later, he was less alarmed than contemptuous: "these damned huckster parties" is what he called them in conversation with Traubel, remarking that real democracy and brotherhood were things that at the best they never even dreamed of. Years earlier, in *The Eighteenth Presidency*, he had relieved his mind of his moral contempt for parties and party politicians: now, however, his distrust of them was taking a sharper and more conscious form. The actual role of politics in the American economy was more evident to him, at least at moments, than it had been in the fifties.

80

The conventional parties, he once observed to his young friend, had both thrown their heritage away, "starting from nothing good and going to nothing good: the Republican party positively, the Democratic party negatively, the apologists of the plutocracy." It was during the presidential campaign of the late eighties that the old poet who had written in praise of Grover Cleveland made this surprising remark, and it was on another day of that same summer that he reënforced the sentiment on the other side by saying, "As things are the working classes, as such, belong to neither party."

These were not the kinds of things he had said thirty years earlier, and if he had said no more than this now it would be clear that he had "wandered at morn," in the evil times of the seventies, to some real effect. The lessons of the Gilded Age cannot be said to have been wholly lost on him after all. Traubel tells us of Whitman's giving him an old letter of introduction written for him, when he was looking for a job in Washington, by a man who had been mayor of Brooklyn. This person had testified in his letter, somewhat liberally it would seem, to Whitman's ardent Republicanism. "I'm afraid," said Traubel as he read it, "you're no longer 'an ardent Republican.' " The old man laughed. "I'm afraid so, too," he rejoined: "if politics keep on going from bad to worse, from worse to worse again and more of it, I'm in danger of becoming an ardent anti-Republican." An ardent Democrat, in other words, Traubel hinted. No, the alternative was enough to make him shudder. "I'll have to go unsworn," he decided, "until something worthy of my ardor turns up: Japhet in search of a father." And he seems to have been not at all without hope that something worthy of his or his juniors' ardor might sooner or later turn up. "New issues are forming," he once said, "and grave issues (among the gravest)—but they are not yet politically expressed." Just how they would ever be Whitman could not be persuaded to prophesy; on this ground, he was frankly in the dark. But of the necessity of new alignments he was quite certain. "I seem," he said, "to be reaching for a new politics—for a new economy: I don't know quite what, but for something."

"A new politics," "a new economy"—such were the linked possibilities for the American future that Walt Whitman, who had begun by glorying in the American present, was willing to contemplate in his old age. He had come a long way from the time when he had stumped for Martin Van Buren and frequented Tammany Hall and written in defense of "our good President Polk"; but his country had come still further. Not many men's lives, until the nineteenth century, have spanned such an historical arc as that which measures the space between the America of Andrew Jackson and the America of Grover Cleveland: the most plastic of minds might well have succeeded imperfectly in comprehending both. No other American writer of his generation succeeded so far as Whitman did in doing this: it testifies richly to the strength of his democratic instincts that, with all his lapses, he saw and understood so much. Certainly he saw more and more plainly as time went on how relatively superficial all merely political issues are, how largely they derive their meaning from forces that lie below and beyond them. He had never been indifferent to these homelier, more basic forces; in his fitful and contradictory way, he had grown more rather than less aware of them with the passage of time; and what he had made of them, early and late, we must now consider.

Pol issues made up of forces that lie below issues such as:

Chapter Three

WEALTH AND ILLTH

A WORLD LIT UP by torchlight parades and patriotic fire-
works; a world tumultuous with campaign speechifying
and election riots and Congressional oratory; a world dominated by lean eloquent men on platforms, by thin-lipped
knowing men in Washington offices, and at certain times
by whiskered or bearded men on horseback—such was the
world in which *Leaves of Grass* was begotten and brought
to birth. The parades and the speeches and the riots, however, were only one aspect of it: they were as characteristic
as possible, but they had less to do with making that world
what it essentially was than the din of the stock-exchange,
the clatter of pick-axes and spades on the road-beds of new
railways, the buzz of spindles and looms, and the gushing
of black geysers in the oil fields. The men on platforms, in
government offices, and on horseback dominated it more
obviously but less tellingly than certain short-spoken men
in counting-houses, in business offices, and in chambers of
commerce; and more was done to mould and transform it
in certain directors' meetings than in all the sessions of
Congress from the Sixteenth, which was sitting in Whitman's babyhood, to the Fifty-second, which was sitting
when he died. The America he "celebrated" was certainly
the America of Polk and Douglas, of Grant and Conkling;

but it was still more truly the America of John Jacob Astor and Francis Cabot Lowell, of Collis P. Huntington and Jay Gould, of Seth Luther and Andrew Cameron: its life was made what it was by the struggle over the Wilmot Proviso, the civil war in Kansas, and the machinations of William Marcy Tweed, but also, and more profoundly, by the building up of the fur trade, the opening of the textile mills at Lowell, and the construction of the Union Pacific.

So much is A B C to the modern historian, if not to the writer of literary history, and it is in this denser medium that we ought to visualize Whitman and his book as far as may be. It is one thing to know how he responded to the slogans of political factions and the demands of partisan journalism; to know where he stood in the clash of sectional interests, and how he felt in the midst of political knavery. It is another thing to know how he responded to all the appeals of a briskly expanding material economy; to know what he made of that unprecedented scene of practical construction, speculation, acquisition, and exploitation; how he judged the men who made it possible and felt about its inevitable frictions and conflicts. With what eyes did he look on at that somehow impressive spectacle of physical development, of industrial progress, of cheerful though certainly intermittent prosperity, of great fortunes and ostentatious spending and bitter poverty? Did he see any good in it? Was he in sympathy with all or any of its essential motives and impulses? How much of its blacker side did he see, and did this seem to him portentous or merely accidental? Is it possible that, on any level, he subscribed to the philosophy of business and the gospel of money-making? Did he have any respect whatever for the morality of enterprise and self-help?

If we were dealing with any of the great European writers with whom Whitman might be compared, we should know very well what the answers to these questions were, and how idle, in fact, it would be to ask them at all. A deep and settled hostility to the aspirations, the ethics, the behavior of the money-making bourgeoisie is what we come very early to expect of the romantic poets and prose-writers of the Old World, however they may otherwise vary among themselves. How much more warily one has to proceed when it is a question of any American born before the regime of Andrew Jackson we should realize beforehand, and in any case we are amusingly reminded of the necessity when, for example, in glancing through Whitman's manuscript notebooks, we come upon a casual entry such as this: "I suppose Franklin is about the fairest, and best representative man of Massachusetts—remembering also Webster, Emerson, and maybe one or two others." Surely there is something more than merely perfunctory in such a note, incidental as it is. Years before Whitman set it down, John Keats had spoken of Franklin, in a letter, as "a philosophical Quaker full of mean and thrifty maxims"; and if nothing could be more one-sided than this judgment of our greatest *philosophe,* nothing could symbolize more pointedly the verdict of the nineteenth-century literary conscience upon the morals of the "Advice to a Young Tradesman"—the morals of "industry and frugality." Beside Keats's contemptuous dictum, Whitman's brief observation seems reasonable and just, and certainly he honored Benjamin Franklin for much more than merely his canny and worldly preachments. It will not do, however, to say that Whitman's mind had never been touched by them at all. On the contrary, the individualism he cele-

85

brated was a richly composite product, and into its make-up had entered, in real though imponderable proportions, a pinch or two of the philistine dogma of self-help.

A not too painstaking reading will discover this in the pages of *Leaves of Grass* itself, but there is cruder and less debatable evidence elsewhere, for what interest it may have. The young Brooklyn editor, for example, was sometimes piquantly aware of his inheritance from Poor Richard. It was not uncharacteristic of him to quote in the *Eagle's* columns a passage from a speech to the normal students of Westfield, a speech full of sound practical advice, by Governor Briggs of Massachusetts—that same "Guverner B.," by the way, whom Hosea Biglow regarded as a sensible man. Sensible he must have been, in the almanac manner at least; and Whitman headed the Governor's quite Franklinesque remarks with the urgent line: "Young Men of Brooklyn, Look at This!" "The great element of success in life, for young people to start with," he then continued in his own person, "is, *dependence on one's self alone,* combined with reasonable perseverance." Are not these the classic accents of Samuel Smiles himself? They are echoed, at any rate, by a brief notice Whitman wrote a decade later, for the Brooklyn *Times,* of a book on *Self-Made Men* by a writer named Seymour—a book that, according to the journalistic Whitman, "should be examined and thoughtfully considered by every young and ambitious man in the ordinary ranks of life." Here if anywhere speaks in unmistakable tones the compatriot and contemporary of John Wanamaker and Cyrus Hall McCormick.

He was quite capable, at least in his practical hours as a sober newspaper-man, of preaching the gospel of industry and frugality itself. It comes somewhat startlingly, it is true, from the author of the "Song of Myself," but there in plain print, in the pages of the *Eagle*, is (for example) a tiny apologue on the subject of laziness and diligence. It is called "A Little Paragraph with a Big Moral." " 'I can't find bread for my family,' said a lazy fellow in company" —so it runs. " 'Nor I,' replied an industrious miller, 'I am obliged to *work* for it.' " Not for nothing was Walt Whitman the heir of generations of diligent Whitmans, Van Velsors, and Williamses; not for nothing was he the heir of a class morality that made sin and indolence almost synonymous. It was not a morality to which his nature was essentially cordial, but he had an extraordinary capacity for adapting himself superficially and amiably to a prevailing mode, and he could speak of such matters as these with all the lightness of the simple-hearted philistine. He never spoke of them more lightly or, so to say, more tribally than on one occasion during the first weeks after the panic of 1857. He had raised in the *Times,* on which he was then working, the question who, among the thousands stricken by that disaster, most deserved help, and had gone on to say that in normal years it was easy enough to account for the great mass of poverty and destitution even in prosperous America. "Laziness, thriftlessness, intemperance, and the importation of foreign paupers—these," wrote Whitman, "are the chief causes of the existence of such a state in a country like our own . . . where, unless under the pressure of extraordinary crisis, a comfortable living is within the reach of all." So, too, thought the McCormicks and the Wanamakers; in Whitman's youth there had been a deceptive color of truth in the idea; but reflective Americans were not, even then, etherizing themselves with such comfortable views.

Whitman had failed to listen attentively, as we shall later see, to the gloomier and more realistic utterances of such men as Orestes Brownson, Albert Brisbane, and Theodore Parker; and both early and late, when he was in his cheerful, conventional, affirmative vein, he could speak with respect and even a kind of enthusiasm about types of men and types of conduct which those other writers regarded with anxiety and distrust. Like Emerson, he had an instinctive love of the show of power: "personal force," he once said, was what he looked for; and he did not always inquire too closely into the quality and the aim of that force. It was of course in business that personal power displayed itself most characteristically and most successfully in Whitman's time and place; could he fail to be sometimes impressed by its performances in that sphere? He had been impressed by them in a certain manner, at least, as we realize when we remember that passage in *Democratic Vistas* in which he declares that he cheerfully includes in the social ideal he is there sketching "a practical, stirring, worldly, money-making, even materialistic character"; or another passage in the same essay in which, describing with unmistakable gusto the hurrying and feverish crowds in Wall Street, he dwells on "their complicated business genius," and adds in parentheses: "(not least among the geniuses)."

In the decades that witnessed, after the War was over, the unification of the oil industry, the triumph of American steel, and the building up of the great trunk lines, was it quite unnatural that an impressionable mind like Whitman's should see the tokens of genius in achievements such as these? Of course not—and yet the effect is not quite the expected one when we hear him extolling these things in-

88

directly with an eloquence which does not so much recall Benjamin Franklin as anticipate Elbert Hubbard. Take, for example, certain notes for a lecture, which Whitman planned but never delivered, for a possible Canadian audience on one of the trips he made to Canada in the early eighties. The drift of the whole lecture we can only guess at, but among other things the elderly poet would have spoken at least incidentally, it appears, of what he called "the new word," Business. This word in modern times, he would have observed, had come to dominate society as never before: "Business—not the mere sordid, prodding, muck-and-money-raking mania, but an immense and noble attribute of man, the occupation of nations and individuals (without which is no happiness), the progress of the masses, the tie and interchange of all the peoples of the earth." In ancient and medieval times, he would have gone on to say, the heroic ideal had been ruthless war and arrogant conquest: "Business," on the other hand, "shall be, nay is, the word of the modern hero." With sentiments like these ringing in our ears, it is tempting to recall a certain summer evening in Camden, at about the same time, when, sitting on the steps of the house in Stevens Street while the sultry twilight deepened, the future author of *A Message to Garcia* listened attentively to the gentle, rambling conversation of the author of *Leaves of Grass*, who was sitting in his arm-chair in the doorway.

They were both poets by disposition, vast as was the space that separated the great talent of Whitman from the little talent of Hubbard, and perhaps only the United States in those Saturnian days of Standard Oil and the Southern Pacific and Carnegie Steel could have witnessed such a collocation as this of bard and bardlet. The older

man of course had never dickered for the employment of
his gifts as the younger man was eventually to do, but he
had quite honestly condoned and even glorified, in some
of his least characteristic moments, the vices of his people.
He wished to say Yes as sweepingly as possible, and the
wish inevitably led him astray. It led him at times to pro-
nounce his blessing on a coarse acquisitiveness so foreign
to his real nature that he could only speak of it abstractly
or challengingly. "My theory," he once said blandly, "includes riches, and the getting of riches"; and many years
later, remembering with distaste the captious spirit that
had voiced itself, as he felt, in "Locksley Hall," he declared impatiently that Tennyson's poem had weakly found
fault with everything—"especially," he said, "the fact of
money's being made (as it ever must be, and perhaps should
be) the paramount matter in worldly affairs." To such
lengths a systematic benignity can easily go: it was rather
Tennyson's pessimistic grumbling than his own spontaneous feeling that dictated that sentence to Whitman. The
philistines are sped onward by such language, nevertheless.

Business, money-making, was undeniably the prime activity of the age, and Whitman the optimist, in his moments of mere impatience with fault-finding, was determined to find this activity a splendid thing. Great wealth,
against whatever background, was a fact in the real world,
and hence it too must be viewed as a manifestation of that
beneficent tendency which, according to Emerson, streams
irresistibly through the years and the centuries. "In a free
and just commonwealth," Emerson had also said, "property rushes from the idle and imbecile to the industrious,
brave, and persevering." Could Whitman fail to succumb
at times to this happy economic fatalism? to believe that

the real is in fact the rational, and that somehow good fortune and high deserts are one and the same? "All wealth,
however large," he once wrote in a defective scrap of manuscript, "is inviolable, being the result of previous [??]
and because society and individual interests are more ben-
efited by leaving it inviolable than by taking any from
excessive wealth and giving it to the poor." Here it is
hardly more than the cheerfully rationalizing pragmatism
of Adam Smith that is at work, but Whitman was capable
of rising to poetic heights in speaking of these matters. A
more loftily transcendental apology for great wealth appears in a curious passage which in 1876 formed part of
the poem called "Outlines for a Tomb" but was dropped
from it in later editions of the book. The poem is a tribute
to the great banker, George Peabody, and the passage
reads:

> Lo, Soul, the sphere requireth, portioneth,
> To each his share, his measure,
> The moderate to the moderate, the ample to the ample.

The Whitman who wrote this was hardly the individual-
ized man and poet: he was, so to say, only the generic
Whitman, vocalizing almost automatically the canons of
his class and his time. He was the same Whitman who once
said to W. S. Kennedy that Stedman had made a mistake
about him in asserting that he did not include within the
range of his sympathies "the wealthy, or so-called higher
classes"; and who remarked to Edward Carpenter: "I think
that notwithstanding all set-offs the great capitalists and
masters of private enterprise have, in America at least,
been useful."

He could say these things partly because he rejoiced in

the sight of any extraordinary capacities at work, even unideal capacities, and partly too because he had really been
exhilarated again and again, as men like Thoreau and
Melville had never been, by the great, dissonant, heady
blare of American material prosperity. He loved the bustling spectacle of physical progress with the passion not
only of a voter but of a poet; all that was bold, adventurous, strenuous, and florid in that spectacle intoxicated his
imagination:

> The superior marine, free commerce, fisheries, whaling,
> gold-digging,
> Wharf-hemm'd cities, railroad and steamboat lines in-
> tersecting all points,
> Factories, mercantile life, labor-saving machinery, the
> Northeast, Northwest, Southwest.

Reflection might tell him that all this building and bar-
tering, though certainly the necessary basis, was only the
basis for a civilized life; and he might come to see that its
operations were anything but democratic in their effects:
meanwhile, there were the wharves and the boats and the
warehouses, the mills and the mines and the fat farms; and
the pleasure that Whitman the burgher-poet took in the
sight of these things was as ingenuous, as direct, and as
profane as the pleasure that poets of simpler ages took in
the sight of lordly herds of cattle or abundant crops or the
bright wares of traders. His complicated century might
teach Whitman many second thoughts, but natively and
spontaneously he associated opulence and true well-being
in a manner that recalls the gift-giving and the palace-
building and the herd-protecting of the primitive epics
and lays.

When, for example, the young editor of the *Eagle* contemplated the vast tracts of the hardly-occupied American continent, his imagination took fire from the vision of them in the future, filled with flourishing cities, happy homes, stately public buildings, and all "the sights and sounds of national prosperity." "Thirty years from this date," he wrote, "America will be confessed the *first nation* on the earth"; and without pausing to dally with fine distinctions he went on: "We of course mean that her power, wealth, and the happiness and virtue of her citizens will then obtain a pitch which other nations cannot favorably compare with." Even now, in the forties, the omens of this fortunate culmination were not to be misread. One October morning found Whitman at Castle Garden on the Battery, wandering about among the carpenters and porters who were getting the place in readiness for the great fair of the American Institute. Spread out there on every hand were the splendid products of American agriculture and industry—big turnips and fat-looking grapes, little mountains of fine cheap cotton and worsted cloths, innumerable farming implements and wares of glass, leather, and iron —and as he viewed these things, the proud thought came to Whitman that, if ever a people had been blessed by God with inexhaustible physical resources and dowered in themselves with the enterprise necessary to develop those resources to the utmost, that people was the American. Yet the Whigs could babble about "protecting" energies such as these!

He had little patience with protectionists and still less, on one level, with the Hoseas who saw something ominous in all this national and public affluence. A decade after his visit to the Institute fair, in the summer of 1857, warnings began to be sounded in various quarters to the effect that

93

the record-breaking good times, the feverish expansion of the previous few years, could not last much longer; and that a painful day of accounting was at hand. To the editor of the Brooklyn *Times* this was nothing but lugubrious folly. "Without fear of failure," he wrote, "we venture again the opinion that, for the next year at least, our country is destined to enjoy unusual prosperity." The laborer, he declared, might rely upon an increased, not a diminished, demand for work and the manufacturer and the merchant upon increasing trade. A month later than this, however, a series of portentous landslides in the banking world echoed through the community with a dismal, inescapable sound; and even the confident editor of the *Times* did not fail to hear it. "At the same time," he wrote, "we cannot see the slightest ground for adopting the theory of the panic makers, that these isolated failures will lead to anything like a general confusion." The whole thing, he declared, was confined to the Stock Exchange anyway. Only at the end of September, when the economic ruins lay smoking all about him, did Whitman reluctantly confess that the smash was general and that nothing like it had been seen since the terrible days of '37.

He was neither much dejected nor much instructed by the difficult months that followed. For him the hard times had no such meaning as they had, for example, for Henry Thoreau, to whom they only demonstrated that justice was not to be dodged. If most of the merchants and bankers did not fail, wrote Thoreau to a friend, his faith in the laws of the universe would have been staggered; and the statement that ninety-six out of a hundred men in such businesses were sure to break down, seemed to him "perhaps the sweetest fact that statistics have revealed." There was a being in Whitman who could understand such reflections, but it was not the man who wrote editorials. This individual at least was not induced in the fifties to think critically about a system of things in which such disasters could recur as frequently as they had already done in his lifetime. So early as December of the panic year he was citing the statistics of American agricultural and industrial productivity, and observing that, in the presence of such bracing facts, Americans might well be assured that no commercial or financial catastrophe that overtook them could be "other than evanescent and temporary in its duration"; that there was "no fundamental unsoundness" in their position as a nation; and that they were justified in their "most sanguine expectations of permanent prosperity." The next summer he was pleading with his fellow-citizens of Brooklyn to see to it that the city assumed "that commanding position which rightfully belongs to her" by developing their extraordinary manufacturing facilities, by substituting "life and enterprise" for what was then "coldness and indifference," and by remembering that "perhaps" "profit and interest is the best awakener." Undismayed by a year of depression, he became apocalyptic over the day when "this great city's wharves" would be crowded with shipping and its streets "vocal with the clash of machinery."

With such habits of thought, exercised on the superficial layers of his mind, and still more, with such a capacity for taking pleasure in the sights and sounds of prosperous activity, it was inevitable that Whitman should sometimes be thrilled by the manifestations of national opulence in the lush days that followed the Civil War. The author of *Democratic Vistas* might sound the note mainly of grave alarm, but Walt Whitman the government clerk, a simpler person, could not wholly resist the general infection of high spirits over the crude facts of economic expansion and progress. There is a serious sense in which all this was wise and healthy enough on his part: it was certainly wiser and healthier, in itself, than the fruitless negations of the Thoreaus and the fastidious aversions of the Henry Jameses. It was the tough-minded and far-sighted Whitman, as well as the philistine, who insisted on welcoming the mere material advances of the country, at least for what they were worth. It is only in their tangible setting of social and class relationships that his enthusiasms have the mocking overtones that, as it is, accompany them.

We are bound to hear such overtones in many of his expressions in those later years. When, on a visit with friends in Providence, Whitman was taken through some of the great textile mills of the vicinity, his most articulate thought appears to have been that, as he said in a letter to Pete Doyle, "some of the owners are men of immense wealth"; and when he later described to Pete the new buildings on Broadway, so tall that they seemed "to almost reach the clouds," he could not refrain from noting that "some of them cost millions of dollars." All this fever of productivity was more than justifying the young prophet of the Brooklyn *Eagle;* and when, to his surprise, he was invited in the early seventies to write a poem for the fortieth annual exhibition of the American Institute in New York— the Institute whose fair he had visited that October morning a quarter of a century earlier—few commissions could have been more welcome to the singing journalist in him. His recitation of the "Song of the Exposition" seems to have been wholly satisfactory to Whitman's sponsors, as well it might have been, with its buoyant evocation of a great cathedral for the New World, a cathedral lifted not in the name of some archaic faith, but in the name of "sacred industry," and designed to illustrate, in its manifold bays and wings and "large calm halls," not the dogmas of antique or medieval superstition, but all the skillful processes of modern technology. There was grandeur and freshness in the conception, of course, and much of the feeling of that poem can well be carried over into other social circumstances; but with our sense of all the terms on which American industry was conducted in 1871, can we fail to be uncomfortably aware of unintended ironies in it?

It received, at any rate, the kind of rude commentary that history loves when, two years later, another financial panic sent a terrifying shudder through the whole economic structure; and the widespread misery of the half-decade that ensued threw a sardonic light back upon the glass and iron of Whitman's great cathedral. Those years coincided, however, with the dreariest days of his own illness and solitude in Camden; he had had his first serious breakdown late in the winter before the panic; and he was perhaps only dully and intermittently conscious—he was certainly not wholly unconscious, as we shall see—of what the crisis of the seventies meant to millions of Americans. By the time prosperity had returned, at the end of the decade, his own health had recovered a little of its old vigor; companionship and recognition had come to him in increasing measure; and his unquenchable powers of enjoyment were disposing Whitman, as much as ever, to revel in the brisk bustle of the streets, the mills, and the fields. What could be more characteristic of him, on this level, than the hobbling walk he took, along Chestnut Street in Philadelphia, one fine spring afternoon late in the seventies? "Doubtless," he said in speaking of it, "there were plenty of hard-up folks along the pavements, but nine-tenths of the myriad-moving human panorama to all appearance seem'd flush, well-fed, and fully-provided"; and quite forgetting that he was a half-paralyzed old man of sixty, he recorded with a boy's gusto his pleasure in the spectacle of peddlers selling buttons and canary-bird whistles, of rare flowers in the window of a mansion near Twelfth Street, of poultry and fish and china and costly books in the sumptuous show-windows of the fine shops. On such a day, in such a street, how easy for a Yea-sayer to forget the "social problem"!

We linger over a point that needs no great insistence, but it is a temptation to extract their full flavor from the paradoxes of Whitman's later years, and in that process neither his spontaneous affirmations nor his deliberate optimism can easily be overstated. "My belief," he said to a reporter for the New York *Sun* in the middle eighties—"my belief is that things in our time—politics, religious investigation, sociology—the movements of all are going on as well as possibly could be." Does not something in the fatuity of this remind one of the complacencies of Whitman's great admirer, Andrew Carnegie? "If asked what important law I should change," wrote Carnegie at about the same time, "I must perforce say none; the laws are perfect." Few men knew better than Whitman that the laws, in 1885, were less than perfect; and the abyss between him and the steelmaster of Homestead need not be described here. Nevertheless, in his least premeditated, least reflective outbursts of satisfaction over the state of things materially, there is more than a touch of the philistinism that struts across every page of Carnegie's *Triumphant Democracy*—a work, incidentally, which Whitman admired and of which he gave a copy to his sculptor friend, Sidney Morse.

There is something that almost beckons forward to George F. Babbitt in the Whitman who, in the eighties, rewards our hastiest glance at him. On a visit in New York he hovers, as if under a spell, about the regions of Fourteenth Street, Union Square, and lower Broadway, fascinated by the movement and color of thousands of well-dressed, good-looking people, and convinced that on such spring afternoons it is as if New York itelf were trying to show what it could do "in its humanity, its choicest physique and physiognomy, and its countless prodigality of locomotion, dry goods, glitter, magnetism, and happiness." In Boston for the first time since the days of Frank Sanborn's trial, he is struck by the city's immense material growth—"commerce, finance, commission stores, the plethora of goods, the crowded streets and sidewalks"—and notes with gratification the "evidences of copious capital." In the Middle West and the Mountain States he purrs over the impersonal facts of growth and activity as comfortably as Mark Twain was to do, very shortly afterwards, in the prosy concluding chapters of *Life on the Mississippi*. St. Louis rejoices him by its position, "its absolute wealth," and the ample spaces around it for future expansion. Lawrence and Topeka are "large, bustling, half-rural, handsome cities." The advantages of Denver—and its mint— enrapture him: "And cash! why they create it here." At the smelting works he is engrossed by the sight of workmen pouring silver into large bricks worth $2000 each; he "rolls

99

over" what he calls a sweet morsel for a poor author's pen and ink—the fact that the silver product of Colorado and Utah, with the gold product of four other states, "foots up an addition to the world's coin of considerably over a hundred millions every year."

Nothing could well be more innocent, of course, or more disinterested than this expression of pleasure in visible and tangible prosperity by the abstemious invalid of Camden. That pleasure, however, could hardly have been so unalloyed if Walt Whitman's imagination had more habitually dwelt on every aspect of the social picture of which all this brilliant prosperity was only the sunny foreground. We have yet to see with what results he did dwell on those other aspects when he was in his graver moods, but for the moment the unction of his affirmations is the salient thing. Whitman travelled through the Middle West during years when thousands of American farmers were living on the bitter terms of poverty, of tenancy, of indebtedness, and of personal degradation which his young friend Hamlin Garland was very soon to put down so pitilessly on paper; but if he ever heard of tenancy or the burden of farm-mortgages, of the exactions of railroads or the struggles of the Farmers' Alliance, he left no record of it in his jubilant remarks on the glories of the Prairie States. Enchanted—very naturally—by the vast parturient stretches of Illinois, Missouri, and Kansas, he was conscious of little but the physical stupendousness of the prairies and their apparent fruitfulness. "Even their simplest statistics," he murmured, "are sublime"; and while the passionate outcries of agrarian rebellion filled all the air, he composed a little poem about the happy states of the Great Valley:

Dense, joyous, modern, populous millions, cities and
farms . . .
. . . freedom's and law's and thrift's society,
The crown and teeming paradise, so far, of time's ac-
cumulations,
To justify the past.

"Freedom's and law's and thrift's society"! How realistic
an image is that of the Middle West or indeed of all America in the days of Populism and the Knights of Labor, of
Ignatius Donnelly and General James B. Weaver, of Albert Parsons and T. V. Powderly? It might almost be a sardonic epigraph upon that world, but of course nothing
could have come more naturally from the pen of the Camden householder who wrote letters to the *Herald* and gave
interviews to the *Sun*. Whatever implications there might
be in Whitman's bardic utterances, however widely his
imaginative sympathies might range, or wherever his intuitive perceptions might carry him—and much is still to be
said on these scores—his conscious, prosaic, and merely ha-
bitual thought about social problems never moved very
far from the hopes and needs of the middling Americans among whom he had spent his cheerful boyhood and
youth. Conscious and prosaic thought, as we shall see,
curbed him far less than it curbs most men, even most
poets; but so far as it took him, it was the thought neither
of the patriciate, so to say, nor of the proletariat; it was the
thought of the plebs; neither that of the magnates nor that
of the workers, but of the independent farmers, the shopkeepers, and the humbler professional men who had made
the Suffolk County and the Brooklyn of his early years the
kind of places they were. The Ketchams and the Brushes
of Huntington, Mr. C. E. Bill (who ran a dry-goods store

in Brooklyn), Dr. Vanderhoef (who kept a drug-store on Fulton Street), John Phillips the Brooklyn baker, Dr. Ball, Judge Johnson—these were the people with whom young Walt Whitman had the most obvious if not the most real affiliations, and these were the people to whom, on one plane, he remained consistently loyal. "The most valuable class in any community," he wrote in the fifties, "is the middle class, the men of moderate means, living say at the rate of a thousand dollars a year or thereabouts." It was certainly the class whose social ideals he most effortlessly understood.

He knew how much these people valued their small independence as producers, how tightly they clung to the sense of security and possession in what they had earned and acquired, how eager they were too that a rough equality and a general decency in standards of life should prevail among Americans; and he spoke of these things as one of them. The real culmination of our national life, he said in the days when the first great monopoly—the first "trust"—was about to be formed, would be "the production and perennial establishment of millions of comfortable city homesteads and moderate-sized farms, healthy and independent, single separate ownership, fee simple, life in them complete but cheap, within reach of all." Democracy, he had earlier said in *Democratic Vistas,* "asks for men and women with occupations, well-off, owners of houses and acres, and with cash in the bank"; and as if the number of such men and women were mounting in the late sixties, he declared that, asking for them, democracy "looks with suspicious, ill-satisfied eye upon the very poor, the ignorant, and on those out of business." The number of the very poor and certainly of those "out of business" was hardly declining in the decades that followed, and Whitman did not fail to take note, intermittently, of that fact; but there was something preternatural in the tenacity with which he could maintain a position he had once assumed, and the wreck of worlds could hardly budge him permanently from verbal allegiance to the social philosophy he had acquired as a young man. "The creation of a large, independent, democratic class of small owners," he said to Edward Carpenter in the eighties, "is the main thing"; and when a few years later Horace Traubel, to whom he had remarked that he was not satisfied with things as they were, asked him what, then, he looked forward to, Whitman answered him, without the blinking of an eyelash, quite as if Andrew Jackson and not Grover Cleveland were in the White House—quite as if the struggle against Biddle's Bank and the Whig protectionists, and not the struggle against monopoly, were the burning issue. "I look forward," he said, "to a world of small owners." Positively, and on the humdrum logical plane, this may be taken as his last word on the subject. On other planes a different story may have to be told.

II

In that exciting summer and fall of his twenty-second year, when the Log Cabin campaign was in full swing and the hard cider flowing abundantly down Whiggish throats, Walt Whitman was not only stumping for Van Buren in Queens County; he was also writing a series of quite unpolitical little essays for a country newspaper, the *Long Island Democrat*. He was boarding at the time at the house of James J. Brenton, the editor of the paper, at Jamaica,

103

and as he had been teaching school in the neighborhood somewhat irregularly during the previous year, he called his essays for the *Democrat* "Sun-Down Papers from the Desk of a Schoolmaster." All the evidence suggests that young Whitman was anything but the usual sort of pedagogue, and not many educational desks on Long Island at that moment could have yielded just such a crop of papers as these. They are hardly the work of a precocious genius, to be sure, but how many country schoolmasters in 1840 would have written, for example, the seventh paper in the series? In this essay the young boarder whom Brenton's wife was to remember as dreamy, lazy, and impractical, imagines himself composing a "wonderful and ponderous book" in which, among other things, he would deal with the nature and peculiarities of men, the diversity of their characters, the means of improving their state, and the proper mode of governing nations. An ambitious project, he grants with a smile, but one for which he will not be so falsely modest as to deny his capacity. "Who knows," he asks, "but that I might do something very respectable?"

The large designs and the self-assurance of the author of *Leaves of Grass* were, as we see behind the youthful humor, no sudden and mysterious growth. What is more interesting at this point, however, is the extraordinary discovery which the young writer declares to be the basis for his principal claim to a place among the great philosophers, and an account of which would take up the larger part of his imaginary volume. "I have found out," he says, "that it is a very dangerous thing to be rich." After much meditation, and after he had long supposed that wealth was an important object of desire, this new conviction has become fixed and unalterable in his mind. If his readers wish to

know some of the reasons for his change of opinion, he
begs them in fancy to look yonder at a man with a wrin-
kled forehead and with sweat pouring down his face. This
individual, says the ex-schoolmaster, is "a poor, miserable,
rich man." Out of bed since an hour before sunrise, he has
been toiling and moiling for many weary hours as if only
in constant motion were there any safety for his soul. "He
is worried from day to day to preserve and take care of
his possessions. He keeps horses; and one of them is by
him. Look at the miserable brute (the horse, I mean). See
how his sides pant. I warrant me, the animal has no rest
for the soles of his feet."

It may be that Mrs. Brenton, who had a very low opinion of her boarder's diligence, would have thought that his
objections to becoming a man of wealth were only too
characteristic of him: in any case, the picture of the over-
worked and cruelly-driven magnate has an unintended
quaintness. There were other objections than this to getting rich, however, in the mind of the warm-hearted young
journalist Whitman, and months later, in another "Sun-
Down Paper," he returned to the attack. Now it is the
folly of being on terms of enmity or even of cold indifference toward other human beings that brings him back to
the subject of wealth and the struggle to gain it. In every
heart, he says, there are fountains of affection that need
only to be touched in order to gush forth. "Yet there are
hundreds and thousands of men who go on from year to
year with their pitiful schemes of business and profit, and
wrapped up and narrowed down in those schemes, they
never think of the pleasant and beautiful capacities that
God has given them." Such men he can only pity for their
gross conception of happiness, and he urges them to de-

velop if they can their disposition for kindness and their faculty of affection. "To be sure," he adds, "it may not bring in a percentage like bank stock, or corporation scrip, or bonds and mortgages, but it is very valuable, and will pay many fold."

Such were the unfledged sentiments, among the earliest he expressed in print, of the poet who was afterward to say that his theory included riches and the getting of riches, and that business is an immense and noble attribute of man. He speaks, in these apprentice essays, far less in the manner of Keats's "philosophical Quaker," Benjamin Franklin, than in that of George Fox, the Quaker shoe-maker, or of John Woolman, the Quaker tailor, or of Elias Hicks, the Quaker farmer. His imagination had been pow-erfully moved, in his boyhood, by the unworldly teachings of these great Friends: was it only this influence that, lin-gering into his early twenties, guided the pen that wrote the "Sun-Down Papers"? Is it only the last echo of a benev-olent and self-denying quietism that we make out in these "impractical" utterances? Did Walt Whitman then, plung-ing into the turmoil of city life which Hicks had so fear-fully deplored, abandon his boyish views about the danger and the folly of becoming rich, and succumb body and soul to the philistines? Did he simply, in those later days, say Yes, stridently and uninterruptedly, to the whole prag-matic program and all the questionable practices of that robust young industrialism which was transforming Amer-ica in his day? Was he to become simply the bard of the shopkeeper and the steelmaster?

These are idle and artificial questions, in any serious sense, as everyone knows who has even dipped into *Leaves of Grass* or *Specimen Days,* and one might well apologize for asking them. Those books have never been taken as manuals for the man on the make, nor are they likely to be. Yet responsible writers have viewed Whitman as a spokesman for the middle class and little more, and we have seen in how many ways he himself supplied a basis for that view. At the very least, if we consider all that he wrote and said, there is a disconcerting ambiguity in his work. So there was, for that matter, in the whole complex of American culture in the nineteenth century, and this fact lifts the singular contradictions in Whitman's outlook from the personal and capricious level to one on which they become highly representative and vital. A lesser writer, by taking in fewer realities than Whitman did, would have achieved a tidier uniformity; perhaps a greater writer, by imposing his own sense of things more imperiously on the disorder about him, would have blended his contradictions into a somewhat richer and subtler unity. Neither would have for us just the interest and just the meaning that Whitman has. Ambiguous his work and his career may be, but it is because there was so constant, though on the whole so quiet, a clash between what he really saw and what he wished to see, between his untrained and half-developed critical sense and his genial temper, between his instinctive loyalties and his superficial complacencies. In his own way, however, he too was at odds with the public and official morality of his time, and in his least uniformed moods, he watched some of the developments of American practical life with a deep if unclarified distrust.

With what feeling but distrust, indeed, could Walt Whitman look on at the flashy spectacle of money-making that spread out all round him? It is true that when it was a question of rebuking the conservative and pessimistic

Tennyson, he could speak with momentary sincerity as if money-making not only must be but perhaps ought to be the paramount matter in worldly affairs; but this comes as hardly more than a pleasant paradox from the man whose whole life had been a good-natured but stubborn protest against the importance attached by his contemporaries to money. He might speak of their acquisitiveness with a conscious indulgence, but it was the indulgence with which a broad-minded water-drinker might speak of chronic alcoholism. It was certainly not the indulgence of spontaneous fellow-feeling. He spoke out of no strong personal conviction or remembered personal experience. Even among poets, Walt Whitman is almost singular for his easygoing thriftlessness, except perhaps among the perplexities of old age, ill health, and approaching death. The evidence is unimpeachable. "He had an idea," said George Whitman, "that money was of no consequence"; and Pete Doyle, who knew him intimately, was even more emphatic on the subject. "Dollars and cents," he declared, "had no weight with Walt at all. He didn't spend recklessly, but he spent everything—mostly on other people. Money was a thing he didn't think of as other people thought of it. It came and went, that was all there was to it." This might be a curious way of putting Poor Richard's lessons into practice, but there is no doubt that it is the way Whitman followed.

He followed it naturally and almost effortlessly because he preferred living to gathering and hoarding, and not because he had taken any grim vow of poverty or aimed tb set an example to more sinful men. If he suddenly abandoned his own little enterprise as a house-builder in the middle fifties, at a time when he "bade fair to be a good business man"—when he was "worth some money and 'doing well' "—we can be sure it was in no spirit of self-chastisement: money-making was certainly a bore to him, as to any artist, and he enjoyed life almost too intensely on easier terms. Incapable as he was, however, of that superciliousness for which he not unjustly blamed Thoreau, he too, like Thoreau, could not help being revolted by the greedy scramble for gain that often passed itself off as enterprise and progress. He was not simply intoning boyish commonplaces when he wrote those "Sun-Down Papers": he was expressing his really spontaneous and untutored feelings about the way to live well and wisely; the language was the language he always used, early and late, when he hearkened to his own instincts and not to the jangling uproar about him. He was a heretic, in that bourgeois carnival, say what he might.

He intended that his approval should fall like the rain upon the just and the unjust, but with the best will in the world, Whitman could not consistently keep the note of scorn out of his voice when he spoke of the money-makers. Listen to him as he speaks, even in the exposed areas of the *Eagle's* editorial page, of what he has the effrontery to call the "morbid appetite for money" among his countrymen —those countrymen of whose practical energies, on other and more conformable days, he boasts so ingenuously. However wild a scheme may be, he says, if it is a scheme for making quick and easy profits, it counts its dupes by the hundreds, and then goes its inevitable way to oblivion. "But the mad passion for getting rich does not die away in this manner. It engrosses all the thoughts and the time of men . . . It enters into their hearts and reigns paramount there . . . The unbridled desire for wealth breaks down the barriers of morality, and leads to a thousand deviations

109

from those rules, the observance of which is necessary to the well-being of our people." This it is, he continues, this "feverish anxiety after riches," that constantly leads to the establishment of those great moneyed concerns that, even in democratic America, practise their frauds and injustices so shamelessly. And he ends with a warning to "the great body of workingmen" against succumbing to the evil contagion.

As for Business being "the word of the modern hero," what of that magazine article he had written in the fifties, for a series of essays on New York life, to describe Broadway and its typical crowds? After picturing the workers and the shop-girls and the clerks who appear along the great street at successive hours in the early part of the day, Whitman proceeds to picture their employers—"the 'solid business community' "—who somewhat later begin to crowd the sidewalks. "A grim and griping generation are they," he continues; "some fat and sturdy; most lean and dried up; all with close, hard faces, and even in the fresh, early morning air, after the kindly gift of sleep, their brains full and throbbing with greedy hopes or bare fears about the almighty dollar." In language such as this it is surely not the eulogist of George Peabody or the precursor of Elbert Hubbard whom we hear speaking: it is much more recognizably the poet who wrote:

> *I have loved the earth, sun, animals, I have despised riches.*

There was a mingling of strains in Whitman's maturest sentiment about wealth and the restless struggle for wealth: something of the plain old Quakerish asceticism had indeed entered into it, as the passage from the *Eagle* editorial hints, and much too, as we shall see, of the common man's distrust, the radical Jacksonian distrust, of everything that leads to economic top-heaviness and extreme social inequality. He was not merely, however, one more Jacksonian among others, and he was not really an ascetic or a Quaker: on the contrary, he had in his nature all those qualities of receptiveness and curiosity, of naïve interest and love of "aimless" experience that we try to pretend are rarer than they are by crediting them to the poetic temperament. In kind, they are not rare at all, but in degree Whitman had them more than most men, and he gave them free rein instead of fearing and suppressing them. It was these traits, more than anything else, that made his attitude just what it was toward the busy, fretful, avaricious, buying-and-selling careers of his fellow-Yankees: for the life of him he could not think of the process of getting ahead in this world as anything but an appalling waste of priceless hours and beautiful faculties. He was never more spontaneously eloquent, therefore, than when he spoke, in the first preface to his book, of "the melancholy prudence of the abandonment of such a great being as a man is to the toss and pallor of years of moneymaking with all their scorching days and icy nights and all their stifling deceits and underhanded dodgings," and declared that all this was "the great fraud upon modern civilization and forethought."

Better do "nothing" and get "nowhere," his instincts told him, than throw away the best of life in doing to so little purpose and getting to so worthless a goal. Whatever Poor Richard or Governor Briggs or Charles C. B. Seymour might say, the native Walt Whitman had no genuine respect for mere hard work, for mere diligent and mechan-

111

ical activity; and he did not need to have heard of Friedrich Schlegel in order to write his own "Idyll on Idleness" in the form of an essay for the *Long Island Democrat*. "The highest and most perfect life," the author of *Lucinde* had written, "is reached by simple vegetating"; and the author of the "Sun-Down Papers," who had probably not yet heard of either Schlegel or his book, would certainly have applauded the sentiment. "How I do love a loafer!" wrote Mrs. Brenton's incorrigible boarder. "When I have been in a dreamy, musing mood, I have sometimes amused myself with picturing out a nation of loafers. Only think of it! an entire loafer kingdom! How sweet it sounds! Repose, —quietude,—roast duck,—loafer. Smooth and soft are the terms to our jarred tympanums." How free from hurry and bustle, from banging and clanging, would an island wholly inhabited by such fellows be! "Talk about your commercial countries, and your national industry, indeed! Give us the facilities of loafing, and you are welcome to all the benefits of your tariff system, your manufacturing privileges, and your cotton trade." How early and how easily Walt Whitman had learned to loaf and invite his soul!

He had not learned it, as I say, from Friedrich Schlegel, and in a sense he did not need to take over from his great romantic contemporaries their deep antagonism to the whole ethic of utility and possessiveness, of aggression and worldly success. The roots of this antagonism were in his own nature, but in a very different intellectual and cultural setting, would they have found the soil and the nourishment they did find? All the while, as it happened, that he was frequenting Tammany Hall and working for the true Democracy in Brooklyn, he was also taking advantage of the stacks of printed matter that came his way as a journalist and reviewer—exchange copies of all the British and American magazines and review-copies of all the new books, good, bad, and indifferent; and he read a little of everybody, from the Hon. Mrs. Norton and G. P. R. James and Martin F. Tupper to Goethe and Lamartine. He read *Sartor Resartus* and at least some of *Modern Painters;* he read the *Biographia Literaria* and Schiller's *Homage of the Arts;* he read over and over a French novel named *Consuelo,* digested thoroughly its views about the artist as a prophet, and came to think of its author, George Sand, as "the brightest woman ever born." Of course, too, he was reading all along and hearing about his fellow-Americans of a similar persuasion—Channing, Emerson, Margaret Fuller. Not all this reading, as we shall later observe, was to have the happiest effect upon Whitman's intellectual development, but whatever else it did or did not do, it undermined—for the poet Whitman—his never very firmly-based respect for the values of the philistines; it troubled, even if it did not destroy, his enthusiasm for material achievement and tangible prosperity; it confirmed him in his far more natural allegiance to an idealistic ethic and the free, beneficent, disinterested career of the creative artist.

It was one thing, for example, to visit the fair of the American Institute at Castle Garden, and when he did so he was accompanied by the shade of Benjamin Franklin; it was another thing to visit the exhibit of paintings at the Brooklyn Art Union, in the winter of 1851, and now it was Ruskin and George Sand who walked by his side. Walt Whitman's taste in the graphic arts might be undisciplined and eclectic, but for all that he could not be unmoved by the spectacle of a group of young painters organizing among themselves for mutual encouragement—as the Art Union members had done—in an atmosphere chilly with indifference and incomprehension; and in a news article on the subject for the *Evening Post,* he seized with evident delight the opportunity to say a good word for this little group, typical as he felt its members to be of thousands of gifted young Americans. How much might be done, he reflected, for the growth of "a grand and true art here, fresh and youthful, worthy this republic," if only these youths might be systematically cheered upon their way! "These thousands of young men, idly as the business world too generally regards them," he declared, "are in the main, composed of the nobler specimens of our race." Wild and thoughtless they might be, but never mean or sneaking; and if their natures contrasted in some striking ways with those of their sober fellow-citizens, so much the better for them! "A sunny blessing, then, say I, on the young artist race! for the thrift and shrewdness that make dollars, are not every thing that we should bow to, or yearn for, or put before our children as the be all and the end all of human ambition."

Apparently the members of the Art Union were encouraged by these generous words to invite young Whitman to address them, in the manner of that age of lyceums; at any rate, address them he did, a few weeks later, with some remarks on the subject of "Art and Artists." It was an excellent chance for him to put down in words his clearer and clearer convictions on the question, and he took what was then called high ground. Among a people like the Americans, he observed, "viewing most things with an eye to pecuniary profit—more for acquiring than for enjoying and well developing what they acquire—ambitious of the

physical rather than the intellectual; a race to whom matter of fact is everything, and the ideal nothing—a nation of
whom the steam engine is no bad symbol," among such a
people that man is a true benefactor who pauses to teach
the feverish crowd that "in the life we live upon this beautiful earth, there may, after all, be something vaster and
better than dress and the table, and business and politics."
To teach this, to inculcate reverence for the great and the
beautiful, is the grand mission of the arts, and the artist
whose solemn sense of this mission had ennobled his whole
nature, is the highest specimen of manhood. Compared
with him, what of the conventional citizen of the age? "His
contempt for all there is in the world, except money can
be made of it; his utter vacuity of anything more important to him as a man than success in 'business,'—his religion what is written down in the books, or preached to
him as he sits in his rich pew, by one whom he pays a
round sum, and thinks it a bargain"—what a wretched figure he cuts! Not from such men need one expect great
thoughts or heroic deeds: these are reserved for the artist
or for the hero with the soul of the artist in him.

In short, Walt Whitman had gone over, perhaps not
body and soul, but with all that was most personal to him,
to the camp where in that generation one would expect to
find him, the camp of the romantic idealists; and though,
in the general confusion, he sometimes dealt blows *for* the
enemy rather than *at* them, even this was in the best of
faith. David himself had wandered among the Philistines;
Emerson had sometimes given them comfort; and Whitman denied, from their point of view, far more than he
ever affirmed. He might really believe, in his mundane
role, that democracy asks for owners of houses and acres,

115

with cash in the bank; he might cling to his petty bourgeois ideal of a world of small owners; but could anyone seriously doubt that the drift of his work as a writer was violently against a crass possessiveness? Would Mr. Bill the dry-goods dealer and Dr. Vanderhoef the druggist really have found much to reassure them in the poet of *Leaves of Grass?* It was just as well that they did not even dip into his book: it was certainly as well that they did not have a glimpse of those preparatory notebooks in which he was sometimes even more vehement than in his verse. "The ignorant man," he had written in one of them, "is demented with the madness of owning things"—and the phrase was to recur, of course, in a famous passage. But the notebook had been more explicit than the "Song of Myself" was to be. "The orthodox proprietor," it went on, "says This is mine, I earned or received or paid for it,— and by positive right of my own I will put a fence around it, and keep it exclusively to myself." How little such a man understands of the true nature of things!—"that dismal and measureless fool not to see the hourly lessons of the one eternal law, that he who would grab blessings to himself, as by right, and deny others their equal chance —and will not share with them every thing that he has"— that fool is doomed to some painful awakening which the unfinished sentence conceals from us but which we can easily enough make out for ourselves.

As unreliable as this, then, from the point of view of A. Lawrence & Son or the Commercial Bank of New York, was the apparently right-thinking editor of the *Eagle* and the *Times!* Whatever that editor might say about "permanent prosperity" or "life and enterprise" or "profit and interest," once he had left his desk and his office behind him he did not really seem to believe that man was made for the Sabbath—the Sabbath of property—or that outward success was the token of an inward grace, or that the heroes of his time were those self-made men who had managed to transform cotton-goods and pig iron and common stocks into great mansions on the Hudson and stables full of fine carriage-horses. How few "successful" men, after all, appear in those poems of his in which one comes upon so many deck-hands and firemen, carpenters and boatmen, plain mechanics and soldiers of the rank and file! And what disturbing questions, from the philistine point of view, Whitman was given to asking in his verse!—

> *(Who goes for men and women showing Poverty*
> *richer than wealth?)*

It was the kind of question Henry Thoreau was always asking—Henry Thoreau, who had enjoined himself to cultivate poverty like sage, like a garden herb. They were snapping their fingers, both men, at the tablets of the law; and worse than this, they conducted their own lives as if a man could be both poor and honorable. Moreover, they both questioned whether a man might not be "successful" without inspiring respect and "unsuccessful" without shame. Walt Whitman could speak his word even for failure:

> *Have you heard that it was good to gain the day?*
> *I also say it is good to fall, battles are lost in*
> *the same spirit in which they are won . . .*
> *Vivas to those who have fail'd!*

III

It was true, as the young Whitman felt, that thousands of Americans in his time were entirely absorbed with their

117

schemes of business and profit; it was true that the morbid
appetite for money, which he castigated in the *Eagle,* was
riding more and more of his countrymen like an incubus,
and that the lust to acquire, rather than to enjoy or develop what was acquired, was becoming, as he said to the
young painters of the Art Union, the great representative
vice of the American people. As a poet, as a romantic,
Whitman rejected, from his earliest youth onward, the
morals of utility and the practices of profit-making, even
while, as a yea-sayer, he gave his assent to the general tenor
of modern life and the broad program of These States. In
rejecting such morals and practices, he was at one with all
the disinterested spirits of his age, at home and abroad:
did he, as only certain of the others did, perceive that anything else was at stake? that, in addition to the coarsening
of manners and the corruption of morals, the actual tendencies of American economy were threatening the political and social program of democracy? Did he perceive that
the undisputed sway of economic individualism was also
menacing thousands of men and women with poverty and
social servitude?

As a romantic idealist, Whitman need not have paid
much heed to these gloomy realities; as a radical Jacksonian democrat, he was bound to be profoundly troubled
by them. Even in his boyhood the actual workings of the
American social system were not producing the fine equality that was his and so many other men's ideal: a world of
small owners might possibly be the true goal, and the most
valuable class in any community might be the middle
class; but in Whitman's youth it was already true that the
rewards which, as a result of putting economic liberty into
practice, accrued to Mr. Bill and Dr. Vanderhoef and their

like were more and more paltry when compared with the
rewards which somehow accrued to Stephen Girard and
Amos Lawrence, to John Jacob Astor and A. T. Stewart.
The old class of independent farmers and artisans, to
which Whitman's family belonged, and even the class of
small shopkeepers, to whom they were so close, were not
holding their own against the aggressions of the great
merchant-princes and bankers or of the profiteers from
real estate; and this, not merely because these men were
unromantic philistines, but because the political and social institutions of the land made all that inevitable.

Already in the forties, too, it was becoming clear that
the ideal program of equality was to be seriously modified
and perhaps thwarted by a new kind of ownership, the
ownership of spinning jennies and mechanical looms, of
steam-engines and sewing-machines. The center of economic power was rapidly shifting to the new class of industrial magnates, and if a few men like Moses Brown and
William Sprague, Francis Cabot Lowell and Cornelius
Vanderbilt had derived great wealth from such ownership,
it was equally true that more and more Americans were
passing most of their waking hours in textile mills, in iron
mines, and on railroad beds—to far less splendid effect. To
be a free American workman no longer meant generally
what some men in the late eighteenth century had hoped
it would mean: it often meant working with a hammer or
a pick-axe from sunrise to sunset for a master-builder or a
contractor; it meant working for fourteen or fifteen hours
a day at a spindle or a loom; it meant earning wages that
ranged from four or five "shillings" to one or two dollars
a day; it meant living in temporary shacks or company
tenements or in the increasingly crowded and miserable

areas of the North End, the East Side, and their like. Hundreds of Americans might be practising the virtues of industry and frugality, and demonstrating the beneficent effects of laissez faire and individual enterprise; other hundreds, and indeed other thousands, at the least, were being drastically educated in the iron law of wages and the length of the working day.

All this presumably had a bearing on the realization of that humane program to which American democracy was officially and solemnly committed. However the transcendentalist might protest against the crazy pursuit of dollars and the enthroning of "things" in the saddle, the equalitarian democrat could hardly avert his gaze from the parallel phenomenon of harsh exploitation and the widening cleavage between classes. Here were realities even more ominous than the Mexican War and the Fugitive Slave Law: how conscious was the young Barnburner editor Whitman of their existence, and how clear a voice, if any, did he raise against them?

Certainly, despite his inclination to linger on the brighter aspects of the national life, and even in the piping times of Polk and Cass, Whitman was far from unaware that there were classes in the community whose share in the general prosperity was something less than it might have been, and whose control over their own lives and labors was hardly, in the fullest sense, democratic. Whatever conclusions he might or might not draw, in those cheerful decades, from facts such as these, he could speak of them only with instinctive indignation. That American men and women, even on the humblest social level, should be forced to work for wretchedly low wages or at inhumanly long hours; that the terms on which they must work should be dictated to and not by them; that opportunity should be denied them to develop and cultivate themselves as dignified human beings—these things seemed to the young Whitman, when he brought himself to consider them, quite as intolerable as that the Whigs should strive to push up the tariff or that slaveholders should dominate the national policy. He expressed that sort of feeling earlier and more strongly than has been supposed.

New York and Brooklyn, for example, were prosperous and progressive cities, as everyone knew who had ever walked along Broadway or Fulton Street. Yet in those very communities, as the editor of the *Eagle* once reminded his readers, "hundreds and hundreds" of working girls and women—seamstresses and the like—made "from *fifty cents* (!) to two dollars per week—very few in the neighborhood of the latter sum, however"; and how could any reasonable or charitable person deny that the "evils and horrors" of "this miserable system" were chiefly to blame for the prevalence of vice and crime among women of the working classes? Nor were girls and women the sole objects of this callous exploitation. When a group of Brooklyn workers once gathered together to form a "benevolent association" and hold out for wages of seven "shillings" a day, the editor of the *Eagle* pointed out that sixty-four and a half cents was a not uncommon wage for a working day in Brooklyn that lasted from sunrise to dark, and that, with potatoes at a dollar a bushel, an income of less than four dollars a week came dangerously close to the edge of decency. "Let our philanthropists," he went on to say, "not go to oppressed England and starving Ireland for samples of scanty comfort; if these things are so, we have enough ground for indignation in our very midst." All the associated workers ask for, he observed a few days later, is eighty-seven and a half cents a day—"and we do say . . . that the man, or set of men, who refuse to give that price, show a most heartless meanness, and that if the curse of ill gotten profits does not attach to their wealth, it will not be because it is undeserved!"

Low as wages often were, however, the phenomenon of wage-cutting was not a rare one; and especially when it was resorted to by Whig industrialists for the purpose of discrediting the low Democratic tariff of 1846, it stirred Whitman to ironic comment. When, in September, the carpet-weavers of Thompsonville, Connecticut, went out on strike against a wage-cut attributed by their employers to the tariff, he noted the fact of the protest with undisguised satisfaction. A month later he observed that anthracite coal was then selling in Philadelphia at from a dollar to a dollar and a quarter a ton more than it had sold at, just a year earlier. "At the same time," he continued, "the coal merchants of Pottsville are attempting to reduce the wages of the miners on account of the 'reductions of the tariff.' " During the same October, the wages of forty or fifty unskilled workers in the white lead factories of Brooklyn were cut twelve and a half cents a day—"by which," the *Eagle* remarked, "the *economically* disposed *poor* manufacturers will save the enormous sum of thirty-seven and one half dollars per week! We hope the country may now be considered safe!"

That extra "shilling" a day had more to do, if not with the safety of the country, at least with the progress of the new industrialism than Whitman, who was no economist, realized; but in any event his comments were not confined to the niggardly wage-scale that so generally prevailed: he could be equally indignant or ironic when he considered the intolerably long hours at which most American work-ingmen and workingwomen labored. When it was an-nounced, early one December, that the dry-goods stores of Brooklyn would be closed, during the following winter, at eight in the evening instead of at nine or half-past nine, as hitherto, he welcomed the change as a happy one, and took the occasion to observe that it might well be made permanent and extended to all the retail stores of the city. The life of a clerk, he pointed out, had many disadvan-tages, of which not the least was the necessity of working fourteen hours or more in a day that usually began at seven in the morning; a necessity that left little time or energy for the pursuits that help to make human beings something more than mere appendages to brooms and wrapping-paper. "It is sometimes suggested," the *Eagle* went on, "that by letting the clerks of stores have their evenings, they may spend them badly." It was a line of argument by no means unfamiliar then and it had still a long life ahead of it. To Whitman it had little appeal. "Similar logic," he observed, "would suggest that by let-ting a man have the use of his legs he might run off the dock, and get drowned."

With such sentiments, it might be supposed that the edi-tor of the *Eagle* would have gone to the support of the movement, then in full career, for a ten-hour law: in fact, as we shall see, he had a doctrinaire predisposition against the legal enforcement of even such standards as this. But it is evident that his doctrines were at war, on this head, with his sympathies. It was not the Jacksonian doctrinaire who, when the journeymen carpenters of Nashville struck for a ten-hour day, quoted in the *Eagle* the statement of

123

their purposes in the strike—a statement that made much of their desire for the decent leisure without which self-cultivation is impossible. Nor was it the doctrinaire who, when the legislature of New Hampshire passed the first ten-hour law—a law, it is true, that was to prove a delusion in practice—observed that if ever an exception might be made to the general principle of non-interference by the state, it would be in favor of such laws as this. A whole-hearted sympathizer with the ten-hour movement might certainly have written this sardonic little paragraph in the *Eagle:* "The queen bees in the Lowell hives we perceive have *magnanimously* allowed the workers to take *three-fourths of an hour* for breakfast and dinner—this generosity, it is said, is unexampled in the mills of New England."

Sanguine, indeed, as Whitman overwhelmingly was in his views of the republican social order and what it boded for the future, there is evidence that he did not always look without apprehension at the more and more rapid development of the factory system and the harsh industrial discipline, with all they signified for the independence, the health, and the morale of the factory worker. In part, to be sure, it was the Jeffersonian in him who, with the ancestral acres of farm land in his memory, eyed with suspicion the multiplication of the mills and the machines. But Whitman was far from being a dogmatic agrarian; he would not have echoed Thoreau's remark that "the fall from the farmer to the operative" is "as great and memorable as that from the man to the farmer"; and it was on broader and firmer ground than this that he protested, intermittently and as it were under his breath, against the cruel physical strain of factory labor and the autocracy under

124

which, even in republican America, the workers, as workers, often lived. It was not simply the scion of the Suffolk County Whitmans, it was the humanitarian democrat who thus expressed himself.

This was the Whitman who, noting that a "female operative" in a cotton mill at Medway was reported to have saved some two or three thousand dollars in a working life of forty years, remarked that the sum—a paltry week's profit for the "manufactory lords"—had been dearly earned at that. "Forty years work in a cotton mill! in the close air, and deafened by the rumbling of machinery, and the freeness of the limbs all cramped by the restraint! Ah, are not the two thousand dollars dearly earned indeed!" Moved by a similar emotion, no doubt, the young editor one day reprinted on his first page a pitiful tale from the *Herald of Freedom,* a come-outer paper published at Concord, New Hampshire—a tale about the sufferings and wretched death from over-work of a young workingwoman in a textile mill. Calling attention to the story in his editorial columns, Whitman took occasion to say: "Though about Factory life, it affords a view of a different sort of 'ruin' from that so much harped about on the part of the great Capitalists." This, too, was the vein in which, a few years later, Whitman philosophized, in one of his notebooks, on the causes of intemperance; and repudiating the crude moralism of the temperance movement, observed that the natural cure for the monotonous, protracted drudgery of so much modern labor was the powerful stimulant of strong drink. "The sense of weariness which follows excessive labor," he reflected, "is almost insufferable. And blame for the drunkenness so common among the working classes

125

of all countries, may fairly be referred back to the task-masters who compel this violation of natural laws, by the repugnant toil they impose."

As task-masters, in fact, when he considered their relations with their employees, Whitman was inclined to think of the very men whose business genius he at other moments delighted to honor. Whatever he might say to Edward Carpenter about the usefulness of the great masters of private enterprise, it is very evident that, at an early stage, he had looked with an at least intermittent distrust at the motives and practices of the new industrial magnates. If certain of his remarks were isolated from their whole context, one would say that Whitman had no illusions whatever about the devotion of the American industrialist to democratic ideals, about his benevolence, or about his concern for the public interest. When he noted one day in the *Eagle* that an order had been issued to the workers on the Concord railroad lines, forbidding the delivery of any daily papers in the workshops, he could not refrain from making the grim comment that "meanwhile the freedom of the press is being recognized in Italy and Prussia." And when, at another time, he quoted from a Boston newspaper an account of certain spinning mills at Bradford in England which were allegedly conducted on humanitarian principles, he added that he welcomed with pleasure "any such evidence of conscience on the part of factory owners—and tremblingly suggest whether it could not be introduced into our 'domestic' manufactories."

Submerged as it may have been in his systematic Yea-saying, the strain of homespun radicalism—the radicalism of the Revolutionary farmers and the Locofoco artisans —was powerful in Whitman, and fortified by his half-

126

developed gift of critical observation, it stirred him to the
firing of occasional shafts of surprisingly sharpened ridi-
cule at the pretensions and the professions of the "domestic" high bourgeoisie. Did the manufacturers of the North
demand the "protection" of a high tariff and claim that it
was for the benefit of the workingman? It seemed to Whitman the most transparent humbug. "Has any one of our
laboring fellow citizens," he asked, with a fine Demosthenic
anacoluthon—"has any one of our laboring fellow citizens
such thin perceptions—does he imagine in his most ab-
stracted dreams—that all this hubbub made by the pale-
fingered richly-housed Whig manufacturers, and their organs, is for *him, the laborer?"* The real workings of a
protective tariff and the real motives of the industrialists
seemed to him obvious enough. "What lots of cents," he
once exclaimed, in his careless journalistic manner, "have
gone out of poor folks' pockets, to swell the dollars in the
possession of owners of great steam mills! Molière, speaking of a wealthy physician, says: 'He must have killed a
great many people to be so rich!' Our American capitalists
of the manufacturing order, would *poor* a great many
people to be rich!" The eulogist of George Peabody was
capable of something like cynicism in contemplating even
the charities of the very wealthy. He had noted once in the
Eagle that the average annual earnings of forty thousand
workingwomen in Massachusetts was $125. "Ah! the munif-
icence," he cried, "of the cotton lords, with their princely
gifts to *benevolent institutions!"* And when John Jacob
Astor once made a gift of five hundred dollars to the fund
for firemen's widows and orphans, the Jacksonian editor
could bring himself only to ask: "How on earth could he
spare it?"

127

Given such sentiments and such perceptions, it is conceivable that, young as he was, Walt Whitman might have found himself in the company of that remarkable group of men and women who, already in the forties, were aware that the movement of American society, directed as it increasingly was by mill-owners, bankers, and the magnates of transportation, was profoundly undemocratic, and that the hopes of eighteenth-century liberals could only be realized now by some fundamental reconstruction. It is conceivable that he might have realized as clearly as Parke Godwin, for example, that, as Godwin had said in the very year in which Polk was elected president, "society tends to a division, more and more distinct, into two classes,—a small number possessing everything . . . and the great mass, possessing nothing." The youth who wrote so caustically of the cotton lords might conceivably have subscribed to the proposition laid down by Albert Brisbane two or three years earlier: "Our evils are social, not political, and a social reform only can eradicate them." Much, in detail, that these men pointed to he saw as plainly as they did, and no one could have shared more unreservedly than he their radical sympathies with the masses. But the habit of hopefulness was much too strong in him to allow him to take, even for a moment, so dark a view of the actual tendencies of the times; and even if this had not been true, he was far too thoroughly imbued with the Jeffersonian dogmas to accept or even, as we shall see, carefully to consider the program of those early socialists. It was in the beneficent operations of an irresistible progress, and not in a consciously worked-out program of any kind, that the Brooklyn journalist put his real trust; and he certainly expressed his dominant sense of such matters when, in his remarks on the poor pay of sewing-women, he confessed that the only remedy he knew of lay in the workings of "an awakened public opinion": once men's eyes are opened to such facts, he declared, "the remedy will somehow or other follow."

A conviction so reassuring as this was likely to be reënforced rather than shaken by the events of the fifties and the conditions of Whitman's own life. The ebullient prosperity that, one-sided as it was, followed upon the discovery of gold in California, appeared to give the lie to the "extreme" views that many men had formed during the lean and trying years of the late thirties and early forties; and Whitman, who of course had never formed such views, inevitably yielded himself to the buoyant mood of the decade. Independently of this, moreover, the initial wave of native socialist thinking was carried under, in the fifties, by the rising waters of sectional conflict; and Abolitionism or the Free Soil movement or Republicanism successfully absorbed whatever energies might have gone into reform agitation or the task of pushing beyond the early Utopianism. If Whitman came to be far more painfully concerned for the safety of the Union than for the present or future lot of the American masses, he was at one with many men who had been more systematically or more analytically radical than he. And the design of *Leaves of Grass,* the execution of which was becoming so large a part of his life, was not consistent, at least superficially, with bitter thoughts or angry criticisms or dubious forebodings. Had not its author, after all, announced that his gait was "no fault-finder's or rejecter's gait"?

How effectively these things, and especially the last, suppressed in Whitman, for the time being, the drastic critic of society, becomes evident when we glance at some of those "rejected lines and passages" which his executors published after his death. Not many of these add anything significant to what we know of him from more available evidence, but one or two of them do at least suggest that the trenchant commentator of the *Eagle* survived, however subterraneously, in the flowering poet of the fifties. This would seem to be the import of such lines as the following, which never appeared in any poem of *Leaves of Grass:*

> *I see an aristocrat;*
> *I see a smoucher grabbing the good dishes exclu-*
> *sively to himself and grinning at the starvation*
> *of others as if it were funny,*
> *I gaze at the greedy hog; he snorts as he roots in the*
> *delicate greenhouse . . .*

> *Have you heard the gurgle of gluttons perfectly will-*
> *ing to stuff themselves*
> *While they laugh at the good fun of the starvation*
> *of others,*
> *But when the gaunt and the starved awkwardly come*
> *for their slices*
> *The quiet changes to angry hysterics . . .*

In such experimental fragments, the right vein of poetic eloquence has not quite been struck, but the poet who wrote them was very soon to be capable of the great declamatory passages in the "Song of Myself," and if he suppressed these lines or any fine revision of them, it cannot have been merely through an artist's dissatisfaction. Even as it is, the emotion in them did not go wholly unvoiced in his book, but it revealed itself, when it did, in quieter and more unobtrusive lines:

Many sweating, ploughing, thrashing, and then the
*   chaff for payment receiving,*
A few idly owning, and they the wheat continually
*   claiming.*

How fully or how explicitly this particular range of
sentiment might have expressed itself if the poet of *Leaves*
of Grass had realized another of his purposes and gone, as
he long hoped to do, directly to the American people with
lectures or speeches, must now be guesswork: certainly he
conceived of himself, in this role as well as in the other,
mainly as the expounder of a new and positive "religion"
and not as a critic or an agitator. At least one manuscript
scrap, however, which appears to survive from the fifties,
suggests that he might not wholly have eschewed, even as a
speaker, the language of protest and denunciation. "I cannot too emphatically remind you," it reads—

I cannot too emphatically remind you that in all countries there always seems to be a settled tendency among
the richer classes and high officials towards breaking down
by sly stratagems or open force the primary and inalien-
able rights of man . . . Real democracy and great riches
are in some sort repugnant to one another. Riches draw
off the attention from the principles of democracy, which
are abstractions, called the rights of man. Riches demand
the use of the house for themselves. And men have frequently to choose whether they will retain one or the
other. My own opinion is that no amount of riches which
numbers can calculate will ever make up to any live man
or any live nation for the deprivation of national liberty
and equality.

Here, perhaps for the first time, the accent of real forebod-
ing makes itself heard in Whitman's voice: did he begin,

even in the fifties, to dread some of the possibilities of the future? If so, he kept his anxieties studiously to himself, and the speech in which these sentences might have occurred was never delivered.

We have seen how cheerfully, meanwhile, as editor of the *Times,* Whitman sunned himself in the strong hot light of national prosperity, and certainly in his public capacity as a journalist he preferred to exult and not to complain. Even in this capacity, however, he was capable of lapsing back into the vehemence of his Locofoco years. Day in and day out, he was only too willing to dwell on such matters as the gradual recovery from the crash of 1857, but suddenly, in the midst of these complacencies, appears the disconcerting editorial he printed one July day during the following summer. His mind dwelling for the moment on the well-to-do and fashionable thousands who were just then making the rounds of the watering-places and summer resorts, he abruptly raised the question whether any of them ever thought of "the elements of woe and crime that are festering beneath their feet." The question was one of those that answer themselves, and so, to some extent, was that which followed—the question whether the "pseudo-philanthropists" with their appeals for alms to be sent to foreign missions, ever consider "the gaunt physical want and heathenish spiritual ignorance that make the city's stews and purlieus hideous." The Tract Society, observed the editor with a curious acrimony, may count its contributions by the millions; meanwhile the Magdalen Asylum and the News Boy's Home are in a sorry financial state. "Nobody knows," however, "and nobody cares about these things. The impudent, the pretending, the tinselled and the superficial—these claim the great world's attention and admiration. Nobody wishes to look deeper—it is unpleasant and inconvenient. It is not pleasant to grope among the muck and the slime. Cover it up! Do you say that pestilence will arise? Never mind—cover it up —never look 'Down below.' "

Obviously, there was a troublesome spirit in Whitman that had to be kept in its place. On the whole, it was kept there during the years just before Lincoln's election; and if there is a singular violence of sarcasm in the passage I have just quoted, perhaps it can be credited not only to spontaneous and simple indignation but to an unconscious self-reproach. However he might rage against the wasters and the pseudo-philanthropists, he himself was little given to groping among the muck and the slime. Unlike the others, however, Whitman knew very well, all along, that the muck and the slime were there; he knew that this was an ugly anomaly in a society in which a few men claimed and received the wheat that other men had sown and threshed; and beneath the layers, no matter how fat or how warm, of his studied optimism, that knowledge lay restless and ready to assert itself. It was wholly silenced, if ever, only by the prolonged strain and the intense excitement of the "impending conflict" and the Civil War itself.

IV

For two days, late in the spring of 1865, the great central avenues of Washington bristled with the bayonets and echoed to the drum-beats of the returning armies of the North as they marched for the last time in formal review before the high officials of the government. Walt Whitman, who had been at home in Brooklyn on the day of

133

Lincoln's assassination, was fortunately back again in Washington, and it is easy to imagine his emotions, as he stood, along with the other spectators, at the sidewalk's edge along Pennsylvania Avenue and gazed at the "immortal ranks" of the returning heroes, with their bronzed and sunburnt faces, their bodies hardened by many marches, and their dusty, war-worn uniforms. He saw President Johnson at close range; he saw General Grant and General Sherman on horseback, General Meade, General Thomas, and many another great military celebrity— but these were not the men who struck and impressed him most. "The *rank & file,*" he wrote to his mother, "was the greatest sight of all." Certainly he was not without a sense of the social drama symbolized by the Grand Review. The common soldiers of the American armies, having put down rebellion and reëstablished the authority of the federal union, were returning—in unprecedented good order—to their farms, their shops, and their machines. Would the destruction of the plantation system and the slaveholding oligarchy prove, for them, to have been worth its incalculable cost?

Whitman was only gradually to put the question to himself in anything like this form. He was by no means, however, to ignore another aspect of the American picture so long or so completely as we have so far seemed to suggest. At the same time that the "million flush'd embattled conquerors" were going back to their old and mostly humble occupations, the groups that behind the lines had quietly seized political power and made themselves masters of the national state, were preparing to harvest the advantages of victory. The close of the war, with all that it implied, was giving a scope to the ideas of "leading capitalists," as John

Sherman wrote, such as they had never attained before. American industry was about to enter upon its great age of expansion and conquest. A taciturn produce merchant in Cleveland, after some hesitation, was committing himself to the brilliant future of the oil business. A young railroad superintendent in Pittsburgh, cannily observing the phenomenal activity in the iron industry, was moving into that promising territory and laying the basis for a huge fortune in American steel. In Wall Street a precious trio of enterprisers were already drawing together and laying plans for the capture and spoliation of the Erie Railroad. The Union Pacific was already under construction; business houses were springing up over night; Colonel Sellers was stepping upon the stage as the grand national type; and it looked as if every hill were a diamond mine and every creek a Mississippi. The great free-for-all was on.

To many men it was an exhilarating sight, and if it sometimes involved the methods of a faro-game or a lynching-bee—if it often meant the massacre of competitors, the swindling of investors, the debauching of legislatures, and the under-payment of workers—well, was not all that the inevitable concomitant of prosperity and progress? Walt Whitman, however, going about his not very strenuous duties as a third-class clerk to the Attorney General, did not actually take it all in this light-hearted spirit. Those four or five hilarious and somewhat ruffianly years that followed the Grand Review inspired certain doubts in him not only about the political machinery but also about the social and economic workings of the reinvigorated Union. He saw the sparkle and the glitter of the new prosperity as clearly as anyone saw them, but *Democratic Vistas* indicates to us that he saw other things too. It is in

that extraordinary essay that, along with certain complacencies, Whitman remarked, late in the sixties, that "society, in these States, is canker'd, crude, superstitious, and
rotten." It is there, too, that he went on to say that never
before had there been so much general falsity, so much
cynical disbelief, as in the United States of those years.
"The depravity of the business classes of our country," he
declared, "is not less than has been supposed, but infinitely
greater." What were the real aims of those classes? "In
business, (this all-devouring modern word, business,) the
one sole object is, by any means, pecuniary gain. The magician's serpent in the fable ate up all the other serpents;
and money-making is our magician's serpent, remaining
to-day sole master of the field." On the strength of such
facts, the author of *Democratic Vistas* decided, with a reluctance that does not have to be underlined, that "in its
social aspects" democracy in the new world was at that
stage "an almost complete failure."

If he had come to such a gloomy conclusion as this so
soon after the victory of 1865, it was not only as a result of
observing the behavior of the speculators, the bribe-givers,
and the "robber barons": other events of those years had
undoubtedly troubled him more than the new editions of
Leaves of Grass ever suggested. Whatever the war may
have done for the men who thought in terms of profits and
dividends, it had done disappointingly and indeed heart-
breakingly little for the men who thought in terms of
wages and hours—or of the price of corn and hogs—and in
fact the very developments that looked so exhilarating from
the point of view of the stock-exchange looked more and
more ominous from the point of view of the workshop, the
mill, and the barnyard. The result was a revival of the

labor movement of the years before the war—of the movement that had been so nearly wiped out by the disaster of
1857—and the stormy beginnings of a long series of farmers' agitations: the increasing use by employers of lockouts, of employers' associations, and of contract labor, was
met and countered by a new movement of workers toward
the building up of trades associations, of national unions,
and even of a national federation of unions. At the same
time, under Ira Steward and his associates, began the long
struggle for the eight-hour day; the farmers of the North-
west and elsewhere began flocking to the new Granges;
and in the first year of Grant's administration the organized workers of the country, perhaps not wholly conscious
of the importance of their step, sent Andrew Cameron, the
Chicago printer, to Basle as their representative at the
fourth meeting of the Workingmen's International.

On Walt Whitman the potential gravity of this sharper
and sharper conflict was by no means lost. Was this a necessary or, at any rate, in republican America a promising
sequel to a war that had presumably been fought in the
interests not of a single class but of an inclusive democratic
union? Whitman could not believe it was, and when he
came to write *Democratic Vistas*—preoccupied as he there
was with another order of facts—he was not willing wholly
to suppress his anxiety about what he called "that problem,
the labor question, beginning to open like a yawning gulf,
rapidly widening every year." He of course made no claim
in that context to offering any solution of the problem,
and indeed, writing perhaps at about the same time a
manuscript note which was put into print only after his
death, he frankly confessed that he saw no clear road
ahead. "The relations," he noted, "between the mass of

employed persons on one side and the employers (capitalists, factories, R. R. organizations, owners, etc.) on the
other side is one of the vast, complicated, unsettled problems of America to-day—one of the problems to which, although I think it will be solved, I confess I do not yet see
any solution or indications of solution." Perfect clarity on
this head, in fact, he was never to achieve and never to
pretend he had achieved, but certainly, from this time
on, he was never quite to lose his sense of the grim ques-
tion-mark in the offing.

Early in the seventies, moreover, he was to furnish a
clue, indirectly and poetically, to some of the emotions
that came to him as he looked on at the social struggle. It
was during the interregnum that followed the decline of
the National Labor Union and preceded the rise of the
Knights of Labor that Whitman published in Washington
the sixth edition of *Leaves of Grass*. In that edition he gathered together for the first time half a dozen short poems—
"To a Foil'd European Revolutionaire" and others—and
gave them as a group the inclusive title, "Songs of Insurrection." This was all, so far as concerns the book that
issued from the print-shop in Washington, but at some
time during his preparation of the edition, Whitman appears to have intended something more. There exists a
manuscript scrap of prose which he must originally have
planned to print at the head of the group or as a note on it.
It is worth quoting in full.

Songs of Insurrection. Not only are These States the
born offspring of Revolt against mere overweening authority—but seeing ahead for Them in the future a long,
long reign of Peace with all the growths corruptions and
tyrannies & formalisms of Obedience, (accumulating, vast

folds, strata, from the rankness of continued prosperity and the more and more insidious grip of capital) I feel to raise a note of caution (perhaps unneeded alarm) that the ideas of the following cluster will always be needed, that it may be worth while to keep well up, & vital, such ideas and verses as the following.

"The more and more insidious grip of capital"! It was just such a phrase as the men of the National Labor Union—Sylvis, Cameron, Trevellick—far as they wisely were from being insurrectionists—might also have used; but the chances are that those men never knew how nearly Walt Whitman was of the same mind with them. The poet and the organizer were at this stage inevitably too far apart for that, and ten years later indeed, in the seventh edition of his book, Whitman somehow saw fit to drop the title, "Songs of Insurrection," and to scatter among other sections the poems he had gathered under it.

If the new leaders of labor, however, who had appeared in that ten-year interval, had happened to light upon the volume of prose, *Specimen Days,* which Whitman published a year later, in 1882, they would have seen at least that one American writer of distinction—at just that moment almost the only one—had been watching their struggles with an anxious sympathy. The intervening decade had been a tragic time for the American people, and part of it had been as unhappy a time as Whitman personally had ever known. Ill as he was, however, and lonely as he felt for two or three years in uncongenial surroundings at Camden, he had not failed, after all, to take notice of the appalling events that succeeded upon the crash of 1873—the crash that occurred so soon after his own paralytic stroke, his mother's death, and his removal to New Jersey.

For hundreds of thousands of Americans, thrown out of work or ruined in their small businesses, the following winter had been one of terrible suffering; and Whitman, with his memories of the two great earlier crises, had not simply ignored the horrors of that third and even greater one. "There is an awful amount of want and suffering from no work, here about," he wrote to Pete Doyle in the February of 1874, and mentioned that he had given "a little" to a young man who, having once seen him in Washington, had come to call on him in Camden and to ask for help. A week or two earlier Whitman had written to Pete of a talk he had had, limping out tentatively into the midst of things, with the "chargé" of the ferry-house on the Delaware, who had told him about the homeless men and women he had been allowing to sleep there on cold nights. It was the sort of thing he could not easily put out of his mind. "God help the homeless and moneyless," he added in his letter, "this weather."

The aid of Providence, as it turned out, proved of little avail to American workers during the depression of the seventies, and when in desperation they attempted instead to help themselves, they sometimes found the forces of "order" arrayed implacably against them. During the month of Whitman's talk at the ferry-house, a demonstration of the unemployed in Tompkins Square, New York, had been broken up by armed police, and hundreds of men, women, and children had been trampled on and beaten. The event had much to do with the radicalization of Whitman's remarkable friend, John Swinton. Less than a year later, the cutting of wages in the anthracite mines of Pennsylvania, almost within earshot of Camden, brought on the grim and protracted struggle which was to be known in mining history as the Long Strike. On the heels of its defeat came the revelations of the terrorist activities of the Molly Maguires and the prosecution of their leaders. Not, however, until the hard times had rounded out their fourth miserable year, not until the summer of 1877, did the intensifying bitterness of the conflict reach its violent climax: then, with the spontaneous revolt of the railroad workers, enraged by repeated wage-cuts—as the round-houses and machine-shops of Pittsburgh and Baltimore went up in flames and federal troops fired for the first time on American workers—the American people realized with profound dismay, as most of them had not done before, that they were perhaps not to be exempt from the embittered social strife that had so long afflicted the old world.

Such, in effect, was the lesson that, with a heavy heart, Whitman himself drew from the events of those blood-stained years: so strong and so painful was the impression they made on him that, late in the seventies, he began to put down a series of notes for a public lecture on what he called "The Tramp and Strike Questions." That lecture, like all but one that he planned, was never delivered, but some of his reflections on the subject must have seemed to him worth preserving, for in *Specimen Days,* two or three years later, he printed a few paragraphs from his notes. These paragraphs make it clear that, unlike many Americans, unlike such writers as John Hay, he could not look upon battles like the Long Strike and the railroad strikes as mere outbreaks of lawlessness and criminal disorder. It was not the view taken by the author of *The Breadwinners* that the author of *Specimen Days* instinctively found himself taking. On the contrary, he sought parallels for those struggles in the epoch-making popular rebellions of mod-

141

ern history. The American Revolution, he declared, was "simply a great strike, successful for its immediate object." So of the French Revolution, which, he said, "was absolutely a strike, and a very terrible and relentless one, against ages of bad pay, unjust division of wealth-products, and the hoggish monopoly of a few, rolling in superfluity, against the vast bulk of the work-people, living in squalor."

It was in this hard historical light that Whitman admonished his countrymen to read the social omens of those later years. Miners and railroad workers, he seemed to imply, might be intimidated by the soldiery and coerced into apparent submission, but not so conveniently as this were the questions posed by their upsurge to be answered. Below the superficial conflicts in the political sphere, he pointed out, lay realities infinitely more disquieting and more sinister than they—"not the abstract question of democracy," as he said, "but of social and economic organization, the treatment of working-people by employers, and all that goes along with it." Out of this really fundamental issue, out of what he called "the Poverty Question," Whitman maintained that all other issues, the tariff, finance, and the like, evolved themselves more or less directly. What, he insisted on asking, did the wealth of the civilized world actually mean as contrasted with its poverty? "A rich person," he answered, "ought to have a strong stomach. As in Europe the wealth of to-day mainly results from, and represents, the rapine, murder, outrages, treachery, hoggishness, of hundreds of years ago, and onward, later, so in America, after the same token—(not yet so bad, perhaps, or at any rate so palpable—we have not existed long enough—but we seem to be doing our best to make it up.)"

How near we were coming to doing so he felt with particular sharpness one winter day, late in the seventies, when on a street in Camden or Philadelphia he had seen a sight that was new to him and that made him, as he said, "serious." It was the sight of three respectable-looking American men, two of them young, plodding along with bags on their shoulders and long iron hooks in their hands, and looking with downcast eyes at the street itself for scraps, rags, bones, and the like. To Walt Whitman, a spiritual offspring of the "strike" he had described the American Revolution as being, there was matter for somber reflection in the sight. "If the United States," he wrote, apropos of all this, "like the countries of the Old World, are also to grow vast crops of poor, desperate, dissatisfied, nomadic, miserably-waged populations, such as we see looming upon us of late years—steadily, even if slowly, eating into them like a cancer of lungs or stomach—then our republican experiment, notwithstanding all its surface-successes, is at heart an unhealthy failure."

A decade or more of life, when he wrote these notes, lay ahead of Whitman. Would the events of those years, more than half of which were prosperous ones, persuade him at last that the republican experiment was a real and not merely an apparent or superficial success? or would they confirm him in his reluctant dread that, with all its actual tendencies, it might prove to be an unhealthy failure? They did neither, in any sharply-defined or ultimate manner: on the contrary, with their own violent contradictions of wealth and misery, of progress and disorder, they heightened the old dualism that had run through his thoughts on such matters more or less from the beginning, until in the end it was as if Whitman had become a kind of unconscious ventriloquist, speaking alternately with the accents of Andrew Carnegie and the accents of John Swinton. Of course they were really his own unmistakable accents in both cases, but the disharmony between them was glaring. He could say to a reporter, as we have seen, that "the movements of all are going on as well as possibly could be." And he could then say to his English admirer, Wallace: "There is nowhere in the world, I suppose, the demonism, the foulness, the corruption, that we have in America." The two personalities that had always existed in Whitman, the yea-sayer and the rebel, had long since ceased to have any real relation with each other, and they now went their separate ways amicably and without disaster. They had become emblems of both the middle-class contentedness of the century's end and the surviving strains of petty bourgeois radicalism which rumbled beneath it.

The rebel in Whitman, at any rate, had not blinded himself to the menacing developments of the eighties—those developments which finally led the mild-mannered Howells to say, in a letter to Mark Twain, that "there is no longer an American Republic, but an aristocracy-loving oligarchy in place of it." Neither Whitman nor Howells had had the theoretical training that would have enabled him to understand the events of the decade in all their significance, and certainly Whitman never saw so clearly as Howells came to see it, that American capitalism (to which he probably never gave that name) was entering decisively upon its monopolistic stage and would soon be ripe for the adventure of empire. He did not see these things for exactly what they were in the rhythm of social history, but even in his old age he was too alert to the stir about him not to take note of the emergence on the scene of powerful "combines" in steel, in packing, in transportation, and especially of the great trusts in oil, in sugar, in whisky. He would not have failed to see that the social and political power of the great industrialists was now at last supreme, and that the enormous productivity of American industry had created a plutocracy such as the American farmers, mechanics, and shopkeepers of his youthful days —with their resentment against patroons and bankers— could never have envisaged. What followed in the wake of all this was almost certainly more present to Whitman than any of his published utterances ever indicated—the bitter revolt of the Western and Southern farmers, for example, the beginnings of Populism, the rush of industrial and unskilled workers into the ranks of the Knights of Labor, the appearance of terroristic anarchism, and the wave of hard-fought strikes that culminated in the eight-hour struggles of 1886. He certainly heard, as almost all Americans heard, on the evening of May 4 in that year, the detonations of a bomb that exploded in the midst of demonstrating workers in Chicago's Haymarket Square— and ultimately sent four men to the gallows.

He had his reasons, good or bad, for keeping what he heard and saw mainly to himself: he had never seen his way clear to giving such perceptions a conspicuous position in the pattern of *Leaves of Grass,* and it was now much too late to modify that pattern radically. Nor did he feel any "leading," as the old Quakers said, to make public in any way his emotions and his thoughts as he observed what was going on about him. Only in conversations with intimate friends, and especially with Traubel, did the Whitman of those apparently serene later years

145

reveal the whole force of his disappointment, his resentment, and his dread. Sitting in his cane-seated arm-chair, however, or lying in bed in the front room upstairs at Mickle Street, he more than once confessed to the young bank-clerk, his most devoted friend, that many things he had hoped for in his sanguine youth had not come about, and that many things he had hardly even feared had become realities.

He had always thought, even in his callow days as a schoolmaster, that the scramble for wealth was a great folly and a great waste, and had probably hoped that it was a passing phase in the life of his fellow-Americans. The sequel of the Civil War had already forced him to abandon that hope, and now, as the century approached its close, the mania raged more violently than ever. The spectacle dejected Whitman in spite of his serenity. "Every man," he declared with a kind of anger, "is trying to outdo every other man—giving up modesty, giving up honesty, giving up generosity, to do it: creating a war, every man against every man: the whole wretched business falsely keyed by money ideals, money politics, money religions, money men." He had once written that real democracy and great riches are incompatible with each other: he was now prepared to admit that the latter had won out. "Horace," he said bitterly one day, "we are all under the thumb of the millionaires: ours is a millionaire government without a doubt." If democracy was to survive, all that would have to be changed. "We shook off England," said Traubel to him on another occasion. "We shook off the slave. What will we shake off next?" "Money!" answered the old man—"the dominion of money." And he

added: "Do you suppose you see any better than I do the
menace hanging over our democracy?"

Certainly when he had set out to become the poet of
the New World society he had had the happy confidence
that he was hymning an order of things from which, whatever its incidental defects might be, the class divisions of
feudal Europe had been banished once for all. This confidence, too, had been shaken by the events of the sixties
and seventies, and in the year of Benjamin Harrison's election—the year also of a strike by Carnegie steel-workers—
it had yielded to Whitman's sense of fact. "Against the
things we call successes," he had remarked that spring, "I
see other, counter, tendencies working—an increased indis-
position of certain classes to do the honest labor of the
world, and the solidification of the money powers against
the fraternity of the masses. Either one of these might,
both of them are sure, to ruin the republic if nothing appears to contravene them." One day in the following
September Traubel was telling him of a Japanese friend
of his who had first been struck, on travelling in America,
by the fearful gap between the rich and the poor. "Ah!
Did he say that?" exclaimed Whitman. "Then I am convinced that he put his finger on the sore spot at once. I always come back to the same idea myself: there is the itch—
the trouble: there is no mistake: the fact of the matter is
the situation is growing worse and worse . . . It is seen at
its damnedest in the big cities—New York, Philadelphia,
Chicago: but it is bad no matter where. America has got
to clean house some day!"

He might feel that time had thus given the lie to the
sanguine expectations of his youth, but he also felt that it

147

had justified his early detachment from the two-and-seventy jarring sects of ante-bellum reformers and even from the Abolitionists. "I never could quite lose the sense of other evils in this evil," he once observed of slavery—"I saw other evils that cried to me in perhaps even a louder voice: the labor evil, now, to speak of only one, which to this day has been steadily growing worse, worse, worse." As we know, even the labor evil had cried to Whitman with an intermittent urgency in the forties and fifties: he himself observed to Traubel that the question had not been "up" then as it was in the late eighties, and that that was perhaps the reason why he had not "embraced" it. Now, however, it was up about as pressingly as it could be: some day, he said, it would be *the* live question—"then somebody will have to look out—especially the bodies with big fortunes wrung from the sweat and blood of the poor." On this head, with all his fine obstinacy, Whitman would concede whatever his radical young friend, from time to time, attempted to win from him. "Won't we," asked Traubel one day, when the talk had turned on Tolstoy, "won't we have the European problems just the same here in a little time?" The old man assented briefly. "All the poverty problems," insisted Traubel—"about the land, about machinery, ownership of things—just the same?" Whitman nodded. "Why not? surely?" he rejoined, "what can prevent it? we seem to be travelling the same damnable road." An inevitable road, the young man put in. "Yes—but damnable, too," said Whitman. Would we get out of it? "Yes, we must: money must take second place!"

He had no doubt that money would do this, ultimately, but he saw as plainly as any of his juniors that the plans of the old equalitarians had somehow miscarried, and that

148

their true realization was still to come. "We've got a hell of a lot to learn yet," he said, "before we're a real democracy: we've gone beyond all the others, very far beyond some, but we're far from having yet achieved our dream. . . . We'll get there in the end: God knows we're not there yet." Whatever he may once have thought, Whitman now saw that the long historical struggle for an equal and harmonious society was, even in these states, still in its preliminary stages. "All the real problems, the fundamentals," he said surprisingly, "are yet ahead of us—will have to be tackled by us or by our children or theirs: not skin-ticklers, like the tariff, but life and death challenges which will line us up fiercely on this side or that." He hardly needed to tell Horace Traubel which side, at least in spirit, he would be on.

Chapter Four

SCIENCE AND THE UNSEEN

IT TAKES LITTLE IMAGINATION to see Walt Whitman as the contemporary and fellow-countryman of Andrew Jackson and Abraham Lincoln; it takes hardly more than a second thought and a somewhat closer view to see him as the contemporary of John Jacob Astor and George Peabody. Even then, however, he has not been perfectly focused in his whole setting. There are many things in *Leaves of Grass* that imply the existence of a quite different group of men in the social and intellectual world out of which the book emerged; a group of men whose names one associates not with the rostrum or the battlefield, the counting-house or the mill, but with the laboratory, the botanic garden, the lecture-room. Whitman himself summoned up the presences of such men in that full-sailed preface in prose which accompanied the first edition of his book—the preface in which he declared, with unevadable emphasis, that "exact science and its practical movements are no checks on the greatest poet but always his encouragement and support." To the men of science themselves he made, at the same time, a deep bow. "The atomist chemist astronomer geologist phrenologist spiritualist mathematician historian and lexicographer are not poets, but they are the law-givers of poets and their construction underlies the structure of every perfect poem. . . . If there shall be love and content between the father and the son and if the greatness of the son is the exuding of the greatness of the father there shall be love between the poet and the man of demonstrable science." From the laboratory to the poet's study, from the observatory to the poetic mount, Whitman insisted, the way is direct and open. "In the beauty of poems," he cried, "are the tuft and final applause of science."

How much he consciously meant to say when he said this, how far his book itself realizes the promise and the program thus advertised, these are bristling and many-sided questions. What cannot be in question, if only because he himself thrust it at his readers so plainly, is the importance of the elementary fact that Whitman belonged to the age of Darwin and Helmholtz, and to the country of Joseph Henry and Asa Gray. The "man of demonstrable science" was one of his truest contemporaries, and how well, on one level, he knew it! The toss and drive of the general western mind that made possible *Leaves of Grass* was also making possible, decade by decade, those almost as extraordinary productions, the great illuminating generalizations of nineteenth-century physics and biology. There were men of letters in that century who could and did insulate themselves almost completely from the currents of thought that moved toward these generalizations, but Whitman was not one of them; he was not, because he was too sensitive and too responsive to all the disturbances, especially the powerful disturbances, in the air about him. He may or may not have been the Lucretius of his age: what is important is that he intended to be something rather vaguely of that sort, and this forces us to look at him in the environment created by uniformitarian geology,

151

atomic and molecular chemistry, the biology of natural selection, and the physics that culminated in the two laws of thermodynamics. Something quite definitive appears only when we look at Whitman thus.

All this would have been equally true if he had been a western European writer of the same generation; it would have been much less true if he had lived, for example, in mid-century Spain or Russia. As an American of the middle decades, he was almost as close to the central stream of scientific activity as if he had lived in London or Paris or Berlin. Not quite, of course; but, even aside from the quick American receptiveness, at the time, to what was being accomplished in Europe, no American could be wholly unaware that compatriots of his own had contributed and were still contributing essential blocks to the growing structure of modern science. Walt Whitman may not have known specifically that, without Benjamin Thompson—renegade though he was!—the mechanical equivalent of heat and the first law of thermodynamics would not have been arrived at exactly as they were; but he must have known about Thompson in some general way, and he would certainly have known how much the knowledge of electricity had been advanced by Benjamin Franklin. He may have realized—we can only guess—that the science of electromagnetism owed hardly more to the great Faraday than to the self-effacing Albany schoolmaster, Joseph Henry. No alert American could wholly fail, in those days, to be aware that the men who were surveying Massachusetts and New York State were all but neck and neck with the leaders of European geology, and that there were excellent reasons for Lyell's repeated trips to the United States, as for Louis Agassiz's coming to make his home here. As time went on, all well-informed Americans must have realized that below the towering propositions of *The Origin of Species* lay, among how many other accretions of humble fact, the bones and fossils that Culbertson sent back from the Bad Lands to Joseph Leidy in Philadelphia, the patiently-collected anatomical exhibits of Jeffries Wyman in Cambridge, and the thousands of botanical specimens in Asa Gray's herbarium and garden.

The years of Whitman's youth were years during which, after its fine precocity under Franklin, American science was rapidly coming of age. Leidy and Henry, Gray and Wyman were far from isolated figures. The man with the microscope, the man at the transit instrument, the man with the geologist's hammer—these men were coming to be more and more representative Americans. Whitman was a young schoolmaster in the country when the first permanent observatory in the United States was built at Williamstown, and in the next few years, as Cincinnati, Philadelphia, and Cambridge followed this lead, there emerged a brilliant young school of American astronomers—a school to which celestial mechanics, the knowledge of meteors and comets, the photography of heavenly bodies were to owe a heavy debt. At the time Whitman was getting out the *Long Islander* in his native village, Lieutenant Charles Wilkes set out for the South Seas on that four-year voyage of exploration which, with the blessing of Congress, was to result in so fine an increment to knowledge. The days of Van Buren's and Tyler's presidencies were days that saw the work of the New York geological and natural history surveys, and it was in the year of the Log Cabin campaign that Ebenezer Emmons, James Hall, and others organized the Association of American Geologists—which

153

was so soon to transform itself into the more comprehensive American Association for the Advancement of Science.
Of all this the people were by no means unaware: to make
them aware of it, indeed, was the function of the lyceums,
the mechanics' institutes, the lecture series, which flour-
ished all the while in so many cities and towns. It would
be easy, certainly, to underestimate the number of plain
men and women who, during those years, heard Benjamin
Silliman or Louis Agassiz or some other savant lecture on
the Principles of Chemistry, on Meteorology, or on the
Plan of Creation.

The work of observation and experiment, unostenta-
tious as it was amid the din of electioneering and conquest,
went forward boldly and brilliantly on every front. How
rich in such achievements, for example, was that year or
two of the Mexican War during which Whitman busied
himself at his desk in the *Eagle* office! At about the time
he took up his new duties, Congress was at 'last, after years
of delay, chartering the Smithsonian Institution "for the
increase and diffusion of knowledge among men," and
Joseph Henry, preoccupied now with his batteries and
magnets at Princeton, was being persuaded to become its
first secretary. Warren and Morton, at the Massachusetts
General, were demonstrating for the first time how ether
could be used in a surgical operation; and Whitman himself, a little later in Brooklyn, was to witness the resetting
of a small boy's dislocated thumb under the influence of
that beneficent liquid. James Dwight Dana, the young
professor at Yale, who had been mineralogist on the Wilkes
expedition, was publishing his great report—for he was also
a biologist—on the zoöphytes of the Pacific. A new planet,
Neptune, was discovered that autumn by a Frenchman,

and immediately after the news of Leverrier's achievement arrived on the packets from Europe, William C. Bond, who was shortly to discover the eighth satellite of Saturn and to take the first photograph of the moon, eagerly turned his telescope at Cambridge upon the last major member of the solar system. While the cleavage in New York between Hunkers and Barnburners was growing wider and wider, Matthew F. Maury, the founder of the science of hydrography, published his *Wind and Current Chart of the North Atlantic,* and a famous monograph "On the Fossil Horse of America" appeared at Philadelphia over the signature of Joseph Leidy. The "increase of knowledge" was proceeding apace.

Of all these developments on many fronts the young Locofoco editor was probably not immediately aware: the central field of his vision lay elsewhere. But, absorbed as he might be by the progress of the agrarian empire, or by his reading of Carlyle and George Sand, he had too eager a thirst for information, too lively a curiosity about all the triumphs of his age, not to find time, casually and unsystematically, for the work of the "atomist," "chemist," "geologist," and the rest. Without even crossing the river to New York, Whitman could get a real stimulus to such scattered inquiries in Brooklyn itself. The old Apprentices' Library there had evolved, after a period of decline, into the Brooklyn Institute, and through that organization the shopkeepers and artisans might now listen to lectures or to courses of lectures not only on morals and religion but on the natural sciences. At such sessions, if we are to judge from occasional notices in the *Eagle,* Whitman was a not infrequent attendant. There he probably heard a lecture by one Professor Gray on Galvanism; there he may have heard a certain Dr. Newcomb expound the science of conchology; there he certainly listened—at first skeptically and then more and more responsively—to Professor Fowler on Phrenology; and there he no doubt sat in the audience of the great Agassiz as he lectured on the transportation of boulders, "particularly by Swiss glaciers." How much Whitman was probably conscious of owing to such substantial discourses as these we may gather from his remarks in the *Times*, ten years later, on the emptiness and triviality of so many lectures of the day—a fact, he felt, so much to be regretted since "there is hardly a science on which much may not be told, in an interesting shape, which persons of ordinary intelligence do not know."

Undoubtedly, at any rate, he was proud of the work done by the Brooklyn Institute, so proud that he wanted his city to move on into further domains where other American cities had preceded her. It was the decade of the new observatories, the decade when the wonderful improved telescopes were being imported from Munich, and Whitman could not bear to see Brooklyn left behind by Cincinnati and Cambridge. He had been stirred by the account of how O. M. Mitchell, the Ohio astronomer, had labored to persuade the citizens of Cincinnati to raise the money for building an observatory on one of the hills that encircled the city; and how, when he had at last succeeded and the new building was about to go up, Mitchell had travelled to Niagara Falls to find John Quincy Adams, and there had prevailed upon the aged statesman, despite his dread of a long and toilsome journey, to go by stagecoach and canal-boat to Cincinnati and lay the cornerstone of the observatory. For all his Locofocoism, Whitman felt nothing but respect for Adams's lifelong espousal of public support for the sciences: he was himself genuinely, if informally, interested in astronomy, and when the project was set on foot of building an observatory in Brooklyn, he repeated the story of Mitchell and Adams in an editorial on "That Observatory in Brooklyn which We Must Have." "Had it not been for Professor Mitchell," he wrote, a little hyperbolically, "Cincinnati might not have had an observatory for centuries to come; and many years might have rolled round before the people of Brooklyn would have 'thought of it,' too."

It had not been his good luck to study under Silliman at Yale or under Gray at Harvard or, as Hawthorne had done a decade or two earlier, under Parker Cleaveland at Bowdoin; and he was to have none of those opportunities for European travel that had made it possible for Emerson to pay his eagerly inquiring visits to the Hunterian Museum and the Jardin des Plantes. But probably few of the literary men of his generation made more use of the sources of information within their reach than Whitman did. If he could not visit the great gardens or observatories, he could go back again and again to Dr. Abbott's Museum of Egyptian Antiquities on Broadway, and he could pump his friends or acquaintances for whatever knowledge of the natural world they might have. He could and did talk with Elias Pierson, whoever Elias Pierson was, about "a very low kind of human beings" he had seen in one of the Ladrone Islands. He talked with Mr. Maher, an old whaleman, about whales, and learning that the cow of that species has but one calf at a birth, amended a line in the "Song of Myself" to make it conform to the facts. He got a certain Mr. Arnold to tell him about Joseph Priestley, and then made a note of the fact that the Englishman had been the discoverer of oxygen and a proponent of "philosophical necessity": "he must have been a *real man,*" added Whitman on his own. Years later, when he was living at Camden, he counted among his friends of the ferryboats the astronomer, Henry Whitall, author of a treatise on the principal fixed stars and constellations, "who posts me up in points about the stars by a living lesson there and then, and answering every question."

As for books, it was certainly not in the literature of the sciences that he did the bulk of his reading, and he may never have read through, studiously and systematically, even one of the scientific classics of the past or his own time. One does not see Whitman mastering the *Principia* or the *Mécanique Céleste* or the *Principles of Geology,* and it is a question how well he was ever to know *The Origin of Species* at first hand. But he undoubtedly dipped into, and he may have read with a certain care, a good many more or less primary, more or less substantial, works of a scientific nature. He noticed in the *Eagle* such books as Denison Olmstead's *Letters on Astronomy,* Mrs. R. Lee's *Memoirs of Baron Cuvier,* and—on the borderline between science and pseudo-science, of course—O. S. Fowler's *Physiology, Animal and Mental.* One book, an epoch-making book in fact, he must have read in part with some diligence, if his outburst of enthusiasm for it is any guide. The book was Justus Liebig's *Chemistry in its Application to Agriculture and Physiology,* one of the Pentateuchal books of organic chemistry, and it led the *Eagle's* editor to break out in the following terms: "Chemistry! the elevating, beautiful study! which only the vulgar think technical, because they have not delved into its capacious recesses. Chemistry—that involves the essences of creation,

158

and the changes, and the growths, and formations and de-
cays, of so large a constituent part of the earth, and the
things thereof. We can well imagine how a man whose
judgment leaps over the mere artificial, can be an enthusiastic, life-devoted, student in this noble science."

He was never to become such a student himself, but the
poet of "This Compost"—

> *What chemistry!*
> *That the winds are really not infectious . . .*
> *That all is clean forever and forever . . .*

> *Now I am terrified at the Earth, it is that calm and*
> *   patient,*
> *It grows such sweet things out of such corruptions—*

this poet had perhaps learned more from Liebig's account of
organic decay and renewal than the impressionistic reader
might suppose. In any case, it was less from books than
from the magazines and newspapers which all his life he
read so eagerly, that Whitman probably derived most of
what he knew about the scientific progress of his time. In
that mass of old papers and mementos that billowed about
him almost threateningly in his upper room at Mickle
Street, there was, as Dr. Bucke discovered after Whitman's
death, a heap of old newspaper clippings and ripped-out
magazine articles, dating back even to the forties, on the
most catholic variety of subjects. They are prevailingly
literary and historical in their bearing, these pieces, as one
would suppose beforehand, but dozens of them bear witness also to that curiosity about the physical world and its
phenomena that Whitman came by so naturally. Here belong the old articles—now from the *Democratic Review*,

159

now from the *Living Age,* now from one of the British quarterlies—on "Botany," on "The Physical Atlas," on "Sir John Herschel," on "Lyell's Geological Tour." Here belong the much larger number of newspaper pieces— pieces on astronomical matters ("Comets, their History and Habits" or "Physical Constitution of the Sun"), on geology (a review of Hugh Miller's *Testimony of the Rocks*), on biology ("Lowest Class of Animals" or "Scenes on the Ocean Floor"), on travel and anthropology ("Barth's Discoveries in Central Africa"). Here belong those clippings that suggest how closely Whitman followed the Albany meeting of the American Association for the Advancement of Science in 1856, and how much he may have absorbed from these newspaper reports of papers read at Albany by the great American savants—by Joseph Henry, for example, on acoustics, by Agassiz on viviparity and oviparity, by Benjamin Peirce on tidal currents in Neptune's ring, by Dana on the geological history of North America, or by Schoolcraft on the Algonquin language.

These were the men who were fostering the scientific sense of things in that otherwise mainly evangelical or romantic or philistine America of the mid-century; and those aged scraps of periodical literature, preserved during so many decades, are eloquent of the interest with which Whitman followed the work of such men—an interest so much sharper than most of his literary coevals were capable of. Was this interest, however, as it might have been, only that of an alert journalist to the newsworthy developments of the day? Or was it only the interest that, in a rather special sense, a poet, a man of letters, might take in the marvelous, the picturesque, the half-incredible? It was both these things in part, certainly, for the journalist in

Whitman was as active here as elsewhere, and the singer in him—rather than, to use his own antithesis, the Poet, the Answerer—was simple-heartedly entranced by the terrifying grandeur of comets, by the weird life of "the world below the brine," by the thought of the flowing and shifting hills. But the Answerer was at work too, and this lecture-going, this querying of travellers, this cutting up of newspapers, all sprang from a certain awareness—however crossed and confused, earlier or later, by other impulsions —of the possible meaning of these things for the philosophic spirit; of what they might say about the world and the status of human beings in it. In short, Walt Whitman had had, and was never wholly to abandon, a genuine bias toward a rigorously naturalistic view of things.

He was so powerfully worked upon by the romantic mood of his generation that it has largely been forgotten or ignored how much he had been affected, in boyhood and earliest youth, by an older and tougher way of thought; yet in fact if he was the child, as of course he was, of nineteenth-century Transcendentalism, he was the grandchild of the Age of Reason. It was not from the idealistic poets and romancers of his own generation that Whitman acquired—it was from the men of the Enlightenment that he inherited—his respect for "the man of demonstrable science" and his leaning toward a vital materialism. He inherited these things in an almost literal and personal sense, in the sense at least that the echoes of rationalistic agitation had been audible even in that simple Brooklyn household in which he spent his early days. The attitudes of the elder materialists had penetrated the Jeffersonian masses more deeply than is always remembered now, and the Whitmans appear to have been close to some of the channels of the old Free Thought. Walter Whitman, the poet's father, had had some sort of acquaintance with Thomas Paine as an old man; and in the days when young Whitman himself was frequenting Tammany Hall, he had seen a good deal of the elderly Colonel Fellows, a man of mark who had been a friend of Paine's and from whom Whitman heard much—but nothing that was not wholly favorable—about the personality of the man who wrote *Common Sense*. He was never to forget these impressions or to cease to honor the memory of Thomas Paine: he was to feel, into his latest old age, that the man had been the "chiefest" of "three of the superber characters of my day or America's early days"—the other two being Elias Hicks and Frances Wright—of whom he had long felt that it was his duty to write something by way of vindication. The sustained essay on Paine which he planned was never put down on paper; the page or two about him in *Specimen Days* alone remain; but who can doubt that *The Age of Reason* had been one of the controlling books of Whitman's boyhood?

It had been, in that case, only one of a little group of free-thinking books that had come his way. Another was *The Ruins,* by Jefferson's friend, the French radical, Volney, whose presence in this country was said to have had much to do with the haste with which, in John Adams's time, the Alien and Sedition Acts had been pushed through. *The Ruins* was of course the book on which Shelley, the atheistical Shelley of *Queen Mab,* had drawn so freely, and which Lincoln was later to read thoughtfully at New Salem. It was another of the books, as Whitman told Traubel, "on which I may be said to have been raised." Still a third was a daring little book, ostensibly about Epicurus,

called *A Few Days in Athens,* the work of "this bold and
forcible female," as the Boston *Gazette* called her, Frances
Wright. The book had once been daily food to him, Whitman said, and the copy he had with him in old age he
urged upon his young Camden friend for his own reading.
But it was not only in this way that Whitman had fallen
under the spell of Frances Wright's imperious personality.
During the late twenties, when the Scotswoman was active as a lecturer and journalist in New York, Whitman's
father had subscribed to the *Free Enquirer* which she and
Robert Dale Owen were issuing, and the family read it reg-
ularly. Moreover, either at that time, when he was a boy
of hardly ten, or in the late thirties and early forties, when
Frances Wright was again in New York, Whitman had
gone repeatedly to her public lectures and received from
them a profound personal and intellectual impression
which nothing was ever to efface; an impression the
strength of which he described in language of peculiar ex-
travagance. "Her very appearance seemed to enthrall us,"
he told Traubel, and he confessed that he had never felt
"so glowingly" toward any other woman: "she possessed
herself," he said, "of my body and soul." He failed to write
the essay he planned on "glorious Frances," as he failed
to write at any length about Paine, but Traubel has preserved for us Whitman's conviction that Frances Wright
was "one of the best [characters] in history though also
one of the least understood."

No doubt it was chiefly as political liberals that writers
such as these exercised their sway over the youthful Whitman's spirit: no doubt it was the Paine of *The Rights of
Man,* the Volney whom John Adams had feared and hated,
the Frances Wright who helped to build the Working-

men's Party—no doubt it was these whom the young Locofoco most consciously venerated. But how could he make
daily food of such books and papers as theirs—how could
he listen to lectures such as Frances Wright's—and remain
wholly immune to the powerful virus of rationalism that
also pervaded them? How could he be untouched by their
assaults not only on kings and aristocrats, but on priests
and theologians; not only on injustice and inequality, but
on religion, on churches, on superstition? Priests, Volney
had said, are "enemies to the rest of society"; the whole
history of religion he had declared to be that of the falli-
bility of the human mind; and Frances Wright, in her
book about Epicurus, had described religion as "that dark
coinage of trembling ignorance." Such were the sentiments on these subjects that at least gained an entrance
into the carpenter's household on Cranberry or Tillary
Street; how easy to imagine their impact on the mind of an
impressionable boy!

There were counter-forces, even then, as we shall see, at
work upon him; but in any case it was not merely a hatred
of priests and churches, not merely a set of iconoclasms,
that he would have imbibed from *The Ruins* and *A Few
Days in Athens*. Volney and Frances Wright, like Thomas
Paine, were the heirs of Locke, of Voltaire, of Holbach;
and "the sacred principles of heaven-born reason," as
Volney called them, were the principles they quite positively—if sometimes too mechanically and ingenuously—
espoused. A sanguine sense of the capacities of the human
mind, of its actual and potential triumphs in deciphering
the book of nature, was the luminous obverse of their distrust of faith: it shone with a steady radiance through all
they wrote. It was a rationalism in which intuition, mysti-

164

cal insight, innate ideas, played no part: all true belief, according to Frances Wright, is based on "the evidence of one or more of our senses," and Volney, in the same empiricist vein, had insisted that men acquire no ideas except through the medium of eyes and ears. The world, moreover, of which men thus become aware is a world whose essential reality is not that of impalpable spirit but of tangible and material substance—"this beautiful material world," as Frances Wright called it—and vitality itself is but a subtle manifestation of the physical energy of nature: "life," as she also said, "is another quality, or combination of qualities, of matter."

It is a world, moreover, these rationalists of the old school held, in which all events have their adequate causes and their inevitable effects; a world in which no mere accidents, no inexplicable miracles, whimsically interfere with the intelligible movement of phenomena; an inherently orderly world of which the principles of order are accessible to the inquiring reason. It is a world, as Volney said, "governed by *natural laws*, regular in their operation, unerring in their effects, immutable in their essence." They hold sway, these natural laws, not only in the sidereal heavens, not only in the behavior of gases, not only in the vegetable and animal kingdoms, but in human experience, in the relations between man and man, as well. It was at this point that these early rationalists were betrayed by an excess of zeal. Morality, declared Volney sweepingly, is *"a branch of the science of physics"*; and it was as "a branch of general physics" that Frances Wright also had somewhat too simply described the philosophy of mind and conduct. At any rate, the methods of the natural sciences they held to be the methods by which all true

knowledge, of whatever kind, is to be acquired; the physicist, far from being a mere investigator of the laws of
mechanics, is the pace-setter for the moralist, the statesman, the philosopher. "Natural philosophy," Paine had
said—embracing as it does "the whole circle of science"
—is "the true theology"; and the Almighty himself, "the
great mechanic of the creation," was "the first philosopher
and original teacher of all science." In saying this, he said
nothing that Volney and Frances Wright would not have
echoed enthusiastically.

Such, in any case, were the strong if over-simplified materialistic views that, living on after the ebb of the Enlightenment, could still be aired, however riskily, in the
America of the twenties and thirties, and work upon the
minds of boys and young men like Abraham Lincoln and
Walt Whitman. How deeply they worked upon the mind
of Walt Whitman, how faithful he remained to the spirit
behind them, how much of Volney and Frances Wright
and Paine can really be discerned in the finished whole of
Leaves of Grass—these are considerations that must be left
for a later page. What can be said now is that, standing behind the lyceum lecturers and the newspaper writers,
Paine and Volney and Frances Wright furnished the intellectual setting for that genial and general hospitality toward natural science in which Whitman went beyond
most of the other American writers of his generation. He
had given voice to it as a young journalist, and it had
found eloquent expression, as we have seen, in the first
preface to his book; years later, in his old age, with all that
had happened in the interval, he was to reaffirm, sometimes in the strongest language, his youthful enthusiasm.
In the last long preface he wrote he was still greeting "the

splendid day-rise of science"; and when Edward Carpenter, a little earlier, remarked to him that Europe and America had much to learn from the wisdom of the East, his host replied: "I do not myself think there is anything more to come from that source; we must rather look to modern science to open the way."

He himself had said things that might well have led Carpenter to expect another sort of response, but certainly the response he did make was not merely disputatious. Horace Traubel could have testified to that. "I stand in awe before the men of science," Whitman once said to his young friend: "they hold the key to the situation: they are the true discoverers: they are—they with their utter abandon, honesty." And one October evening, while they talked of George Eliot and of Heine, he broke out into a kind of conversational hymn to science and the scientific spirit. It was the best gift to the age so far, he declared: it was "the crowning glory of our time," this "new evangel," and only in it—with its humility, its appeal to things as they are, its whole-hearted surrender to facts, its universal acceptance and assent—only here was there any real salvation. It was the agent that, more than any other, was making for truth and simplicity and profound sincerity everywhere, in literature as much as in the laboratory and the field: Heine had understood it, fundamentally, and without this spirit *Leaves of Grass* would have lost who could say how much? "The whole mass of people are being leavened by this spirit of scientific worship—this noblest of religions coming after all the religions that came before." No matter what happens or fails to happen, he went on with greater and greater fervor, what science tells us is to say yes. "That's where science becomes religion—where the new spirit ut-

167

ters the highest truth—makes the last demonstration of faith: looks the universe full in the face—its bad in the face, its good—and says yes to it." His face was shining as he finished, and he regarded his companion "with great love."

So much—so unexpectedly much, perhaps—had the lectures and the conversations and the newspaper stories meant to Whitman, to his imagination if not to his intellect. They had convinced him, on one level, that a fresher and truer way of looking at all things had come into human affairs with the telescope and the retort, and that the poet of the new time would ignore at his peril not only the findings but the methods, the spirit, the mental habits, of the man who used those instruments. Almost alone among American writers of the middle decades, he saw in the large if not in detail what a difference it would all make, would have to make, to the poet of the future; almost alone he hailed what he called "the entire revolution made by science in the poetic method." He himself may not have appreciated the full bearing of his words; it remains for us a question whether or not he did; but he at least said, when the thing was not yet a commonplace, that the real poems of the present "must vocalize the vastness and splendor and reality with which Scientism has invested Man and the Universe"; that "the true use for the imaginative faculty of modern times is to give ultimate vivification to facts, to science, and to common lives, endowing them with glows and glories and final illustriousness which belong to every real thing, and to real things only." He felt, moreover, that in *Leaves of Grass* he had essentially done this himself; that, without being (as he said) a scientist, he had thoroughly adopted the conclusions of the great scientists of his time, and that "they have interiorly tinged the chyle of all my verse, for purposes beyond."

Had he in fact, however, adopted those conclusions as thoroughly as he maintained he had? Had his verse really assimilated them with the physiological completeness he claimed for it? These are questions that ought to be answered before we undertake to define Whitman's meaning for us and for the immediate future, but before we answer them we must consider the effect on his mind and imagination of other and contrary currents in the mental air of his period.

II

Whitman's America was capable of the Smithsonian Institution and the Association for the Advancement of Science; it was capable of the Cambridge Observatory and the lyceum system and, in his later years, of the *Popular Science Monthly*. Whitman's class, the American middle class, was able to produce such men as Joseph Henry and Asa Gray and Edward Youmans. His America and his class —the one so largely defined and dominated by the other— could conceive and make realities of the Pennsylvania Canal, the Mohawk & Hudson Railroad, the Patent Office, the magnetic telegraph, and the Atlantic cable. The culture of that youthful capitalism, commercial and growingly industrial, to which his life belonged, made room for "pure" and certainly for "applied" science as no culture before it had done: it had its uses and therefore its respect for the physicist and the botanist, the learned society and the serious popular journal. What that culture proved unable to do was to maintain the intellectual and philosophic

169

gains of its great century, the eighteenth; to preserve, without relaxation of grip, and then to enrich, to humanize, to make dynamic, that bold if too mechanistic materialism it had attained during the Enlightenment; to move on unfalteringly from dogma and mysticism and the supernatural to the high and open levels of a mature naturalism. It could achieve a momentarily workable compromise between faith and knowledge; it could not achieve a synthesis on a superior plane.

The mind of the middle class in Whitman's time shrank back from the austere implications of its own advance toward the understanding and the mastery of nature, physical and biological, just as, politically, it shrank back from the radical implications of its own liberalism, its own battle-cries of equality and brotherhood. It could no more make the full transition from belief to science than it could make the full transition from feudalism to social democracy. It yielded ground, for strategic reasons, to its preachers and its poets; and just as it had elevated its Websters and then its Grants to the moral posts once occupied by Samuel Adams and Thomas Jefferson, so it elevated its Henry Ward Beechers and its Lyman Abbotts to the posts once occupied by Benjamin Franklin and Thomas Paine. The determination to make the best of both worlds went hand in hand with the determination to reconcile democracy and economic individualism.

Just how difficult the preachers and the poets, after all, would have found it to enter wholly into the new intellectual world, becomes evident when we listen to their contemporaries, the great scientists themselves. Almost to a man, these scientists succeeded in "reconciling" their inherited Calvinism or Arminianism with their Newtonian or their Darwinian knowledge. Almost to a man, they persuaded themselves that the exact study of nature was in essence a reverent study of the great works of God. No one in his time did more than Benjamin Silliman to diffuse among Americans an understanding of chemistry and geology, and Silliman held that physical science "everywhere demonstrates both supreme intelligence and harmony and beneficence of design in the Creator." Asa Gray, for whom Darwin entertained so high a regard, was "religiously an acceptor of the 'creed commonly called the Nicene.'" Perhaps the leading American geologist of his time was James Dwight Dana, and Dana believed that "the whole Universe is not merely dependent on, but actually is, the Will of one Supreme Intelligence." Religion, we are told, was one of the chief interests of Lewis Henry Morgan, the great student of primitive societies, who is said at times to have been deeply troubled lest his ethnological writings should be detrimental to religious faith. And what of Edward Youmans, the tireless propagandist of Spencer's and Darwin's ideas, an acquaintance of Whitman's too, who maintained that "the inflexible order of the universe . . . bears the loftiest witness to its Divine Creator"? At a time when men of "demonstrable science" —and men, moreover, of an eminence so real—could remain such good theists as this, could anyone fairly have impugned the consistency of a poet who could reconcile what he knew of Hegel with what he knew of Darwin?

The years of Whitman's childhood had coincided with the lingering twilight of the elder Free Thought; his extreme old age was to coincide with the slow dawn of a newer naturalism, a naturalism that had been heralded by *First Principles* and *The Origin of Species*. The intervening years had been dominated, intellectually, by the liberal Protestant preacher, the metaphysical idealist, and the romantic poet. In their various ways, these men had been occupied in repairing the dykes which the materialism of the preceding century had broken through; in protecting the soil of middle-class life from the ravaging waters of disbelief. They had been justified in part by the crassness, at many points, of the older materialists themselves, and in part by the general difficulty, for the troops of human culture, of moving forward unbrokenly on every front at once; and Whitman was both a product and a creator of the mood which the preachers, the philosophers, and the poets had conjured up. He had hardly become familiar with the names of Thomas Paine and Frances Wright, he had hardly had time to digest the ideas in *The Ruins* and *A Few Days in Athens,* before his mind began to be played upon by the contradictory teachings of quite different men and quite different books.

Even in his childhood, indeed, there had been influences of this other order at work. The family that cherished the name of Thomas Paine and subscribed for the *Free Enquirer* seems not to have had any of the usual religious affiliations, and if in fact the boy Walt was exposed to a certain amount of Sunday-schooling at the old gray Dutch Reformed Church on Joralemon Street, its lessons can hardly have worked their way much below the surface of his attention. The important fact was that, without being actual members of the Society of Friends themselves, his father and especially his mother leaned strongly in the direction of Quakerism: his mother, indeed, came partly of Quaker stock, and what her son was to call "her fundamental emotional tendencies" were all of that sort; his father, having broken (it seems likely) with whatever early religious training he had had, was a friend and almost a follower of Long Island's own heresiarch, the Quaker preacher, Elias Hicks. That tall, straight, large-browed, glowing-eyed old farmer-prophet, whose mystical preachings had wrought a disastrous schism among the Friends of his time, was certainly one of the most salient characters of that whole locality, and except for Lafayette and Jackson the most imposing personality whom Whitman was to have sight of in his boyhood. It was within a few months of Hicks's death and at the height of his power and influence that Walter Whitman, coming home from his carpenter's work toward sunset of a winter's day, threw down an armful of kindling-wood with a bounce on the kitchen floor, and said laconically, "Come, mother, Elias preaches to-night." That evening, in the singularly un-Quakerish setting of the ball-room at Morrison's Hotel, the boy Walt, who at the age of ten was old enough not to be sent off to bed, sat in the midst of Brooklyn fashionables, town dignitaries, officers from the Navy Yard, and others, to listen, still and absorbed, to the "magnetic stream of natural eloquence" that flowed from the lips of the Jericho farmer.

In his old age, not unnaturally, he was unable to reproduce even the outline of the discourse he had heard as so small a boy, but he felt sure that it had been one of Hicks's many appeals to "that moral mystical portion of human nature, *the inner light.*" Undoubtedly it had been; undoubtedly Elias Hicks, when drawn by the leadings of the Spirit, would have uttered the old Quakerish call, revived by him now in an extremer form, to what he himself described as "the inward manifestation of divine light," that transcendent faculty within man to which, as he held,

173

spiritual truth is immediately and overwhelmingly evident, without regard or even respect for the voice of the carnal reason. What spoke through him that night in the late twenties was the spirit of Quaker individualism at its purest and deepest, but it was also the spirit of Quaker obscurantism at its most persuasive and most misleading; the spirit that had set itself against the intellectual conquests of the seventeenth and eighteenth centuries, and was to remain aloof from those of the nineteenth; the spirit that had led Hicks himself, for example, to warn his hearers against Thomas Paine and his "dark insinuating address." It was to exercise a dangerous sway over the imagination of Walt Whitman; to encourage him in a flaccid irrationalism to which he and his generation were to be sufficiently prone at the best; to encourage him in an easy habit of saying with the Quakers, as he himself put it, "this is so or so because of some inner justifying fact—because it could not be otherwise." For the poet whose book was allegedly to be pervaded by the conclusions of the great scientists, this was hardly the wisest habit to form. In any case, Whitman as "a young fellow up on the Long Island shore" seems seriously to have debated with himself whether he should not become a real Quaker: he decided, it is true, once and for all, that he "was never made to live inside a fence"; but the fact of the debate itself is full of meaning.

It was too late in the day for a youth of genius like Walt Whitman to be attracted to any formal association with a sect whose best life was already in the past, and the drab austerities of Quaker morals must quickly have repelled the poet who was to write the "Children of Adam" poems. What really affected him in the Quaker discourses he heard and the Quaker books he read was very much what affected Emerson at somewhat the same time: it was a strain that had never been exclusively Quakerish, and was now more and more congenial to the imaginative temper of the whole age—the rejection of rites and offices and ecclesiasticisms in favor of "the religion inside of man's very own nature," the spiritual independence and self-trust that this implied, and the assertion of immaterial truths that evaded analysis and could not be supported by logic. Insensibly, as the Brooklyn school-boy grew into the adolescent printer's-devil and then into the country school-teacher and the youthful journalist, the charms of Quakerism were blending into and fusing themselves indistinguishably with the charms of something fresher and in the long run more influential on his spirit; something that must have touched him at first almost as bodilessly and anonymously as the air he breathed and the light he saw by; something expressed unphilosophically and only half-deliberately in the verse he would read in the newspapers and magazines, in the plays he would sometimes see in the city, in the music he would hear at the opera, and the pictures he would see when he saw pictures at all; something that would only gradually come to him in tangible and verbal form through the words of great contemporary writers as he found them in famous books.

This "something," of course—for it is an old enough story now—was, on the simplest level, the sentimentalism that, becoming conscious of itself a generation or two earlier in Europe, had hardly grazed the surface of our own colonial mentality, and was only now, with the gift-books and the tender engravings, coming into its own among us; but it was also, and far more importantly for Walt Whitman, the stronger and deeper idealistic romanticism into which sentimentalism had gradually sublimated itself. The undernourished sensibilities and over-disciplined emotions of the middle class were in full revolt against the hard-headed practicalities of the middle-class way of life: at the same time, and paradoxically, they were in revolt against the humanistic rationalisms which the culture of the merchants and mill-owners themselves was increasingly to repudiate. All that was affirmative and life-giving in romanticism came on arm in arm with all that was sterile and regressive in it; the voices that rose more and more bravely in behalf of feeling and imagination were also crying down logic and analysis and "exact demonstration" more and more truculently. What wonder if Walt Whitman, already divided between Frances Wright and Elias Hicks, should listen to these newer voices without discriminating very sharply among their tones?

Certainly, in that rather raucous and over-strenuous America of Van Buren's or Polk's administrations, the voices of the sentimentalists, the romancers, the idealists, would have fallen upon his ear with an alluring sweetness or an impressive sonority. The spirit they represented came to him first, in his boyhood and adolescence, in its simpler and naïver forms; came to him—to speak only of the printed word—through the work of the ingenuous poets and the half-boyish story-tellers of historical fiction. What romanticism earliest signified to Walt Whitman, as to any imaginative and healthy boy of the time, was the songs of Robert Burns (those songs of which the very titles, he said, had a "native spice and untranslatable twang"); or the melancholy, reverent nature-poems of the New York editor, Bryant, with the "clear nameless beauty" that

176

pervaded and overarched them all; or the endlessly "racy"
and "vigorous" Leatherstocking tales of the New York
squire, Fenimore Cooper, who was always to seem to
Whitman so "fresh, robust, noble"; or—almost beyond all
the others—the romances and verse tales and *Border Min-
strelsy* of Sir Walter Scott, "an inexhaustible mine and
treasury" over which he pored for years, and of which he
came to feel—anti-democratic though he thought it all
was—that its influence had permeated him through and
through: "if you could reduce the Leaves to their elements," he once said, "you would see Scott unmistakably
active at the roots." Freshness of feeling, certainly, un-
guardedness in expression, boldness and bigness in work-
manship, enthusiasm for daring and heroic action, contempt for mere prudence and calculation—these were some
of the things that the song-writers and balladists and romancers had taught the future poet of *Leaves of Grass*.

As time went on, however, and the boy who gobbled up
The Spy and *Kenilworth* gave place to the editor and
book-reviewer of the *Eagle*, Walt Whitman began to tun-
nel deeper into the sub-surfaces of romanticism. Scott and
Cooper, though he never ceased to relish them, yielded
ground in his interest to a series of more reflective and
more philosophic writers; the story-tellers yielded to the
ideologues; and now it was a question of such books as
Goethe's autobiography, in Parke Godwin's translation,
which hinted to him how profound and profitable a book
a man could make out of the growth of his own individuality; or the *Confessions* of Jean-Jacques Rousseau, which,
"frivolous" and "repulsive" as it struck him, still seemed
to him to have "a great lesson" in its pages; or Friedrich
Schlegel's *Philosophy of Life and Philosophy of Language*,

177

with its "disquisitions," as he called them, "on the most solemn subjects that can engage human thought." Unsophisticated by the academies, unequipped with the literary training so many of his fellow-writers enjoyed, forced back upon translations by his innocence of every language but his own, the Brooklyn carpenter's son was finding his own almost instinctive way to the head-waters of European romanticism.

Of the great French and German writers he came to know in this unforced, unsystematic manner, one of them —and again a woman—was to excite his imagination perhaps more fruitfully than all the rest. George Sand's was not a name to bandy about in the genteel circles of the forties, and many a respectable reviewer of the time had warned his polite readers against the depravity of her books. Like Frances Wright, George Sand was known to have made the institution of marriage the subject of critical discussion, and there was no health in her. The emancipated spirits of Brook Farm, however, had seen that there was something else, something not at all immoral, in her extraordinary books, and some of them had asked Francis George Shaw to translate, for serial publication in their paper, the *Harbinger,* her *Consuelo* and its sequel, *The Countess of Rudolstadt.* Reprinted in book form a year or two later, these two novels fell into the hands of Walt Whitman of Brooklyn and cast over him a spell he was never afterwards to break. Again and again he went back to the singular adventures of the beautiful Venetian singer Consuelo and her lover, the mad young Bohemian count; read them and re-read them so untiringly that thirty years later he was able to reproduce and even to enact little scenes from the book, and after forty years was

178

still to have about him, battered and half-unbound, the five old volumes of *Consuelo* and its sequel. He thought it the noblest book George Sand had written, "the noblest, in many respects, on its own field, in all literature"; it displayed, he said, the most marvelous verity and temperance; and George Sand's heroines—but particularly Consuelo— seemed to him far superior even to any of Shakespeare's own. The woman who had achieved such a masterpiece had contradicted with "a supreme affirmation" the old denial that women as creative artists could ever be the equals of men. George Sand, Whitman declared, "redeems woman."

What had there been in the book, in addition to its luxuriance just as narrative and in spite of its extravagances, to exert this sorcery over the young poet's mind? The answer is partly suggested by a remark John Sullivan Dwight had made in introducing the novel to the readers of the *Harbinger*. The central purpose of *Consuelo*, Dwight had said, is "to hold up an ideal of the Artist's character, especially in Music . . . and to show how genuine Art flows only from, and leads always to, the Moral; how all inspiration, alike of Saint or Artist, must come from devotion to the 'first Good, first Fair.' " George Sand, in short, had embodied in *Consuelo* a conception of the artist and his art profoundly antithetical to the conception held by the materialists and the utilitarians, a conception according to which the mere pleasure, fleeting and sensuous, that a genuine artist can give is abysmally inferior to and often inconsistent with "the revelation of the infinite" which has been vouchsafed him and which, if his spirit is pure, he may transmit to his audience. There is an incommensurable difference, Consuelo's old master tells her, be-

179

tween "a material talent," entertaining or astonishing, and that "genius of the soul" which ennobles and exalts: music, the young Count of Rudolstadt later assures her, far from being a mere gratification of taste, is a "divine art," and the true musician, far from being a mere skilled performer, is a kind of priest or priestess. So much, according to George Sand, for the hedonistic calculus of the Baron d'Holbach and Mr. Jeremy Bentham!

It was certainly a serious and lofty attitude toward the artist and his art which the novel inculcated, and when it is set beside the rather dry instrumentalism of the rationalists, there is little cause for wonder that the young poet found it irresistible. Its philosophic underpinnings, however, were of course in an extreme and enthusiastic idealism, and all this was to have a far more dubious effect upon his thinking. It was the impress of Elias Hicks's gospel and not the impress of Volney's that *Consuelo* overwhelmingly confirmed. When the nobly-gifted heroine of the novel becomes involved, at the court of Frederick the Great, with the workings of a mysterious secret society—a kind of Transcendental Free Masonry—it is to learn not only that its members are dedicated to the establishment of political freedom and social equality among men, but that, as the Initiator explains to Consuelo, "it is a religion that we wish to reconstruct." Of this new, undogmatic, purified religion Consuelo's lover and husband, Albert of Rudolstadt, is one of the hierophants: it is he who gives utterance to such propositions as that "Man is an emanation from God," that "God alone is Being, absolute Being," that "we gravitate towards the ideal, and this gravitation is infinite as the ideal itself"; it is Albert too who denounces the low, earth-creeping notions of the materialistic scientists: "Do you believe," he asks, "that the natural philosophers can now-a-days really understand nature? Despoiled by them of the living God who fills it, can they feel it, know it?" The high romantic could give but one answer, and Whitman was to learn only too quickly to give it.

His learning was sped along by *Consuelo* more than by most other books, but he was not to remain unaffected, as he could hardly have done, by the writings of the great English ideologues of romanticism also. Like so many thoughtful young Americans of the thirties and forties, Whitman was having his influential encounters with such writers as Coleridge and Carlyle. Not that Coleridge, to speak only of him, was ever to mean to Whitman what he had meant to Channing and Emerson or such younger Unitarian divines as Clarke and Hedge: there is nothing to indicate that he ever wound his way through the entangled logical underbrush or the drifting metaphysical fogs of *Aids to Reflection* and *The Friend*. But he dipped far enough into the *Biographia Literaria* to feel that it was a book which would reach "the deepest thoughts of the 'choice few' among readers who can appreciate the fascinating subtleties of Coleridge," and that its author—the old mystagogue of Highgate!—was "like Adam in Paradise, and almost as free from artificiality." Was it only the chapters on poetry and poetic language, on the imagination and the fancy, on Mr. Wordsworth's style, that charmed Whitman—and suggested to him this very inept analogy? Did he have the patience to puzzle out also those chapters which refute Hartley's mechanistic psychology or denounce "the impious and pernicious tenets defended by Hume, Priestley, and the French fatalists or necessitar-

ians"? Did he have the requisite preparation for taking
in those chapters which celebrate "the illustrious sage of
Koenigsberg"—Immanuel Kant—and his disciples, Fichte
and Schelling, and defend a philosophy that, in its highest
perfection, "would consist in the perfect spiritualization
of all the laws of nature into laws of intuition and intellect"? It seems hardly likely that Whitman mastered these
passages, to say the least, but the thoughts in them may
have brushed his mind contagiously, however lightly.

He was much more vividly and lastingly affected by the
books of Thomas Carlyle, by *Sartor Resartus,* by *Heroes
and Hero-Worship,* by *Past and Present* and *The French
Revolution.* Noticing these books in the *Eagle* as they appeared or re-appeared, Whitman confessed to liking Carlyle the more he communed with him, to finding a sort of
fascination about the man, to feeling that many noble
thoughts were placed—"we may almost say *hidden"*—under
that weird, wild, perverse style of his, and that, after one
had grown used to it, that style became "strangely agree-
able." The Carlyle manner, in fact, was to color his own
expression strongly, especially in prose, and all his life he
was to be more steadily "fascinated" by Thomas Carlyle's
personality than by that of any other Victorian, even Tennyson. Years after the *Eagle* days, the news of Carlyle's
illness and imminent death affected Whitman so strongly
that, as he strolled about on a fine, clear, magnificently
starry winter night, the thought of the dying Titan mingled itelf inextricably with his sense of the solemn beauty
of that "silent indescribable show." Bitter as the old Scot
had been, Whitman reflected, and contemptuous as he had
shown himself of all the best hopes of democracy, what
would the whole picture of British life in those fifty years

SCIENCE AND THE UNSEEN

have seemed like without him? It would be, he thought, like an army with no artillery.

In these later years, it is true, he had come to see how dangerous to the democratic future was Carlyle's harsh disdain for average humanity, and to get wholly out of patience with "the green envy and devilish venom of his growl"; but the Carlyle of the early books had made an ineffaceable impression on his mind. In part, it was fortunate that he had. Fortunate, so far as Carlyle strengthened in Whitman his own increasing antagonism, on one level, to the morals of money-making—to that "Mammon-gospel" which, as Carlyle said, holds cash payment to be the sole nexus between man and man, that "brutish godforgetting Profit-and-Loss Philosophy" which the Carlyle of *Heroes* and *Past and Present* had so unsparingly cried down. Fortunate too, perhaps, though more doubtfully, so far as Carlyle inspired in Whitman his scorn for the "gross, steam-engine Utilitarianism" of the Benthamites, for that "Benthamee utility" which had seemed a fruitful philosophy to Frances Wright and so many other Radicals. For a young American who had his own bias toward a too mechanical pragmatism, there was doubtless a wholesome corrective in Carlyle's onslaught upon the "Greatest-Happiness Principle."

What was far less wholesome than all this, however, was that Carlylean obscurantism with which an impressionable reader of these books was so likely to be infected. The Carlyle who stormed against the "Unbelieving Century" of Gibbon and Voltaire, with its "withered mocking Philosophisms," its "Mechanical Atheism," its "Sceptical Dilettantism"; the Carlyle who had nothing but sneers for "painful Logics and Baconian Inductions," for "that progress of Science, which is to destroy Wonder, and in its stead substitute Mensuration and Numeration"—this Carlyle was a far more questionable guide than the other. From him, as from Elias Hicks and George Sand, Whitman had imbibed a romantic metaphysics that was to prove a more and more uncomfortable bed-fellow for his naturalism, for that "Scientism" which he yet felt it his duty to espouse. Wonder and reverence and a mystical faith that based itself upon them, this—and not respect for demonstrable fact—was what the young book-reviewer would have taken in from the explosive chapters of *Sartor* and *Heroes*. "It is the spiritual always that determines the material," he was assured by the persuasive lecture on "The Hero as a Man of Letters"; and how, in the frame of mind in which he naturally approached them, could he have resisted the recurring burden of Professor Teufelsdröckh's meditations?—"All visible things are emblems; what thou seest is not there on its own account; strictly taken, is not there at all: Matter exists only spiritually, and to represent some Idea, and *body* it forth." There was a siren music, at that moment, in such strains as these, and Walt Whitman was of no mind to stop his ears against it.

Similar strains had been reaching him even earlier from a source less remote than Highgate and Cheyne Row. *Sartor Resartus* itself had been published in Boston three years before it appeared in book form in London, and the ideas set forth in it had had a prompter and more wholehearted reception among a group of young and early-middle-aged New Englanders than they had had at home. The New England mind, set free by the thawing out of the Calvinistic ice chains and, more lately, by the warming of the chill Unitarian waters, had been evolving, with foreign assistance it is true, its own characteristic romanticisms; and Walt Whitman was probably teaching at some Long Island village such as Babylon during that autumn of 1836 when a group of rebellious and aspiring spirits gathered together at George Ripley's house in Boston to form what came to be known, chiefly by outsiders, as the Transcendental Club. New York was to catch only slowly the contagion of Transcendentalism: it was never in fact to make a home, comparable with Boston or Concord, for "the latest form of infidelity," as Andrews Norton called it; but one young New Yorker showed himself peculiarly receptive to the emotional and intellectual currents that came to him from the north and east. Walt Whitman was a good enough Long Islander to regard all Yankees with a certain sectional aloofness, but these Yankee romantics were to mean far more to him, in the next decade, than any Knickerbocker writer, even Cooper, had meant.

He fell under the sway, for example, as all the New Englanders had fallen, of the lofty spirit of Channing, who had done more than any other man to open the way for Transcendentalism. The exhilarating address on "Self-Culture" which Channing had delivered at the Franklin Lectures, calling upon young Americans to be true to their own highest convictions, seemed to Whitman "an unsurpassed piece, either as to its matter or manner"; and once, when the subject came up of political patronage for literary men, he could not help raising the question whether any gift in the power of government to bestow could have repaid Channing for "the great anchor he has built for mental independence in America." Certainly the poet who wrote the "Song of the Broad Axe" ("the beauty of independence, departure, actions that rely on themselves") had

185

gone to school, at least for a brief spell, to the man whom
Emerson called "our bishop."

He had probably not been powerfully affected by any
one of Channing's followers, with a single momentous exception, but he had unquestionably been alertly aware of
them all and of that "high-toned" idealistic frame of mind
they were all, in the forties and early fifties, evoking. No
such inveterate reader of newspapers as Whitman could
have missed Margaret Fuller's literary pieces in the *Tribune;* when some of them appeared in a volume—*Papers on
Literature and Art*—he welcomed them in the *Eagle* "right
heartily." He was particularly impressed by Margaret's
essay on "American Literature" and her sharp warning
against the folly of supposing that, because the United
States printed more books and periodicals than all the rest
of the world, it therefore really had a literature. Many
years later he was to quote this warning—"unquell'd for
thirty years"—in *Specimen Days.* Like virtually all Northerners, too, he had heard that "wicked and blasphemous
monster," Theodore Parker, preach or lecture—though
almost certainly not, as he recollected, in Boston. He could
easily have heard him elsewhere, however, and have had a
basis for that parallel he later drew between Parker's powers as an orator and Daniel Webster's. Parker, he said, was
incomparably the bigger and sincerer man of the two; in
every important way he left Webster in the lurch; where
the godlike Dan shone, intellectually, Parker was a brilliant luminary. The preacher who, along with Bushnell
and Beecher, had done most to liberalize and latitudinize
Christianity in America, had quickened the mind of Walt
Whitman just as, more indirectly, he had quickened that
of Abraham Lincoln, and Whitman was long to think of

him as "built for mountains and seas—for might, for loyalty."

Had Whitman also been one of the tiny number who bought and read *A Week on the Concord and Merrimack Rivers?* Had *Walden* fallen into his hands during that pregnant year that preceded the first appearance of his own book? If so, the fact went unrecorded, and certainly Whitman was never to feel for Henry Thoreau the same unreserved enthusiasm he felt for the other New England seers. Heartily as he admired Thoreau's lawlessness, his intransigeance, the dissidence of his dissent, and much as he relished the tang of Thoreau's outdoorishness, he could not conceal his disappointment at the man's supercilious disdain for average, ordinary people, and on one occasion he had even to confess that Thoreau's love of nature itself seemed to him too bookish and intellectual. Wide of the mark as this judgment may have been, there had been a real bond of respect between the two men, though the overtures, for once, had come from Thoreau and not from Whitman: like Emerson, Alcott, and Conway, Thoreau, who had read the first edition of *Leaves of Grass* with half-reluctant admiration, sought Whitman out in Brooklyn of his own accord and came away from their interview with a still livelier sense than before of both the strength and the sweetness of the new poet. To sympathy of this sort Whitman was the last man in the world to be unresponsive, and for years he cherished the story Emerson had told him of Henry's going about Concord carrying *Leaves of Grass* defiantly like a red flag and challenging the townspeople's violent disapproval of the book and its vicious author. With all their differences the two men were chips off the same spiritual block.

In a large sense they were both products of one deep urgency in the higher life of their time: in a more limited sense, they were both disciples of one spell-working master. Whitman had not walked through the Concord woodlots with Waldo Emerson or skated with him on the frozen Musketaquid, but hardly less entirely than Thoreau had he succumbed to the strong, fine charm of the Emersonian prophecies. Scott and Cooper had meant incalculably much to him; he had yielded himself wholeheartedly and irrevocably to the *Drang* of *Consuelo* and *Sartor Resartus;* but more than by any of these other books, the whole power and pressure of romanticism had been sharply, simply, and finally concentrated for him in the utterances of Ralph Waldo Emerson. The voice that decisively won him over to idealism was the voice that reached him in *Nature* and the first and second series of *Essays.* The time came when Whitman was apparently to resent, with not uncharacteristic caprice, that this had been so true: the role of disciple he might once have accepted, however uncomfortably, but he would not, if he could help it, have that role imputed to him; and he was not at his strongest or sweetest when he wrote, early in the eighties, that as a youngster he had had a touch—"though it came late, and was only on the surface"—of "Emerson-on-the-brain," and that "for a month or so" he had thought of Emerson as master. He had certainly been more than a youngster when he began to compose *Leaves of Grass,* but as an old man he could write impatiently to W. S. Kennedy that, unimportant as it was whether he had read Emerson before that time or not, "the fact happens to be positively that I had *not."*

The fact "happens" to be, if not positively then almost
188

irresistibly, that he *had,* and a truer as well as more admirable side of his nature had revealed itself when, during the war-times, he freely admitted to J. T. Trowbridge that Emerson had helped him to "find himself" in a way that made his book possible: "I was simmering, simmering, simmering," he said; "Emerson brought me to a boil." Certainly it would have been a feat, even with less omnivorousness than Whitman's, if in the forties and early fifties he had managed to remain deaf not only to Emerson's fame but to the basis for it. He would have had to read magazines and newspapers less avidly than he did to avoid, for example, that piece in the *Democratic Review* in 1845, only a few months before one of his own tales appeared there, on Emerson's essays by "a Disciple," in which "the abhorrent theory of the materialists" was set over against the "affirmative and oracular" views of the author of *Nature.* A quotation in the *Eagle,* a year or two later, from one of Emerson's "inimitable" lectures suggests that the editor of that paper was beginning to dip into the Emersonian waters directly, and indeed nothing is more likely than that Whitman had seen and heard Emerson in the flesh as a lecturer at a time when *Leaves of Grass* was still in a fetal state: he himself recalled, in extreme old age, attending two or three addresses by Emerson at the Historical or the Athenaeum Society's hall on Broadway, and one line in a very early unfinished poem that was to have been called "Pictures" has both a pleasant and a convincing concreteness:

> *And there, tall and slender, stands Ralph Waldo*
> *Emerson, of New England, at the lecturer's*
> *desk, lecturing.*

189

The unknown young poet, moreover, who sent Ralph Waldo Emerson a copy of his first edition and addressed him as "dear Master" in a letter appended to the second, a year later, had probably already written the scrap which Dr. Bucke found affixed to a magazine article of 1847 and in which Whitman had observed that Emerson "pierces the crusts that envelope the secrets of life," that he "joins on equal terms the few great sages and original seers," and that "his words shed light to the best souls; they do not admit of argument." Something like this had surely been his feeling from the beginning: surely for him Emerson had been almost what Epicurus had been for Lucretius or Spinoza for Goethe, and if he was sometimes to make light of that debt, and even to be critical of Emerson's limitations—his coolness, his caution, his excessive decorum—his truest feeling remained a grateful veneration that was only this side idolatry. When, toward the very end, Whitman was asked what his last word about Emerson would be just before he "shut up shop for good," he laughed mildly. "It will be loyal," he then answered: "after all the impatiences, loyal, loyal."

It was in the mental soil that had been harrowed and seeded by the poets and novelists, by the preachers and lecturers and essayists, that *Leaves of Grass* took root and sprouted: it was a soil that had its own latent and beautiful fecundity and needed only to be impregnated by the potencies of Scott and Cooper, of Carlyle and Coleridge, of Hicks and Emerson. After all this had been done, and the book itself began to appear in its successive and expanding forms, its tone and its direction continued to be affected not only by the development of Whitman's individual life and by such tremendous events as the Civil

War, but by intellectual influences of a sort to which, unsystematic as he was, he had his own genuine sensitiveness.
At some indeterminate period—though the chances are
that it was after two editions of *Leaves of Grass* had appeared and perhaps mainly during the sixties—Whitman
began looking more closely and more curiously into the
significance of certain stupendous names that had recurred
invitingly in so much that he had heard and read, in Coleridge, in Carlyle, in Emerson too; and these were the
names of the great German metaphysicians of idealism,
Leibniz, Kant, Fichte, Schelling, Hegel. American thought,
on its professional and formal levels, was more and more
taking its account of these "critical" and dialectical philos-
ophies, not simply as diluted through Coleridge or Cousin
but at the sources themselves, the great, craggy, arduous
"Critiques" and "Systems" and "Encyclopaedias"; and
even Whitman, who was certainly neither a professional
nor a formal thinker, was responsive enough to these activities of the ideologues to go into the subject at his own
leisure and in his own way.

His way did not consist, any more than Emerson's or
Thoreau's had done, in toiling painfully and analytically
through the *Critique of Pure Reason* or the *Philosophy of
History,* even at a time when translations of such books
might have lain at hand: for that sort of intellectual mining he had, needless to say, neither taste nor talent, and
in spite of his own implied claims to a capacious learning—

> *Having studied the new and antique, the Greek and
>   Germanic systems,*
> *Kant having studied and stated, Fichte and Schelling
>   and Hegel—*

191

we may be pretty sure that he knew little more of these writers at first hand than he could have found in such an anthology as Frederic Hedge's *Prose Writers of Germany,* of which he owned a copy. Whitman's way with metaphysics, as with science, was to make out what he could from the popular or half-popular treatments, and he had no scruples whatever about trusting to the *Britannica* for his knowledge of Kant and Fichte, or to Ripley and Dana's *American Cyclopaedia* for Schelling, or to Joseph Gostick's *German Literature* for Hegel. An article on Leibniz in the *Atlantic,* which came his way as editor of the *Times,* was doubtless quite as useful to this particular poet as the *Théodicée* or the *Monadology* themselves would have been.

What was important was that these names had acquired, in the western world of the mid-century, an almost preterhuman prestige: that, in itself, would have been enough to arouse Whitman's curiosity and to kindle his imagination; and when he learned, from Gostick and the encyclopaedias, that Kant and the others had brought up the heavy artillery of metaphysics, of logic, of "scientism" itself as he gathered, in defense of faith, of intuition, of vision, of the romantic frame of mind, he threw himself into an attitude of veneration along with the other devotees. "Taking their whole philosophy," he wrote in some notes for a projected lecture, "it is the most important emanation of the mind of modern ages and of all ages, leaving even the wonderful inventions, discoveries of science, political progress, great engineering works, utilitarian comforts etc. of the last hundred years in a comparatively inferior rank of importance—outstripping them all." The contribution that Kant had made to metaphysics, was it not "probably the most illustrious service ever rendered to the human mind"? Was not the character of Fichte, peaceful though his life had been, as noble and heroic in its way as that of "the best and bravest warrior in war's campaigns"? As for Schelling, the palace of idealistic pantheism that he had begun but never completed, sounded nevertheless to Whitman like "one of the most beautiful and majestic structures ever achieved by the intellect or imagination of man."

Dazzled as he was, however, by the resplendence of these names, it was what he learned about Hegel that captivated Whitman most powerfully. Very possibly he had actually read, in this case, the selections from the *Philosophy of History* in Hedge's book; if so, they would certainly have carried him up into dizzy and exhilarating regions; and in any event his enthusiasm for "the Hegelian formulas" during a few years was extreme. To the perplexing question of the relation between human personality and the objective world of matter it seemed to him that Hegel had given the deepest and most substantial answers so far given, and had done so "with a more consoling scientific assurance than any yet." The phrase has its ironies, and there are others in Whitman's odd conviction that what Hegel had to say about metaphysics, about theology, about history and politics was more applicable to the destiny of These States than to that of his own Prussia: Hegel, he would have it, is the philosopher for us even more than for Germany: only Hegel is large enough and free enough for America, and those formulas of his are "an essential and crowning justification" of the democracy of the western world. "Humanity's chiefest teacher"—so he described Hegel at what was certainly the high point of his zeal—"and the choicest loved physician of my mind and soul."

Without much doubt Whitman exaggerated, when he spoke in these swelling terms, the effect that either Hegel or the earlier idealists had had on his development as a poet. The bent of his genius was already taken, almost certainly, before he began to ransack the encyclopaedias, and even otherwise it is only too obvious that what he would find in Kant and Hegel, especially at second-hand, would be a large and general but very august confirmation of his romantic bias and never a close-knit logical rationalization of it. His own breezy summaries of German philosophy make amusingly evident what anyone could predict beforehand. His veneration for Kant, it is scarcely worth saying, drew none of its warmth from Whitman's having conquered the transcendental deduction of the categories or the antinomies of pure reason or the unknowableness of things-in-themselves. For Schelling's transformation of the proposition $A = A$ into the proposition $I = I$ he could have felt little natural enthusiasm. And so, at one stage, he might honestly think of Hegel as his dearest teacher, but it would hardly be because Hegel had held that the laws of logic are the laws of being, or had seen the antithesis endlessly negating the thesis, or had distinguished between *Existenz* and *Wirklichkeit*. In one word, there was a sizable element of bluff in Whitman's characterization of himself, in a Camden newspaper, as "the greatest *poetical* representative of German Philosophy."

Just the same, the Whitman of the period especially after *Drum-Taps* owed much that was less tangible and literal than this to the sway of the idealist metaphysicians

SCIENCE AND THE UNSEEN

over the thought of the time: for better or for worse his later poems, like his later prose, would not have taken just the form they did take if it had not been for the Kant, Fichte, Schelling, and Hegel whom he claimed to have "studied and stated." The attitudes that the men and women of letters had made attractive to him, had encouraged him to adopt, were consecrated and somewhat formalized by the authority of the illustrious Germans. He might know little or nothing of Kant's super-subtle dialectics, but he understood well enough that Kant had checkmated—or was alleged to have checkmated—the skeptics and rationalists with a stunning exhibition of their own logical techniques; that in his own words he had proposed to "abolish *knowledge,* to make room for *belief*"; that he had bolstered men's faith in God, freedom, and immortality by "demonstrating" that the pure reason could no more disprove than it could prove their reality. Similarly Whitman might have little bias toward Fichte's overstrained moralism, but the poet who had written the "Song of Myself" knew how to make his own use of a philosopher who had concocted the whole material universe, as well as the whole duty of man, out of the demands of the arrogant Ego. That poet could never have followed the later Schelling in his tortuous defenses of Lutheran orthodoxy, but how could he fail, even at a certain distance, to delight in the earlier Schelling's eulogies of spontaneity and intuition, in his doctrine of the profound identity of real and ideal, in his view of Nature as a living organism, expressing and symbolizing in its infinite upward strivings the clearer and clearer aspirations of the human soul?

And what of Hegel? Condensed and approximated as the Hegelian formulas were by those literary or encyclopaedic summaries, it need never have been evident to Whitman that their tendency was toward an empty rationalistic fatalism, or that with all their "scientific" pretensions they gave aid and comfort to the most bigoted obscurantists, or that, far from being large enough and free enough for American or any other democracy, they were quite sufficiently authoritarian for the reactionary Prussian monarchy. Of these noxious elements in his "loved physician's" system Whitman was never to be unhappily suspicious: he was never to see the need that Marx saw for setting Hegelianism right side up. What he found in that system was something very different from all this and much headier. For Hegel, he gathered, had demonstrated with irrefutable logic that the whole universe and all human history are the work, as Whitman summarized it, of an "endless process of Creative thought," that the tireless change and becoming of things is held together by "central and never-broken unity," that all the varieties, contradictions, and paradoxes of experience are continually reconciled and sublimated in higher and higher syntheses, that the history of the world is nothing but the progress of the consciousness of freedom, and that true freedom harmonizes in some transcendent way the individual's rights with the claims of society and order. Not the Hegel who thought Napoleon "the World-Spirit on horseback" or who raged against the Revolution of 1830: not he, but the Hegel who spoke out for spirit and for intelligible progress and for good emerging out of evil and ostensibly for freedom and unity, this was the Hegel whom Whitman urged upon his countrymen as a teacher. The great mass of his countrymen, of course, were never to heed this counsel, even less than they were to know Whitman himself

as a prophet, but it was profoundly indicative both for
their own situation and his that the poet who had begun
life under the aegis of Thomas Paine should end by becoming, on one level, an apologist for the "Germanic
systems."

III

In an intellectual environment so full of contradictions
as this—an environment bounded at one extreme by Volney and Darwin, at another by George Sand and Hegel—
it is little wonder that so impressionable a temper as Whitman's should express itself artistically in a confusing and
paradoxical manner. He was not a mere smooth and passive surface, reflecting mirror-like the images and the ideas
cast upon him by his complicated age: his sensibility was
too highly characterized and his plastic power too robust
for that. But his sensibility itself was a complicated one
and his plastic power had its natural limits: the result was
a body of poetic work almost as divided within itself as the
culture of Whitman's America was. Sincerely convinced
that the poetry of the new day should bring itself into
harmony with the most advanced thought and knowledge,
Whitman was able to stride forward a certain distance—
a remarkable distance—into the regions still so largely un-
explored by men of letters; but he could outstrip his fellows, his audience, and one side of his own nature, so far
and no farther. Like Shelley, like Heine, like Baudelaire
—and more than any of them—he was able to spell out the
first invigorating syllables of a naturalistic credo; like them
too, however, he recoiled from its full and final exactions,
and fell back, if not upon Platonism or the Old Testa-

197

ment or Swedenborg, then upon an intuitionalist theism that was for him the more natural equivalent. As the bard of Scientism, he gave very generously with his right hand, and then took back with his left something of what he had given.

Something, but by no means all. Whitman had learned too much from the rationalists and the popularizers of science ever to forget his lesson entirely, and his work as a whole, verse and prose, could certainly not have been produced by a poet before the Enlightenment. Its strain of bold and positive naturalism is too pervasive ever to be successfully minimized. For one thing, Whitman had early acquired a passionate anti-clericalism, a vehement antagonism to churches and "preachers," and from this, in spite of the all-inclusiveness he later cultivated, he was never to recede. It reveals itself in *Leaves of Grass* rather by indirection than otherwise, but it is unmistakably there. No doubt Whitman had found encouragement toward a certain sort of religious heterodoxy even in Carlyle and Emerson, but the quality of his anti-clericalism is much less theirs than it is that of Paine and Volney; much less the romantic repudiation of the Transcendentalists than the fiery hostility of the Jacobins. It dated back to a period in his life before Transcendentalism had affected him in the slightest. At the end of the century old men on Long Island who remembered Whitman in his school-teaching days recalled that he had not been religious in any way, that he had never been seen inside a church, and that in fact he had had a local notoriety as an atheist or infidel. There was something about preachers, as a rule, said his brother George after Whitman's death, that seemed to repel Walt; and though the poet of *Leaves of Grass* usually refrained from denunciation here as elsewhere, that same poet, if he had realized his ambition to become a popular lecturer, might then have been less affirmative. That at least is what certain manuscript notes for lectures suggest to us:

Really [he asks in one of them] what has America to do with all this mummery of prayer and rituals and the rant of exhorters and priests? We are not at all deceived by this great show that confronts us of churches, priests and rituals—for piercing beneath, we find there is no life, no faith, no reality of belief, but that all is essentially a pretence, a sham.

Even in the publicity of print, the early Whitman was capable of a similar harshness of invective: in the open letter to Emerson in his second edition, he dared to denounce the churches of America as "one vast lie," a lie in which neither the people nor the churches themselves believed; and fifteen years later he was to return to the theme in one of the gloomier passages of *Democratic Vistas:* "A lot of churches, sects, &c., the most dismal phantasms I know," he then wrote, "usurp the name of religion." The passage of time might mellow or weaken his feeling about many things, but nothing that appeared in the American churches of the seventies and eighties availed to tone down this early-acquired anti-clericalism. It was part of what lay at the base of his admiring friendship for the famous infidel, Robert Ingersoll, with whom he differed frankly at particular points, and it came out with all the heat of a youthful passion in his conversations with Horace Traubel. For the church as an institution, he told Traubel, he had "the profoundest contempt," and it is clear from other

199

conversations that this contempt, far from being merely Transcendental, still had the older political and social bias. On one occasion, when he had been denouncing the priests of religion and the priests of the arts, Traubel interjected: "We still have the priests of commerce to contend with." "So we have," answered Whitman: "doubly so: the priests of commerce augmented by the priests of churches, who are everywhere the parasites, the apologists, of systems as they exist." This was hardly the literal truth about the church and the priesthood everywhere, at all times—nor even of the American church and the American ministry in Whitman's day—but it testifies to the strength of his antagonism that he should have struck this old deistic note even in his latest years.

It was a note he had virtually never struck explicitly in *Leaves of Grass,* though even there, first in his original preface and then in the poem ultimately named "By Blue Ontario's Shore," he had announced the disappearance of priesthoods in a line which he never dropped from the book: "There will shortly be no more priests, I say their work is done." With rather different phrasing Emerson or Carlyle might also have written that line, and certainly the poet who did write it had long since thrown in his lot with the romantic visionaries. The first thin copies of *Leaves of Grass* that reached the men in Concord made that clear enough to them: nevertheless, the new prophet-poet whom they welcomed so hospitably was to espouse, during his first phase of four or five years, an idealism in which the elements were not mingled quite as they had been by the idealists of the pure tradition. There was something singularly earthly and man-centered in the form of the spiritual philosophy expounded by the writer of the first preface and the earliest poems and certain lecture notes of the period. When this Whitman spoke of the supernatural, of God, of the soul, it was in a manner that might have led his readers to question the real bent of his idealism. He could reject supernaturalism with what was not really the Transcendentalist accent: "The whole theory of the special and supernatural and all that was twined with it or educed out of it departs as a dream," he wrote, in almost the vein of his earliest rationalistic teachers; and neither Carlyle nor Emerson would have described the supernatural, in language Whitman used, as "of no account." They might challenge the old simple dualism of matter and spirit, but it was always to assert the superior reality of what lay above and beyond the natural.

This was not quite Walt Whitman's way at the beginning, and when he spoke of deity it was not in the manner of Carlyle—"Love not Pleasure; love God"—or of Emerson —"Idealism sees the world in God." On the contrary, he sometimes spoke at this stage in the tones of a kind of Transcendental atheism. Like Swinburne a few years later, Whitman began by exalting Man at the expense of any omnipotent Maker. The notes for lectures are particularly sweeping:

The whole scene shifts—the relative positions change— Man comes forward inherent, superb, the soul, the judge, the common average man advances, ascends to place. God disappears—the whole idea of God, as hitherto presented in the religions of the world for the thousands of past years, or rather the scores of thousands of past years, for reasons disappears—

God abdicates.

201

It is true that he did not mean this apparent atheism as literally as Swinburne meant his: Whitman would never have cried out against "the supreme evil, God," and almost from the beginning there were the germs of a nebulous theism in what he wrote. His first inclination, nevertheless, was to humble and naturalize and humanize the thought of deity, not to sublimate it, and he came closer than he may have intended to an almost godless pantheism:

> I hear and behold God in every object, yet understand God not in the least,
> Nor do I understand who there can be more wonderful than myself.

> Why should I wish to see God better than this day?
> I see something of God each hour of the twenty-four, and each moment then,
> In the faces of men and women I see God, and in my own face in the glass.

There is little even of the ideal and impersonal Oversoul or Absolute in lines like these, and just as little in the passage in which Whitman declares that the poet worthy of these states is silent in the dispute on God and eternity:

> He sees eternity in men and women.

He certainly did not wish to be taken as denying either God or eternity, though half-wittingly he was emptying those words of most of their serious content, and he certainly did not wish to be taken as denying the soul. But the young poet of the early editions had too robust and too spontaneous a love of bodily life and "this beautiful material world" to insist on the soul and the spiritual world at their expense, as the stricter idealists were always doing. He could not, at the beginning, see the universe of natural objects and physical bodies as a mere evocation of the thinking or willing ego, as only a lovely symbol of transcendent realities, or as the illusory vesture in which Spirit might choose to clothe itself fleetingly. On the contrary, his unschooled and unsophisticated "metaphysics" led him to make spirituality and the soul depend upon the visible and the palpable in a manner that savored strongly of the materialism he disavowed. There is a curious manuscript note, evidently of an early date, in which Whitman charges himself to preserve in his work the balanced truth that the world of matter and its laws are as "grand and superb" as that of spirit and its laws:

> Most writers have disclaimed the physical world and they have not over-estimated the other, or soul, but have under-estimated the corporeal. How shall my eye separate the beauty of the blossoming buckwheat field from the stalks and heads of tangible matter? How shall I know what the life is except as I see it in the flesh?

There were the germs of heresy, of course, in this very material ideality: it leaned much more toward a supernatural naturalism than toward Carlyle's "Natural Supernaturalism"; and Whitman was later, in effect, to abjure it. But the poet of the fifties found no difficulty in having his metaphysical cake and eating it too. "I will make the poems of materials," he cried, "for I think they are to be the most spiritual poems." And there were even more radical implications in a passage of the "Sun-Down Poem" ("Crossing Brooklyn Ferry") of 1856. The poet is addressing all the sparkling, stirring, flowing objects of Manhattan Bay at sunset:

> *We descend upon you and all things, we arrest you all,*
> *We realize the soul only by you, you faithful solids and*
> *fluids,*
> *Through you color, form, location, sublimity, ideality,*
> *Through you every proof, comparison, and all the sug-*
> *gestions and determinations of ourselves.*

He was to drop this passage from the poem many years later, and for obvious reasons; but fortunately he never reworked all the early poems from beginning to end, and he never rejected this equally revealing passage in "Starting from Paumanok" (1860):

> *Was somebody asking to see the soul?*
> *See, your own shape and countenance, persons, sub-*
> *stances, beasts, the trees, the running rivers, the*
> *rocks and sands . . .*
>
> *Behold, the body includes and is the meaning, the*
> *main concern, and includes and is the soul.*

The poet who wrote this last line was the poet who also wrote the "Poem of the Many in One" ("By Blue Ontario's Shore")—

> *All comes by the body, only health puts you rapport*
> *with the universe—*

and the "Song of Prudence"—

> *The spirit receives from the body just as much as it*
> *gives to the body, if not more—*

and he was also, of course, the poet who composed the "Children of Adam" chants for the express purpose of re-vindicating, in the teeth of all corrupt asceticisms, the dignity—he himself said rather the "sacredness"—of the human body, and the high worth—he himself said even the "divinity"—of all its functions and acts. He might be bound not only by the vocabulary but by some of the old mental habits of supernaturalism when he spoke of these things, but the poet who quietly resisted Emerson's suggestion that he drop "I Sing the Body Electric" and its companion poems—this poet owed a heavier debt to the wholesome influences of modern science, of modern physiology and medicine, than to either the Quakers or the metaphysicians. There was a token of this in the very gusto with which he used such words as "physiology" itself or "physiognomy" or "phrenology"; and certainly in all that frank celebration of sexuality Whitman was closer to what was rebelliously naturalistic in the poetry of his century—to Byron and his sensualism, to Heine's "rehabilitation of matter," to Pushkin's defiant fleshliness—than he was to the ascetic Fichte or the atrabilious Carlyle. The biologist and his like would be more at home than the subjective idealist with these dithyrambs of health and physical fitness and procreation.

Naturally there was a temperamental basis, quite as real as the ideological one, for such poems as "Spontaneous Me"; but naturally, too, the personal impulse could have expressed itself so boldly only in a certain environment of ideas and attitudes, and it would not be easy to say just how far "Children of Adam" was prepared for by the "pagan" poets and just how far by the developments represented, however humbly, by Orson Fowler's *Physiology*.

The two, of course, were but different aspects of one general earthward movement of men's thoughts and loyalties, and it was that movement—embodied indifferently, if one will, in Burns and Lyell, in Heine and Liebig, in Diderot and Cuvier—that lay behind all that was most affirmative and acceptant, in an earthly and even an earthy sense, in *Leaves of Grass*. It may have been "Scientism" of the most general and undifferentiated sort, but it was Scientism and not metaphysical idealism that confirmed and abetted Whitman in his early passion for the "divine soil" and the "rolling earth," in the large healthy satisfaction he took in mere air and light and water, in his delighted sense of being in easy harmony with the natural elements, in his conviction that all things, even the meanest or vilest, are there "for reasons" and are good "in their place." There were idealists, to be sure, like Schelling and Emerson, for whom objective nature was precious as the emblem of supernal reality, but for one thing the early Whitman did not speak so characteristically of an abstract "Nature" as of the friendly and substantial "earth," and besides he sometimes exalted it in a manner that would have seemed alarming, theoretically, to the others:

> *I swear there is no greatness or power that does not emulate those of the earth,*
> *There can be no theory of any account unless it corroborate the theory of the earth,*
> *No politics, song, religion, behavior, or what not, is of account, unless it compare with the amplitude of the earth,*
> *Unless it face the exactness, vitality, impartiality, rectitude of the earth.*

A religion that has to compare with the amplitude and

face the impartiality of the earth—or be rejected as of no account—is not the religion that Kant or Coleridge or Emerson had proposed to reconstruct: for them, it would have signified a setting of all such things on their heads, and certainly the "earth" of these early passages is not so much an emblem of anything as a criterion of everything. It is not something flickering, fanciful, metaphorical, and transient, any more than it is something base and sin-ridden: it is a thing immitigably real and good and lasting, adequate in itself to all the physical and spiritual needs of man. "I conjure you, my brethren," said Nietzsche, *"remain true to the earth";* and the early Whitman had anticipated him: "The earth," he had written, "that is sufficient." He had spoken of it as no really consistent Transcendentalist could have done:

> *What can the future bring me more than I have?*
> *Do you suppose I wish to enjoy life in other spheres?*
>
> *I say distinctly I comprehend no better sphere than*
> *   this earth,*
> *I comprehend no better life than the life of my body.*

This passage too—from the "Clef Poem" of 1856—was rejected after twenty-five years, but it had said its say, in all the early editions, for a very geocentric idealism. The emotion it expressed had been so strong that, even after *more* than twenty-five years, the aged poet could recur to it with magnificent unconcern for so much of what he had said in the interval. The important thing, Whitman could say as a very old man, is the present life and the people about us, "the earth struggle" itself; whatever may come later, we need not bother our heads about it: "our responsibilities are on the earth."

When he spoke in this strain, he was justifying, so far as that went, his own claim that he had written in full sympathy with the findings of natural science. There were other respects too in which he was genuinely affected by the spirit of that tradition. "Scientific" rather than Transcendental, surely, was the vivid sense Whitman had, especially at the beginning, of the inexhaustible multiplicity of things and the delight he took in it; the outgoing love of variety that was sometimes so much stronger in him than his meditative conviction of unity; the thing that made him the poet of the Many at least as much as he was the poet of the One. It was in the naturalistic heritage, in the heritage that had celebrated "the plurality of worlds," that Whitman would have found a certain corroboration for his naïve satisfaction in numbers and the pleasure it gave him to contemplate a world pullulating with uncountable stars and comets, with stones and plants and animals, with cities, races, languages, trades, buildings: "always," as he wrote, "the free range and diversity." In the vastnesses of space that the astronomers had opened up, in the dizzy remotenesses of time evoked by the geologists and archaeologists, he found not terror or dejection but exhilaration:

> See ever so far, there is limitless space outside of that,
> Count ever so much, there is limitless time around that;

and with a similar zest:

> We have thus far exhausted trillions of winters and
> summers,
> There are trillions ahead, and trillions ahead of them.

208

Far from rebelling against space and time, indeed, or denying their reality, as the idealists did, Whitman could glorify them—even, paradoxically, in his mystical moments—as "ties eternal"; and far from being obsessed with the Unchangeable, like the orthodox visionaries, he felt a profane enthusiasm for change. Was it not the "tough" side of his mind that enabled him to feel it? Certainly he was no more depressed than a geologist or a chemist would be by the spectacle of a universe in constant motion, involved in a restless process of breaking down and building up:

> *Ever the mutable,*
> *Ever materials, changing, crumbling, re-cohering;*

on the contrary, the fact of change, of movement, of an endless procession of finite events was a congenial fact to the realistic Whitman; it braced him with a sense of the unweariable power and fecundity at the heart of things:

> *Urge and urge and urge,*
> *Always the procreant urge of the world.*

It was partly the tirelessness of the "rolling earth" that inspired his paean to it, and in this virtue he elsewhere proposed to emulate it himself:

> *Let others finish specimens, I never finish specimens,*
> *I start them by exhaustless laws as Nature does, fresh*
> *and modern continually.*

What is the "Song of the Open Road" if not a call to men and women to rouse themselves from their lethargy, to refuse all stops and stays, to move with the free and flexible movement of the world of objects, to "know the universe itself as a road, as many roads, as roads for traveling souls"?

There was undoubtedly something in the idea of the mere flux that stirred Whitman happily in his healthiest years, but even at the beginning of his poetic career he had understood that for modern naturalistic thought the flux is no mere chaos but an orderly process—even if not "designed"—and an intelligible one—even if not consciously intelligent. "I have felt from the first," he said to Traubel, "that my own work must assume the essential truths of evolution, or something like them"; and although the qualifying phrase is more important than he may have realized, it is quite true that even before *The Origin of Species* Whitman, like Emerson, had had more than a glimpse of some of the things that were implied by what was then called the Development Theory. Inevitably all that pre-Darwinian speculation—by cosmogonists, by palaeontologists, by comparative anatomists—had seeped through to him along the public channels; however indirectly, and no doubt partly through the uproar over *The Vestiges of Creation,* he had made out more or less clearly what Buffon and Goethe, Lamarck and Geoffroy, Erasmus Darwin and Robert Chambers had been getting at. With all its rich implications of slow and patient growth, of increasingly complex development, of progressive change, the conception of evolution not only in its biological but in its vastest sense had captured the imagination of Walt Whitman almost from the beginning.

We know how the conception expressed itself most palpably in his verse—in images of a world emerging slowly and serenely out of "deathly fire" and "turbulent chaos," of the "covering waters and gases" that overlay it "before man had appear'd," of the "long slow strata" that had accumulated for his own embryo to "rest on," of the "long-threaded moss" and "esculent roots" he himself "incorporated," and of the birds and quadrupeds with which he was "stucco'd all over." We know too that the "evolutionism" Whitman considered himself to have voiced was of a highly teleological and sometimes egocentric sort; that he could say with a curious subjectivism, "All forces have been steadily employ'd to complete and delight me"; and that his evolutionism was rather early given a bias that brought it nearer to Hegel than to Darwin. When all deductions are made, however, the idea of progressive development on the natural level is potent and productive in *Leaves of Grass*.

There is a final sense in which, more than any comparable book, Whitman's is affirmative of what physical science had made possible, if not of its philosophic substructure. Most of the poets of his time, even in America, were either indifferent to the machines which applied science had brought into being or bitterly hostile to them. It was an attitude that, in view of much that those machines had done to human life and human personality, it is easy enough to understand and condone. To distinguish between the necessary and the actual effects of the machine—under the social circumstances in which its use began—was evidently more than many men of great gifts were capable of doing. Unlike most of them, on the other hand, Whitman did feel that distinction, even if he had never made it consciously; and characteristically he saw in the machine not only a delight to the eye of the craftsman but an intrinsically constructive agent in the civilizing of mankind, the freeing of it from the primitive bonds of dis-

tance and inflexibility and weight. Thoreau's fear that the
railroad might ride upon us instead of our riding upon it
Whitman virtually never shared, though he sometimes
said loosely comparable things; and he told Traubel that
he had no patience with such protests as Tennyson's
against the introduction of a railroad near him on the Isle
of Wight, or with Ruskin's thinking himself constituted to
object to all modern improvements.

It was in a very different spirit from theirs, certainly,
that the editor of the *Eagle* remarked, apropos of a visit to
the engine-room of a ferry-boat, that "there are few more
magnificent pieces of handiwork than a powerful steam-
engine, swiftly at work!" Or that, on another day, he
gloatingly described a new printing-press the paper had acquired as "about as pretty and clean-working a piece of
machinery as a man might wish to look on." This was the
young writer whose verse, after a few years, was to be so
unprecedentedly full of steam printing-presses, telegraph-
wires, sewing-machines, forge-furnaces, steam-whistles, and
even drain-pipes and gasometers. He was the poet for
whom a locomotive was to be—not, as for the romantic
poets generally, something ugly because it was useful, but
—a "fierce-throated beauty," a "type of the modern"; the
poet for whom steamships were to be "splendid resistless
black poems," and the reapers and threshers that crawled
like monsters over the fields of the West to be "human-
divine inventions." If he had done nothing else in *Leaves
of Grass*, Whitman would have done an important service
to culture by opening men's eyes to the unhackneyed if
"unromantic" beauty of the machine and to the imaginative grandeur of much that men of mechanical genius had
achieved. Nothing came easier to him than to praise "the

212

strong light works of engineers," and it was quite in the spirit of a subsequent and, in this respect, bolder generation than his that Whitman proposed, in a late prose sketch, to take as a symbol of America "some colossal foundry," flaming, smoky, dust-clouded, disordered, and clangorous. When he wrote in this vein—as in the others we have alluded to—Whitman was richly bearing out his proud claim to be the poet of modern Scientism.

IV

In much of its purport, in much of its characteristic grain, *Leaves of Grass* by no means failed entirely to be the book that Whitman maintained it was: there are real senses in which "the tuft and final applause of science" may be found, as he felt they ought to be, in the beauty of his verse. Few poets of a later time could be said to belong even so truly and positively as he did to a culture that had produced Benjamin Franklin and Joseph Henry and Asa Gray. In an age when poetry generally was oriented only negatively toward what was implied by natural science, *Leaves of Grass* was splendidly exceptional. But to maintain, as Whitman did, that the conclusions of the great scientists had seeped and soaked into the vital tissues of his book, was to translate excellent intentions into tangible achievements. For much that was fundamental to the physical studies of his century he had little feeling and, to tell the truth, little respect. Partly through temperament, partly under the sway of other modes of thought, he could not bring himself to accept the universe of wholly unideal objects that science assumed, to bow to the unappealable reality of material forces in that universe, to face the full rigor of the truth that events follow one another in a necessary sequence of causes and their effects. Still less could Whitman tolerate the assumption that the physical universe is in itself indifferent to human wish and purpose, that life is a product and not a transcendent condition of the natural order, and that the real freedom of the human will lies not in a defiance of physical causation but in a clearer and clearer knowledge of it. Least of all could he consistently appreciate the austerity of scientific method, its rejection of bias and desire and "purpose," its reliance on experiment and analysis, its elimination of all possible sources of subjective error, its readiness to submit to the demonstrated. Responsive as he might be to whatever was earthly and humanistic and hopeful in science, Whitman was too good a romantic to yield his whole mind to its difficult discipline.

It was the reason why, in his poems themselves, he hardly went farther in the appropriation of what scientific knowledge was available to him than to draw upon it for imagery and color and allusion; why he who was so much more richly gifted a poet than Erasmus Darwin wrote no poem that might have outdone "The Botanic Garden." It is not at all inconceivable that Whitman might at least have attempted something very broadly of that sort: in point of fact he projected, at some early date, a series of ambitiously scientific poems. A manuscript note is the evidence:

Poems identifying the different branches of the Sciences, as for instance: Poem of the Stars—? Astronomy—? Suns, planets and moons. Poem of Geology—not a good word—? the processes of the earth.
Poem of Chemistry.

Unlike others of his projected pieces no one of these poems ever came to completion, unless indeed the "Song of the Rolling Earth" and "This Compost" are two of the poems there foreshadowed: if so, then their dependence on Denison Olmstead or on Liebig, real and interesting as it is, is strikingly loose and general. No, even while the first installments of his work were in preparation, it was later than Whitman thought: too late for him to break fully out of the hypnotic Transcendental spell and write a group of poems that would endow with imaginative grandeur and humanize with all the resources of poetic eloquence the cold facts established by sidereal astronomy or the geology of denudation and deposition or the chemistry of carbon compounds.

To do this he would have needed a greater patience than he ever had in the presence of the facts themselves, a greater willingness to pause and consider the potential poetry that lay in them. But he had little patience or willingness of that sort, and he had early fallen into the insidious Transcendental habit of Indian-giving, of paying the most prodigal tributes to the achievements of the scientists and then negating his tributes with an all-too-ready "but." "Hurrah for positive science!" he could exclaim in his first long poem, "long live exact demonstration!"—and then, after calling for wreaths and bouquets to bestow on the chemist and the geologist, he could add at once:

Gentlemen, to you the first honors always!
Your facts are useful, and yet they are not my dwelling,
I but enter by them to an area of my dwelling.

Twenty years later, in the Tufts commencement poem,

the "Song of the Universal," he could be similarly anti-climactic:

> *Lo! keen-eyed towering science,*
> *As from tall peaks the modern overlooking,*
> *Successive absolute fiats issuing.*
>
> *Yet again, lo! the soul, above all science. . . .*

And in the preface he printed during the centennial year, Whitman could say, with perhaps still blander inconsequence, that though he joyfully accepted modern science and followed it loyally without the slightest hesitation, for him there always remained "still a higher flight, a higher fact, the Eternal Soul of Man, (of all Else too,) the Spiritual, the Religious." Something of what lay behind this speech was of course profoundly important, but the language itself suggests that Whitman would follow modern science as far as he chose to follow it and no farther.

In doing so, he was far from being eccentric or solitary: the attitude he was taking was that of the overwhelming majority of the intellectual leaders of his day and of the great numbers who hearkened to them. It was the attitude taken by the liberal preachers, by men like Parker and Beecher, and as we have seen it was not essentially different from the formula adopted by the men of science themselves. It found striking expression in the uneasy mixture of Whitman's feelings about evolution, especially in the years that followed *The Origin of Species*. He had always been sensitive to the imaginative connotations of the pre-Darwinian development theory, as we have seen, and when the whole subject was dramatically reinvigorated and lifted to a higher level of scientific assurance by Darwin's great book, it was not for Whitman suddenly to drop out

216

of line. No word of his exists, it is true, to suggest that he took in exactly what was Darwin's special contribution to the discussion, that he ever appreciated the significance of natural selection as a means to evolution. But the stunning prestige of the book itself could not fail to have its effect on him, and he counted himself a good Darwinian. The old theory, he felt, had been revived with "all-devouring claims" by *The Origin of Species,* and had thus become a priceless counterweight to many a tenacious and degrading superstition. "I believe in Darwinism and evolution from A to izzard," he said in the middle eighties to the interviewer for the *Sun* whom we have already quoted; and certainly, however he may have felt about the theory, there could be no question of his veneration for the man. The exaltation of Darwin's name after his death seemed to Whitman a "deserv'd apotheosis," and all that he heard of the Englishman's beautiful personal qualities made a strong impression on him: "the sweet, the gracious, the sovereign, Darwin" he called him in conversation: "Darwin, whose life was after all the most significant, the farthest-influencing, life of the age."

Strong words—and he meant them with that particular sort of sincerity that is quite consistent with half-comprehension: he had not weighed them in any tediously accurate balance when he uttered them. Thoroughgoing as he might profess his Darwinism to be, in fact Whitman shrank back in unconcealed dismay from the real philosophic consequences of the biological theory. He might once have expressed a kind of desire to "turn and live with the animals," and a feeling that in their self-contained placidity they revealed their relations to himself; but he had no serious relish for an hypothesis that pointed to the actual

217

biological affiliations between man and the lower primates. "Nevertheless," he wrote in the next breath after paying one of his tributes to Darwin, "the problem of origins, human and other, is not the least whit nearer its solution"; and only a moment earlier he had given voice to the conviction that some third theory, reconciling evolution with the ancient belief in man's descent from the gods, would sooner or later arise. If this was Darwinism, it was of an extremely Pickwickian order. Whitman always shied, says Traubel, at purely physical theories accounting for life, and he seems sometimes even to have shied at his own Darwinian applications. In a conversation that turned on the subject of conscience, he once remarked that that attribute must have developed naturally as the other organs and faculties had done; and then at once added, as if with a certain alarm at his own daring: "Still—the development theory does not account for it all. Remember: be bold, be bold, be not too bold." In this connection, at least, Whitman could hardly have been accused of recking not his own rede: for all his hospitable gestures toward evolution, he had drawn the line at the Swinburnian boldness:

> *What Newton's might could not make clear*
> *Hath Darwin's might not made?*

To Whitman the name of Hegel would probably have seemed preferable here, and indeed he frankly included his remarks on Hegel in *Specimen Days* partly in order "to counterpoise . . . the tenets of the evolutionists." In all this, as in other matters, he was of course startlingly inconsistent, but against any such charge as that of inconsistency Whitman was perfectly forearmed. His Transcendental masters had done that for him if they had done nothing else. The rationalists of an earlier generation might have set a high price on stiff intellectual responsibility, but their sun had set temporarily, and all Whitman's native capriciousness, all his native inclination to trust to intuition rather than to reason, had been strengthened and sanctified by the contempt of his romantic teachers for "a foolish consistency." From the beginning he had gloried both in his fine and in his lazy contradictoriness:

> *Do I contradict myself?*
> *Very well then I contradict myself,*
> *(I am large, I contain multitudes.)*

It was true that he was too large and contained too much to be satisfied with the tight and sterile consistencies of mediocre minds, but in another intellectual setting he might have been forced to consider the heavy obligations of a prophetic writer to be consistent in a richer sense, and there was much foolish complacency in the way he accepted his own contrarieties. "You give us no consistent philosophy," his friend Brinton, the archaeologist, said to him one day. "I guess I don't," responded Whitman with something like smugness—"I should not desire to do so."

The answer seems not to have dashed Brinton, who later described Whitman as the "profoundest explicator and defender" of evolution, but of course there was not only nothing positively scientific, there was something hopelessly irreconcilable with an even broadly scientific outlook in this willful and self-righteous irrationalism. The method of the poet, it goes without saying, is not the method of the inductive investigator, but that is not to say that the poet who makes philosophic claims for his chants can with impunity set all logic at naught, and there were far more ominous possibilities in Whitman's breezy illogicality than, to do him justice, he ever realized. He may at first have meant only to assert the superior rights of vital experience over mere intellectualism; he may have meant hardly more than this in some of the noble verses of his early poetry:

> Logic and sermons never convince,
> The damp of the night drives deeper into my soul;

or:

> (I and mine do not convince by arguments, similes, rhymes,
> We convince by our presence.)

So far so good. But the germs of a lethal obscurantism were latent from the beginning in this apparently healthy attitude:

> Wisdom is of the soul, is not susceptible of proof, is its own proof.

Here is already waiting, unwittingly to be sure, the justification for all unjustifiable superstitions and inequities, and as always, the appeal to pragmatic action, even to force, rather than to reason, is not very far in the distance:

> How beggarly appear arguments before a defiant deed!

It was no accident that this sentiment was followed almost at once, as it would have been in Carlyle, by the kind of sentiment that can always be turned to advantage by self-interested Supermen and Leaders:

> All waits or goes by default till a strong being appears.

220

How little support Whitman really meant to give to force or to the superman—how powerful in him to the end were the liberal sentiments of the Enlightenment—we shall see before we are through. But the backward drift of his idealism is not to be conjured away, and we need not be surprised to find this anti-intellectualist belittling not merely rational argument but even exact knowledge. It was in his later phase, to be sure, that he did this most frankly. "You must not know too much," he wrote in one of his notes on bird-life, "or be too precise or scientific about birds and trees and flowers and water-craft; a certain free margin, and even vagueness—perhaps ignorance, credulity—helps your enjoyment of these things. . . . I repeat it—don't want to know too exactly, or the reasons why." Could Whitman possibly have suspected into just whose hands he was playing when he wrote these extraordinary and not uncharacteristic sentences?

He wrote them too casually and indeed too parenthetically, in any event, to be fairly open to the charge of systematic and ruthless obscurantism, but such asides as this are straws in the wind none the less. They help to mark the gradual surrender of Whitman's mind to some of the negative elements in romantic idealism—a surrender, moreover, that is marked by a change for the worse that took place in his attitude toward poetic style itself. He had begun by contending that the poet worthy of America will be one whose constant aim is to speak with the utmost plainness and clarity. His earliest ideal of expression had been that of the robust and popular wing of romanticism; its whole emphasis was on the fullest possible communication. What he wanted in his own verse, according to his early "rules for composition," was "a perfectly transparent,

221

plate-glassy style, artless, with no ornaments, or attempts at ornaments, for their own sake," a style of expression "with great severity precluded from all that is eccentric"; and in a somewhat later memorandum on the revision of his poems he enjoined himself to make certain that there remained in them "not one word or sentence, that is not *perfectly clear.*" "What I tell," he maintained in his first preface, "I tell for precisely what it is." Perhaps there were pages even in the first and second editions of *Leaves of Grass* that belied this high claim, but the claim itself is significant.

As time went on, however, and his mind gave itself more and more relaxedly to the prevailing mysticisms, Whitman came, in his thought about style, to make less and less of clear communication and more and more of what he called suggestiveness, "vista," "half-tints," and the like. All those aspects of his work that were to endear him to the symbolists, to the extreme subjectivists, to the poets of solipsism, came to seem more and more valid to him; and he regarded with increasing complacency whatever was ill-defined, misty, and enigmatic in his book. "I have not been afraid of the charge of obscurity," wrote in the seventies the poet who had once striven for perfect transparency; and still later the poet who had striven for artlessness was delighted, as he indicated to Edward Carpenter, when W. S. Kennedy called him "artful." "I think," he added in talking with Carpenter, "there are truths which it is necessary to envelop or wrap up." How far had the mystagogue gained upon the poet of the divine average before he could voice such a sentiment! Yet it was the dominant strain in all Whitman's latest pronouncements on the subject. In the whole matter of Shakespeare's history plays, he said for example, "I should specially dwell on, and make much of, that inexplicable element of every highest poetic nature which causes it to cover up and involve its real purpose and meanings in folded removes and far recesses."

All questions of poetic expression are not disposed of, to be sure, when poets have simply been charged to achieve a transparent clearness or perfect communicability, and it would be preposterous to deny that the "half-tints" in Whitman are responsible for much of what is finest in *Leaves of Grass*. It is true too that these changing views of Whitman's had, in one respect, less effect on the actual language of his verse than a simple view would lead one to expect; on the whole the later poems, inferior as they often are both in lift and in firmness, are no more cryptic than certain passages in the "Song of Myself" and "Calamus." Nevertheless there were the elements of a profitless occultism—there were even hints of charlantry—in all this talk of a poet's enveloping and covering up his meaning; and if it hardly added appreciably to the obscurity of Whitman's later verse, it was intimately associated with the growing fogginess and laxity of his thought, and this had its own effect upon his style. A real loss of virility, in any case, a real decline in muscular tone, had taken place when the writer who had begun by saying that "nothing can make up for excess or for the lack of definiteness" could end by almost boasting, as Whitman did apropos of another remark of Brinton's, that "of all things, I imagine I am most lacking in what is called definiteness, in so far as that applies to special theories of life and death."

There is certainly little enough that is definite, in any philosophic sense, in the attitudes that grew upon Whit-

man with the lapse of time, but their emotional drift is
unmistakable and on its own level consistent. It was a
steadier and steadier drift away from the realistic, the
demonstrable, the purely natural, and toward the wishful,
the unarguable, the dimly and cloudily mystical. Not that
the pattern is simple or one-dimensional: these elements
were in Whitman's work from the beginning, and the
opposite strains were never to disappear from it. The large
tendency, however, is what I have described it as being.

There was not much in the culture about Whitman to
encourage the strong young shoots of a genuine naturalism
in his work: there was a good deal to encourage the more
turgid, more narcotic growths of idealism. As a result,
what his mind might be forced to recognize became less
and less valid for Whitman the bard, and what he wanted
to believe, more and more self-evident. The process was
measured by the increasing emphasis, as time went on, on
the messianic, the evangelistic, the religious import of
Leaves of Grass. There had been little use even of the
words "religion" or "religious" in the first edition of the
book, and not much more in the second: the "faith," the
"assurances," the "miracles" that appear in those earliest
poems are all of an ambiguous and more than half worldly
order. Already, however, in the volume of 1860 the transcendental is gaining the upper hand: the poet announces
that he sings his chants solely in order to drop in the
earth "the germs of a greater religion." "The whole earth
and all the stars in the sky," he declares, "are for religion's
sake." And with the stress of the War behind him, with
the submission of his mind to the Germanic systems and
their like, Whitman began to employ a word that could

hardly have passed his lips twenty years earlier: it is the word "theology." Though science, he wrote in 1872, had cast the Old Theology of the East into the discard, its principal service to mankind might prove to be its having prepared the way for a New Theology, "indescribably grander" than the old, a "supreme and final Science," namely, "the Science of God."

Naturally there was nothing even metaphorically "scientific" in this new science as Whitman practised it: grander than the old theology it may have been, but it was certainly less reasoned and systematic. What he meant by "God" in "Passage to India" was no more clearly defined than what he had meant by the word in the earliest "Song of Myself." But without becoming by any means a more philosophic concept, it had grown measurably more personal, more Biblical, more anthropomorphic as time had passed. The God who had once been for Whitman hardly more than the misty deity of the pantheists or even of the deists, hardly more than a cheerful abstraction from the facts of nature—the God whom he had beheld in every object and about whom he professed not to be painfully curious—had now again become something like the God of the sects, a father, a comforter, an inspiring presence. He was to become at times not merely "God" but "the Lord," and even, in a less conventional, more idiosyncratic phrase, "the great Camerado, the lover true for whom I pine." The Absolute of the philosophers was proving too impersonal for the later Whitman as it had proved too abstract for the young poet, and more and more he was to strike the note—the troubled, yearning, comfort-seeking note—of the erotic mystics:

225

Reckoning ahead O soul, when thou, the time achiev'd,
The seas all cross'd, weather'd the capes, the voyage
done,
Surrounded, copest, frontest God, yieldest, the aim
attain'd,
As fill'd with friendship, love complete, the Elder
Brother found,
The Younger melts in fondness in his arms.

How revealingly the very idiom of this later verse—with its dull archaisms, its inversions, its worn-out images ("seas" and "capes" and "voyages")—betrays the mental flaccidity of a poet who had once known how to find his own un-tarnished metaphors and to make strong rhetoric out of the grammar of men's usual speech!

Not only did his somewhat materialistic pantheism yield slowly to a more primitive theism, but the "faithful solids and fluids" that had once seemed to Whitman the suffi-cient evidence of the soul, came more and more to lose their firm and beautiful reality for him, to waver and vaporize before his vision, to take on the aspect of illusion and unreality. The process, it is true, was never to reach its ultimate: to the end he remained sufficiently the earth-poet to regain at many moments his early powers of pic-ture-making and evocation, and he had a right to say that "the physical and the sensuous" retained holds upon him which had never been weakened and which he himself had "hardly wish'd to weaken." Nevertheless, even before the War and especially after it, his verse abounded increas-ingly, when the objects of the visible world were in ques-tion, in the familiar phrases of mysticism: such objects had become for him "these shifting forms of life," "this en-tire show of appearance," "the ostent evanescent." Increas-ingly the feeling grew upon Whitman that the material

things he had once found so reliable were but phantasms
of the senses, and that the only true reality was the spiritual, the ideal, the unseen. "Here spirituality," he pro-
claimed for America in "Paumanok," "the finalè of visible
forms"; and in the seventies "Thou Mother with Thy
Equal Brood" demonstrated how far he had gone with the
Transcendentalists:

> *The soul, its destinies, the real real,*
> *(Purport of all these apparitions of the real).*

The world of the seen had ended by becoming for
Whitman, at least in his weaker phases, less credible and
less grand than "the unseen soul of me," and meanwhile
another and more obviously negative strain—a strain of
active revulsion from the seen world—had begun to emerge
in *Leaves of Grass*. Not even to the end was this strain to
come decisively to the top: doubts and skepticisms and
despairs were never in any sense to master Whitman's
spirit and they were never to impart their familiar hues to
the bulk of his verse. There was a counter-movement
within him, nevertheless, against the affirmations that were
so fundamental to his nature and to his program: the ten-
sion set up by the conflicting influences and loyalties we
have spoken of, would no doubt in itself have been enough
to account for this, and a force to the same end was perhaps the complexity, even the ambiguity, of Whitman's
sexual nature. In any event he had his own rare moments
of fatigue and gloom and they expressed themselves in
ways that almost suggest Schopenhauer and the romantic
pessimists. The buoyant poet even of the 1860 volume
confessed, in a kind of aside, that he too had known his
"downcast hours," hours when the earth turned to "a

chamber of mourning" and a mocking voice cried in his ears:

> *Matter is conqueror—matter, triumphant only, con-*
> *tinues onward.*

In such terms did his very occasional dejection express it-self—in terms of a fear lest the material world should prove to be the solid reality he had begun by thinking it: in later years Whitman was to recant, even more surpris-ingly, his former conviction that the earth is sufficient; was to lose, intermittently, his old imperturbable sense of "standing at ease in Nature":

> *What is this separate Nature so unnatural?*
> *What is this earth to our affections? (unloving earth,*
> *without a throb to answer ours,*
> *Cold earth, the place of graves.)*

It is true that this mood of distrust was never to be more than intermittent, and true too that, in the same poem, Whitman foretold how "the true son of God," the poet, would, when the symbolic passage to India had at last been opened up, "absolutely fuse" Nature and Man in a per-fect unity. But for the Whitman of the first volumes there had not been so acute a question of any unhappy dis-harmony between them.

There had not been, I say, so acute a question of any such disharmony, yet even for the Whitman of the middle fifties, with all his high spirits, with all his passion for the "divine soil," with all his hardy realism, there had been a lurking question beneath these excellent things—a ques-tion for which he was never to find the strongest and most

228

truly philosophic answer. It was the question of human mortality. Recall those two lines in the poem later called "To Think of Time":

Do you suspect death? if I were to suspect death I
*   should die now,*
Do you think I could walk pleasantly and well-suited
*   toward annihilation?*

And recall the answer that came back in the last lines of the poem:

I swear I think there is nothing but immortality!
That the exquisite scheme is for it, and the nebulous
*   float is for it, and the cohering is for it!*
And all preparation is for it—and identity is for it
*   —and life and materials are altogether for it!*

The fear of annihilation allayed by the soothing assurance of personal survival beyond the grave: it was not the answer given by the courageous naturalism either of antiquity or of modern centuries; it was the answer given by all world-weary and compensatory mysticisms, and Whitman's increasing insistence on it was a measure both of the inner strains that otherwise found so little expression and of his intellectual failure, as a prophet-poet, to reconcile the natural and inescapable fact of death with a fearless and affirmative humanism. Like Browning, Whitman was convinced that a belief in immortality was part and parcel of an optimistic credo, and like Browning too, he failed to realize that, in seeming to identify that belief so largely with his optimism, he was yielding an essential point for the future to the preachers of despair.

The obsession with death grew upon him with time,

and more and more it became clear how inextricably this was entangled with an unconfessed distrust of the "sufficient" earth, with a curiously gloomy and half-theological doubt of the goodness of life, with a pessimistic longing for a future existence unconditioned by the material. The word "death" was to become, for this lover of life, a "low and delicious word"; the touch of death was to become "soothing and benumbing"; and death itself was to be personified, in an image of perhaps unconsciously revealing melancholy, as a "strong deliveress." How beautiful is a material world, how good is a natural life, from which one must at last be "delivered" by a "dark mother"? It was a question with which Whitman was never to be directly posed, and to ask it is not to make light of all that is nevertheless invigorating and positive—and more pervasive—in *Leaves of Grass;* but a single poem of two lines is enough of itself to force the question on our minds:

> *The untold want by life and land ne'er granted,*
> *Now voyager sail thou forth to seek and find.*

Toward the painful personal emotions that lay behind this and other expressions of Whitman's cult of death there can be no valid attitude but sympathy and the desire to comprehend; and the mesmeric beauty of some of the poetry that resulted from it is simply not to be gainsaid. There is a sense too in which Whitman's way of dwelling on the thought of death was the strong and natural obverse of his consuming passion for life. But this—which is partly true—will not account for the sicklier and softer moments of his later verse, or reconcile them seriously with a genuinely modern way of thought. The language of Spinoza—"A free man thinks of nothing less than of death, and his wisdom is a meditation not of death but of life"—reminds us of that. For this reason and the others we have considered, Whitman fell short of being quite the full-grown poet of modern science he wished to be.

Chapter Five

FOR PURPOSES BEYOND

As an evangel-poem of democracy *Leaves of Grass* had its concrete historical basis in the Jacksonianism of the middle decades; its point of departure was democracy as it was conceived by the great masses of plain Americans in the forties and fifties—by the farmers, the small merchants, the lesser professional men, and the artisans, who furnished the indispensable human and social setting for Whitman and his book. It was a democracy still largely envisaged in the liberal, political, individualistic terms of the eighteenth-century revolutions, a democracy that honored the self-relying and self-sufficient virtues, that was undistrustful of the aggressive and acquisitive individual, undisturbed by the threat of class separation, and dependent for its moral ideals on evangelical Protestantism. There are the germs of a more thoroughgoing democracy in *Leaves of Grass,* it is certainly true, but given its actual origins it would be absurd to expect of the book or to claim for it a full imaginative realization of the necessity and the possibilities of socialism. Absurd, however, not because, even before Whitman had written a line, men had not begun to challenge, both in Europe and in America, the workings of a competitive and merely political democracy or to propose a reorganization of society on coöperative lines. Robert Owen and his followers had been active in the United States during Whitman's childhood, and he was a very young newspaper-man at a time when the followers of Fourier were busy with their propaganda and their experiments all about him. It was not simply out of his private consciousness that the Whitman of the fifties would have had to spin at least a primitive vision of social democracy.

He was a poet, however, prophetic and ethical as his purposes were; he was not a political or social ideologue, and ideas of the sort propagated by the Owenites and the Fourierists, before they become available for the needs of poetry, must notoriously conquer far more ground in the common life and feeling of the people than they had conquered when *Leaves of Grass* was on the stocks. The arts, as it seems, can draw fruitfully only upon ideas that, beyond their intrinsic soundness, have become irresistibly relevant to the whole culture that has produced them; and the ideas of the Utopian Socialists were by no means so relevant as that to the American culture of ante-bellum days. The failures of that commercial and early-industrial democracy were far less evident, both to the common man and to the poet, than its successes and its promise: what wonder if the yea-saying Whitman "instinctively" made the latter the theme and the substance of his chants? He composed them in what was a prevailingly progressive phase of capitalism, and it would be a prodigy if they were more overtly and literally socialist than they are. Against what he might know of socialist or quasi-socialist thought, in fact, Whitman was biased, on a certain level, by the tenacious individualism of his class, its distrust of centrality and control; and besides, his ears were closed to

233

much of the appeal that socialism might have made to him by that muffling and soothing idealism which became the literary habit of his time. The heritage of Franklin and Jefferson joined hands with the authority of romanticism to come between Whitman and any close intellectual consideration—imaginative sympathy being another matter— of socialism and socialist naturalism.

Unlike most of the New Englanders who followed Ripley to Brook Farm, the Whitman of the forties was not only a humanitarian democrat but, as we have seen, a zealous member of the actual Democratic Party, doctrinally committed against any extension of governmental activity; and if this meant mainly a passionate hostility to Whiggery, with its "protection" and its "internal improvements," how much harder such doctrines would have borne upon the elaborate and ingenious regulations of the Fourieristic Phalansteries! Far less than that was usually in question in the forties. The true role of government, wrote the letter-perfect young editor of the *Eagle*, is simply to defend the rights of every citizen from imposition: when it aims to go farther than this, it is "intrusive" and "does more harm than good." Far from admitting the desirableness of additions to the functions of the state, the youthful Whitman was disposed to be critical even of those already recognized: the Post Office department, for example, seemed to him the most mismanaged affair in the world, a living argument against the capacity of government to compete with "individual enterprise and quicksightedness." Even for good ends—ends with the spirit of which Whitman was in natural sympathy—he took his stand against the increase of political control: when a New York newspaper, the *Tribune* no doubt, argued that governments ought to protect the general health of the poor, he granted that the result itself was praiseworthy—"but governments," he demurred, "have nothing more to do with it than they have to give 'the poor' new jackets every Christmas."

Simon-pure Jacksonianism could hardly express itself more strongly than in words such as these: the young writer who uttered them might be sensitively aware of many inequities and many miseries in the world about him, but far from attributing them to what George Ripley called "the race of selfish competition," Whitman cried for more purely competitive conditions rather than less. He knew, as we have seen, that the wages paid to American workers were often scandalously low and their hours of labor inhumanly long, but he could persuade himself in the forties that an "awakened public opinion" would change all that, and in any case he was sure that the dangers of political interference were infinitely greater than its possible benefits. The real interests of the workingman, he contended, involved not only such good Jacksonian policies as a low tariff but the rigorous abstention of state and federal legislation from "meddling so much with the relation between labor and its payment"; and when that picturesque character, Mike Walsh of Tammany Hall—now the Hon. M. Walsh of the state legislature at Albany—introduced in this body a resolution declaring it expedient and proper to fix by law the daily hours of labor, the editor of the *Eagle* protested that he had expected better things of Mike than this: "such a resolution," he maintained, "if infused into a law, would violate the first principles of free trade."

With dogmas like these in so complete possession of his

235

mind, it is hardly surprising if Whitman succeeded in insulating himself almost perfectly against the power and push of that early socialist agitation which, with its watchwords of coöperation, of collective action, of "association," blew all about him in the forties. Of the agitation itself he could scarcely have remained unconscious, nor could any literate American of the time, especially one so near the center of things as Whitman was: the dominant gospel of individualism was being too earnestly and too intelligently challenged for that, and Whitman had his opportunities to hear another language than that of self-help.

He attended, for example, some of the sessions of the "World's Convention" which Robert Owen called together in New York in the fall of 1845 and at which so many reformist programs found outlet; he had probably heard Owen himself lecture on other occasions too, and in fact no boy whose family had subscribed to the *Free Enquirer* could quite have missed hearing about Owenism even in the twenties. That movement, however, had more than passed its zenith by the decade of the Mexican War: its place had been taken by the more systematic Fourieristic socialism—or Associationism—which Albert Brisbane of Batavia had brought back to this country from France and which Horace Greeley sponsored for a time in the *Tribune*. As a newspaper-man in New York Whitman could hardly have failed to know of the convention of Associationists which assembled in the city under Brisbane's leadership in the spring of 1844: indeed, neither the propaganda nor the practice of Fourierism could have been wholly unfamiliar to him. The debate, for instance, between Greeley and Raymond over the merits of Association, which ran through many issues of the *Tribune* and the *Courier*,

Whitman may have followed with a languid interest, but he at least noted in the *Eagle* the appearance of that debate in book form.

He knew of the Fourieristic communities, it goes without saying: he could hardly not have known of Brook Farm or the North American Phalanx or the Sylvania Association, though it is true that a reference in the *Eagle* to the prosperity of the Wisconsin Phalanx at Ceresco is almost his sole allusion to any of them by name. When, however, a group of Brooklyn mechanics, distressed by the hard times and stimulated by the preachings of the Associationists, organized what they called the Social Reform Unity and set up a community of their own in Pike County, Pennsylvania—only to come to grief within less than a year—Whitman, who could hardly have missed hearing of the experiment, must have felt that Associationism was coming extremely close to home. Did he ever sit among the large audiences who listened to Albert Brisbane during the days of his greatest influence? We can only guess, but certainly the tall, stoop-shouldered, sack-coated figure of Brisbane walking abstractedly down Broadway was a familiar figure to Whitman in the fifties; and at his friend William O'Connor's in Washington, during the War, he saw more than once and even argued with the now almost forgotten socialist who had once talked with Marx himself in Cologne. Some warmth of feeling must have existed between them, for Whitman gave Brisbane a copy of *Passage to India* when it was first printed as a pamphlet.

He could not very well, in short, deafen himself to all the reverberations of social discontent and reformist agitation in that period when the new industrialism was first

237

disturbing the minds of humane and thoughtful men. But as a mere journalist Whitman knew how to immunize himself intellectually against the infections of Utopianism. He even knew how to patronize such men as Robert Owen and the hard-working organizers of those ill-starred but brave and adventurous "communities." When Owen, for example, returned to this country in the summer of 1846 after a short journey to England, the *Eagle* greeted the father of English socialism as "an honest and enthusiastic old man" from whose hardest blows "the present system of society" had little to fear; and a few weeks later, noting that Owen was again stirring up the people over the need of "a complete social and political revolution," it exclaimed: "Ah, Mr. Owen! when God has ordained that evil shall exist, do you think that *you* can banish it altogether?"

About the experiments with coöperative living or association Whitman could be similarly sardonic. He confessed in the *Crescent,* during his weeks in New Orleans, to knowing little of Fourierism, but with something of Emerson's mild humor on the subject, protested that it seemed to him a great objection to the system that no one was to do anything under it but be happy. "Now who," he asked—in real enough ignorance of Fourier's resourceful arrangements for getting tedious work done—"who would peel potatoes and scrub the floors?" Already he had described the Fourierists in the *Eagle* as men who "preach better than they practice the sublime doctrines of human equality," and quoted in derision of them a phrase of Carlyle's about the Fop being also our brother. With such easy ironies Whitman managed to shut in his horizon during the days of Utopianism, and still more naturally, during the later times when he argued with Brisbane at O'Connor's, we are told that he never yielded an inch of ground to his more far-sighted antagonist. "Our form of government," says his friend Eldridge, "he thought about as good as could be under present human conditions." Perhaps he had come to one of these conversations fresh from the reading of an encyclopaedic summary of the Hegelian scheme.

The communities, at any rate—with the exception of Oneida, a special sort of affair—had "failed" one and all, and their failure, along with the dying down of Utopian agitation, may well have seemed to justify Whitman in his resistance to that whole order of views. They were premature, those views, certainly, and a strong, undefined intuition may have told him that, with all their crudity, their unripeness, their momentary irrelevance to practice, he would espouse them at his peril as a creative writer. There was something precarious, at the best, in his relations with the great mass of Americans for whom he wished to write, and he may well have felt instinctively that he could not afford to endanger them still further by becoming the mouthpiece of a questionable sect. It would be easy too to understand any resistance on Whitman's part to whatever was freakish, mechanical, and humorless in Fourierism; to all those explicit blueprints for grandiose Phalansteries, to that crazily ingenious clockwork of Groups and Series of workers with their Ascending and Descending Wings, to all that lovable insanity about Little Commencers and Little Hordes. It is not wholly untrue to say that Whitman demonstrated a healthy wisdom by remaining aloof from Utopianism.

Nevertheless, there was far more than mere eccentricity

239

and dyspepsia in the social criticism of such men as Ripley and Brisbane, W. H. Channing and John Humphrey Noyes: premature as it may have been in one sense, it was extraordinarily true and clairvoyant in another, and it is eloquent of Whitman's deep dependence on the moral life of the middle classes, of the extent to which in his early years he shared their social illusions, that he was unable to take that criticism seriously at the time and appreciate its more fruitful aspects. It is eloquent too of his surrender to the opiates of idealism that, neither then nor later, did he find it worth his while to make a serious study of Fourierism or any other reasoned social program. "I am old and indolent," he once wrote, "and cannot study (and never did)": it was the plain truth, and it accounts for his easygoing ignorance not only of Associationism but, in later years, of the Lassallean socialism that influenced American workers in the sixties, of Henry George and the Single Tax, and of the Marxism that became an increasing force from the seventies on. If Whitman ever dipped into *The Social Destiny of Man, Progress and Poverty,* or the English translation of *Capital,* the experience left no trace behind it.

The idealists had assured him, and he was prone by nature to believe it, that with social as with ethical and metaphysical questions it was unnecessary to subject oneself to any difficult discipline of study and analysis; that here, too, one could safely rely upon feeling and intuition. He learned perfectly the lesson they taught him, and except no doubt for his early reading in Paine and Jefferson remained to the end, in this sense, a political illiterate. Fortunately, of course, his feelings and intuitions were better worth attending to than most men's. What, meanwhile, aside from programs and theories, had been Whitman's attitude toward the actual struggles of American workers, if not for a better social order, then for such immediate objectives as higher wages and shorter hours; toward their strenuous attempts at organization into unions and federations; toward their battles on the economic front? We have seen how conscious he was, at least intermittently, of the justice of their case: how closely did he follow and how vocally did he sympathize with their endeavors to achieve solidarity and a place in the social sun? Was this journeyman printer himself ever a member, in the thirties, of the New York Typographical Society? Did this practising house-builder take any part in the lively activities, during the early fifties, of the House Carpenter's Union? Mark Twain, only a little later, was to hold a union card in the Pilots' Benevolent Association: had he been anticipated, correspondingly, by the older writer?

The answer, in the absence of evidence pro or con, must be speculative, but it is as nearly certain as such things can be that Walt Whitman was at no time, however briefly, a trade-unionist. His silence on the subject, in all his printed and conversational reminiscences, is sepulchral; and when, on one or two occasions, he did express himself about workers' organizations, it was not in the vein of a convinced and understanding partisan of trade-unionism. He sympathized, as we have seen, with the Brooklyn workers in various trades who, in the spring of 1846, formed a "benevolent association" for the sake of raising their wages to eighty-seven and a half cents a day; but if he respected their aims, he was by no means so sure of their methods. "Organized associations to 'regulate' the prices of labor," he took the occasion to point out, are "the most fallacious

241

things in the world"; and it was only so far as the workers
confined themselves in their struggle to "their individual
influence" that he would commit the *Eagle* to their cause.
A few weeks later the workers on the Atlantic Docks in
South Brooklyn, whose employers had refused to grant the
wage increase, went on strike, and immigrant German
strike-breakers from Manhattan were quickly brought in
to take their places. It was then as "rioters" who would be
"severely dealt with" that the *Eagle* referred to the striking workers, who had attacked the scabs; and when they
and their families were evicted from the shanties in which
they had been living, on company property, it reported
the fact rather with approbation than not. The strikers
had now become "the misguided men" and their strike
"this unhappy matter," and when it was all over, the
Eagle pointed out, with apparent satisfaction, that "the
effect of the disturbance seems to have been to bring no
good for the laborers, but materially to inconvenience
the progress of the work."

It is true that, after a couple of months had elapsed, the
same journal was to remark that, in denouncing the "riots"
of workingmen, it is well to remember that all the wrongs
are far from being on one side, and that "few masses of
men move discordantly and tumultuously against peace
and good order without *some* reason at least"; but the fact
remains that Whitman the individualist—and the old-
fashioned villager—looked askance upon disciplined unionism and its militancy. This skeptical attitude was to remain with him, incongruous as it was with other attitudes,
long after the Atlantic Docks strike was forgotten; he was
to have it by him, ordinarily unvoiced, in the days when
even the Knights of Labor were disappearing from the

scene and yielding ground to the A. F. of L. Sidney Morse,
the sculptor, who spent a few weeks one summer in the
late eighties making a bust of Whitman, records some
rather surprising observations the old poet made to him
apropos of a troublesome call he had had from a labor
"agitator." This person, who tried to persuade Whitman
to introduce him to a Camden audience, may well have
been an opinionated and aggressive bore: he appears to
have been just that, but this is hardly enough to account
for the manner in which, after the man's departure, Whitman chatted with Morse about the whole question of labor
struggles in that decade. So far as he could see, Whitman
said—or so Morse tells us—there was as much "cussed selfish-
ness" on the one side as on the other: the real desideratum
after all was "manhood," and strikes were not likely to
develop much of that. The spectacle of union men setting
upon their non-union fellow-workers "like beasts of prey"
seemed to him an unpleasant one; his own injunction to
the American worker would be to "accept the situation,
and triumph on the side of his manliness in spite of it":
if he did so, he would find that no man could despoil him.
"When the labor agitation," he concluded, "is other than
the kicking of somebody else out to let myself in, I shall
warm up to it, maybe."

Morse wrote out this extraordinary conversation one
day, he tells us, and asked Whitman whether he would
sign the statement as his full and final deliverance on the
labor issue: the old man, however, refused, perhaps to
Morse's surprise, and went on to remark, with quaint self-
knowledge, "You must compare that with something else
I may say some day, if you want the 'final' and 'full.'" Certainly he said extremely different things from these on

243

other days, and it may be reassuringly indicative of his deeper feelings that, after keeping it by him for some time with a view to putting in some "emendations," Whitman should finally have lost the paper on which his friend had written out their conversation. Undoubtedly he regretted and would have liked to suppress the apparent hostility toward the workers, at least the organized workers, in what he had said: a day or two later he told Morse that he wanted him to say, as summing up his thoughts on the subject, that he was for the worker and for every man, but he wanted the worker to make his cause the cause of the manliness of all men: "that assured, every effort he may make is all right." His captiousness, indeed, in the original conversation, may be taken as nothing more sinister than the revulsion of an old-fashioned middle-class American from some of the harshnesses of class conflict in the eighties. Yet could anything but Whitman's own isolation from that conflict and the sedative effects of his Transcendentalism account for that majestic detachment, that momentary blindness to the real issues, that reduction of the whole racking problem to a question of personal morals?

He had of course taken no direct part, at any time, in the struggles between American artisans or factory workers and their employers: he had been a worker himself, to be sure, but it was only as so many Americans of the nebulous middle stratum had been, and though his relations with men and women of the working class were richer and more intimate than those of any other American poet, they were personal and companionable relations, undefined and undirected by the practical demands of class life. Nevertheless, even in Whitman's youth, a struggle had gone on in the economic sphere: it had grown sharper and more conscious as time elapsed, and there is a sense in which it is not irrelevant to ask how fully and fairly *Leaves of Grass* reflects it. Not irrelevant, if only because its author claimed for the book a representative and inclusive quality. In writing it, he himself said, he had aimed to "absorb" and "express" the whole multitudinous life of nineteenth-century America, at least in its significant aspects: he had been willing that the question should be asked of him, as of any poet who would talk or sing to these states, "Are you really of the whole people?" And the answer to these questions is that *Leaves of Grass* does leave out much that was tragically real and intensely present to thousands of Americans in its time.

In the midst of so many pictures of work and play, of battles and disasters even, there is no picture of tired workers in a textile-mill at the end of a fourteen-hour day, no glimpse of over-driven women or children in a factory of any sort, no sudden view of the hell of sweated labor in tenements or of life in the more appalling slums. It is not from *Leaves of Grass* that one would learn of wage-cuts or lockouts, of hard-fought strikes or evictions, of the blacklist or the firing upon workers by militia-men. There are scenes of terror and distress in the book, but no such scenes as those of the New York bread-riots of 1837, the unemployed demonstrations in the terrible winter of '57–'58, or the Tompkins Square incident of '74. It was not because all that is ugly and grim was to be omitted from the scheme of the book: there is more than a little of both. It was because these other things would have threatened its hopeful unity in a far more portentous way.

They would have had too much the air of alarming and not just accidental or transitory shadows over that pure

democracy which it was the purpose of the book to celebrate—to celebrate as already, at least in the large, achieved
in the New World. Even one or two such details, it seems
hardly too much to say, would have destroyed at once the
special tone, the characteristic composition of *Leaves of
Grass;* and a trustworthy literary instinct, though probably
no deliberate reflection, must have told Whitman just
where to draw his lines. When he began it was still democracy the ideal—democracy rising like a sun upon the night
of feudalism and privilege—that had, virtually for the first
time, to find its full utterance in poetry: the nature of
poetry being what it is, it would doubtless have been a
superhuman feat for Whitman to take not only that step
but the step beyond. It was a new political and social program that, broadly and ideally, he had to lift to the imaginative and ethical level: he can hardly be asked to have
versified its failures simultaneously.

With all its wishfulness, moreover, with all its illusions,
with all its unconscious class limitations, that democratic
program was by inheritance and in spirit a radical, a profoundly progressive one; and after all reservations are
made, that fact insists on being re-stated. In his later years
Whitman himself, out of the midst of his inessential surface conservatisms, was determined that it should be understood. He would not allow the role of a systematic conservative to be thrust upon him: the real drift of his book,
he persisted in claiming, was irrepressibly radical. As he
and Traubel chatted one day about wealth and poverty,
and the old poet made some extreme statements, his young
friend broke out: "Why, you're almost radical!" "Almost!"
returned Whitman with some impatience. "Why—I claim

to be altogether radical—that's my chief stock in trade:
take the radicalism out of the Leaves—do you think anything worth while would be left?"

It was when such questions as wealth and poverty were
up, moreover, and not merely political or moral issues,
that Whitman was most likely to say things of this order.
When, on another occasion, Traubel quoted a common
friend of theirs as saying that he thought Whitman was
rather conservative on the labor question, the old man
again demurred—in spite of his conversation with Morse.
On the contrary, he protested, he was a radical of radicals;
he only did not belong to any sect. "After I got done with
it," he added, "there wouldn't be much wealth left in private hands—that is, if my say was final." It was a singular
remark, this last, to come from a man who, even during
the same years, had described the goal of democracy in
terms so belatedly Jacksonian. But the time had long
passed when Whitman could understandingly be held to
a stern consistency on any subject, and now that twenty
years and more had passed since those talks with Brisbane
in Washington—now that, as we have seen, the social contrasts of the eighties forced themselves at moments more
and more menacingly upon his attention—he was more
willing than he had once been to yield ground even to the
socialists. It was the details of their program rather than
its spirit that he refused to examine studiously. He might
be dodging their doctrines, he once said to Traubel, but
he was not dodging their purpose. In what they strove for
he was with them—"solidarity, the supremacy of the people: all the people in possession of what belongs to all the
people but has been stolen from them"—he was with the

247

socialists in that; but he could not follow them through all the intricacies of theory through which they made their way.

He was not unaffected, however, by the realization that so many of the younger men who appreciated him and his book most intelligently, men like Carpenter and Traubel, were turning toward socialism: he had always, he said, preferred the radicals to the conservatives as men, and now, as he once observed, it seemed as if all the admirable fellows were getting to be socialists. "Sometimes," he added, "I think, I feel almost sure, Socialism is the next thing coming: I shrink from it in some ways: yet it looks like our only hope." We know well enough what the things were that made him shrink from it: the idealistic individualist, with all his middle-class affiliations, was not to be exorcised like a bodiless wraith at this late hour. We have still to consider on their own level the things that nevertheless drew him in the socialist direction: they were quite as real and vital as the other forces, if they were less tangible and less specific, and Whitman himself could not wholly fail to recognize their bearing. On one occasion, after a visit from Ernest Rhys, the talk ran on William Morris and the other English radicals. Did he have any sympathy, asked Traubel, with the socialism of these men? "Lots of it—lots—lots," answered Whitman; and went on to say that, in the large sense, whatever the political methods, the social goal itself—the goal, as he said, of dethroning things and ennobling human beings—was bound to be achieved. Then, in language that echoes that of a hackneyed wise-crack, but in what we have a right to consider a very different spirit, he added: "Ain't we all socialists, after all?"

II

It ought now to be possible to answer the question we began with, not wishfully or abstractly, but critically and in its own dense historical medium. We ought now to be able to say with some tangibleness how right Whitman was when he observed, apropos of Beckett's article, that "intrinsically," in his "meanings," he appeared to be more of a socialist than he had thought he was. It was no mere conversational complaisance that led him to speak in this manner: he could be concessive enough and vague enough in indifferent matters, but he knew very well how far from indifferent a question of this order was; he had behind him a lifetime of effort, of deliberation, of difficulty as a responsible writer; and he was not likely now to be guilty of lightmindedness or whim. There was nothing fortuitous or aimless in the remarks we have so abundantly quoted—those remarks Whitman made in his old age, to Traubel and others, on the social problem: they point toward one quarter of the compass and no other. The elderly Whitman may have had no more exact a knowledge than the younger had had of socialist theory: he certainly had no understanding of primary accumulation or of surplus value; but he had not been deaf to the progressive and socialist agitation of the seventies and eighties, and he made out at significant moments that in some such terms as these the humanistic purposes of *Leaves of Grass* would in the long run be served. Negatively he saw with undeludable clearness that they not only would not be served but would be thwarted and eventually wrecked by the actual social tendencies of those decades—by monopolism,

249

by privilege, by intensifying inequality. This was what he saw most clearly, it is true; but Whitman did not come to the end of his life in entire unawareness that he and his book between them had been premonitory of a contrary tendency, a far more creative program, a richer and deeper social life.

When all reservations have been made, when all contradictions have been allowed for, it remains true that *Leaves of Grass* belongs among a handful of books of the nineteenth century that reach out, in this constructive sense, beyond the limitations of their own hour, and demand for their full realization in experience, even for their full understanding, an equalized and unified society. In fact it is hard to think of another book of the century of which this is so true—not, however, because Whitman was the most brilliantly endowed writer of his age, but because he "happened" to be the completest representative in poetry of a national and a class culture that abounded, at his particular time, in more of the elements of fruitful change than any other, and underwent less heavily the pressure of the past. Western culture in general during the whole century was big with the possibility of a genuine social democracy in the future, but American culture, at the same time that it was giving wider play than any other to the program of individualism, was also giving freer rein to the drive toward equality: it was even furnishing a more appropriate theater than any other for experiments in coöperative living; and inevitably the most expressive book it produced would be one in which all these prophetic forces would voice themselves more fully than they could hope to do elsewhere. Nowhere else had the middle and working classes emancipated themselves so completely from the social and intellectual trammels of feudalism, and if this meant that no other society was moving with less resistance toward the culmination of capitalism, it also meant that no other was suggesting more boldly the expectation of what was to replace it. *Leaves of Grass,* as we have seen, was the expression of much that was sterile or illusory in the older American way of life; but Whitman's genius was closer than that of any of his fellow-writers to all that was warmest, freest, and most vital in that way of life, and his book, as a result, is fuller than any comparable book of perceptions and imaginings that will seem valid in a socialist culture.

Some of these we have already dealt with by way of tracing the development of Whitman's mind, but they deserve to be re-stated here in more critical language. We have seen to what extent Whitman's spirit surrendered itself, with the passage of time, to the nebulous mysticism of the romantics; how perfectly he typified his class and his generation by floating off more and more narcotically on the pinions of "mystery" and "spirituality." We have not quite done justice to that strong and youthful realism which had been his starting-point and, in spite of everything, a point of reference from which he never drew away irrevocably. In spite of its feeble stretches, *Leaves of Grass* is richer than any comparable book in intimations of what a purely natural, an exclusively earthly existence for human beings may become when the ghost of the supernatural is finally laid and men are freed at the same time from their helpless primeval servility to the forces of nature. It is not here a question simply of what Whitman owed intellectually to the achievements of nineteenth-century science: it is a question of something more radical, more personal, more livable than that; something that can only be expressed by saying that, in spite of every lapse, Whitman did more than all but a few other writers to domesticate the modern sensibility in its natural setting. He could do so because, in all his healthiest creative moments, he felt no corrupt dissatisfaction with his own existence as a natural person, physically constituted at base and blessed with animal vitality; because in those moments he felt no superstitious fears of the natural world about him and had no sense of its malign hostility to him. On the contrary he delighted without shame in the rank as well as in the exquisite functions of the subtly-compounded physical organism, and he approached external nature not as an enemy but as a lover.

If Whitman had done nothing else as a writer, he would have enlarged incalculably the whole aesthetic range of modern poetry by showing how all the strong instinctive powers, all the fine natural responsiveness of bodily life can be endowed with plastic and imaginative value by the secular poet. He was by no means without forerunners in doing so, but none of the passionate poets of the Renaissance or of Romanticism made quite what Whitman made of the natural man's frank pleasure in food and drink ("Joy of the plenteous dinner, strong carouse and drinking"), of the delight in physical motion, of the senses of smell and touch ("The smell of apples, aromas from crush'd sage-plant, mint, birchbark"), of the deliciousness of sleep and indolence, and of the exhilarations of sex. Since Whitman wrote, poetry has been a more expressive medium, more expressive of men's whole profane experience, than it was before; more than that, the conviction that, aside from literature, material life itself may be both sane and poetic in quality has been immensely reënforced by *Leaves of Grass*. If its physicality had been merely that of an unbalanced and unhealthy hedonism, this would not be true; as it is, the book is full of value for men who wish to build up a well-proportioned secular culture.

Contradictory as it is, it embodies on its most characteristic side a fresh creative feeling about physical nature and man's relation to it. The primitive sense of nature as an array of maleficent forces—or its modern equivalent, the sense of nature's subhuman ruthlessness ("red in tooth and claw")—has almost wholly disappeared from this book, though all the elemental terrors have not been complacently banished. Gone, too, is every fastidious revulsion from nature's rankness, every contemptuous sense of its degradedness or meanness ("Dung and dirt more admirable than was dream'd"). Even the typical romantic views of nature are superseded in *Leaves of Grass*, and Whitman does not characteristically render the physical world as an enchanting spectacle or a collection of splendid pictures, as a comforter of the downcast or a monitor for the bewildered; not even as an ideally living presence or an emblem of transcendental verity. There is something of this last, of course, in the book, but it is not what is most idiosyncratic. What *is* is much more a sense of intimate and unreflective harmony with nature as with a perfectly equal and reciprocal life, an identification of the poet's self with natural existences so complete and so tender that it can only be described as the self-surrender of a lover. There is nothing in poetry before Whitman quite like his appeal to the sea to "dash" him with "amorous wet," or like his insistence to the same sea that "I am integral with you"; and it signifies a great deal that one of his erotic poems, "We Two, How Long We were Fool'd," should be the

253

poem in which the thought of entire identity with the life of nature is most sweepingly expressed ("We become plants, trunks, foliage, roots, bark," and so forth).

As a metaphor this sort of thing has become a commonplace in modern poetry; as a deep, spontaneous experience it has become a commonplace neither in poetry nor in life. It belongs to the future much more than to the past, and we can hardly doubt that, as men come to have less and less reason to live in terror of nature, something like Whitman's lover-like emotion will prevail among them increasingly. Something like it, though not quite the same: as Whitman voiced it the feeling is rather too purely the voice of instinct and rather too little the fruit of understanding—informed and disciplined understanding of natural law. There are dangers in any manner of feeling so largely unintellectual as this, and there are dangers in Whitman's merging of himself with vegetable and animal life: we have to remember, however, how sanely he was capable of asserting not only man's identity with nature but his potential supremacy over her. "I know," he wrote,

I know before the fitting man all Nature yields;

and in another poem he addressed his generalized reader—"you whoever you are"—as

Master or mistress in your own right over Nature, elements, pain, passion, dissolution.

This note of humanistic independence, of hopeful strenuousness, is quite as characteristic of Whitman as the note of amorous surrender; and it is another of the strains

254

in *Leaves of Grass* that insures it a long life under social-ism. Its basis temperamentally, of course, was in a pre-dominantly sanguine disposition, though there is more to be said in that connection than is often heard. In another sense the basis of Whitman's strong affirmativeness was in the expectant and energetic life of the class to which he belonged; a class which, in his impressionable years, looked for far more from the future than from the past, which habitually assumed that the course of things was a forward and upward course, and which had no settled fear of move-ment or change. We know very well how delusive and how unfeeling this American middle-class optimism was capa-ble of being, and how full of meaning was the repudiation of it by men like Poe and Melville. The fact remains that it was an intrinsically more creative attitude toward things than its despairing opposite, and that there was a sure wis-dom in the impulse that led Whitman to embody it in his verse. *Leaves of Grass* would have an enduring vitality if only as an evangel-poem of humane hopefulness, of posi-tive struggle, of progressive movement and change.

The poet owed his enthusiasm for change, as we have seen, partly to the incitements of contemporary science, and we have spoken of it in that connection: what is worth adding here is that he lifted to the poetic and even philo-sophic level what might have been a merely sensuous or merely intellectual perception, inspired by the crude flux of things or by the naked facts of the laboratory. Before he could have known even so much of Hegel as he came to know, Whitman had given plastic expression, in the "Song of the Open Road," to the essential spirit of an his-torical and dynamic philosophy:

255

> *Now understand me well—it is provided in the essence
> of things that from any fruition of success, no mat-
> ter what, shall come forth something to make a
> greater struggle necessary.*

It goes without saying how congenial such a thought is,
when realistically conceived, to the ethics of socialism,
with its rejection of the fixed, the final, and the static, and
its assertion of the reality of time, the value of struggle,
and the dignity of conscious development.

How far this was from being a mere "thought" with
Whitman—how deeply his imagination was tinged by the
vital sense of process, of movement, of endless becoming
and growth—we have already observed briefly, but we
must come back to the point here. We are vividly aware
of its bearing when we recall how marked and visible a
seal this feeling of Whitman's set upon the language, the
imagery, the very titles of his poems. Did any other verse
ever abound as Whitman's does in the verbs and partici-
ples of motion?—was any other verse ever so full of the
sense of things "rocking," "gliding," "tossing," "ascending," "soaring"; of things "sprouting," "swelling," "growing," "ripening," "expanding"; of men "starting," "roaming," "wandering," "marching," "traveling," "journeying"?
Perhaps no poet ever found his imagery more naturally
than Whitman did in the onward drive of vessels by sail
or steam, in the tireless heaving of the waves of ocean, in
the rolling of the "apple-shaped" earth through space.
Nothing could be more characteristic than the recurring
image of a procession, a march, a journey, a pageant, a
passage. And what of the titles themselves?—what of "The
Ship Starting," "Starting from Paumanok," "Ages and
Ages Returning at Intervals," "Roaming in Thought,"

"A March in the Ranks Hard-Prest, and the Road Un-known," "Unfolded out of the Folds," "To Soar in Freedom and in Fullness of Power"? Could such titles testify more eloquently than they do to Whitman's love of the mobile and the mutable?

Do not some of them, moreover, point unmistakably to the strenuous, the voluntaristic strain—as contrasted with the passive or spectatorial—in Whitman's nature and in his credo? Certainly there was a strain of passiveness, of indolence, of languor even, in both of them; but the verbs to float" and "to flow" are actually less characteristic of this poet than the verbs "to arise" and "to stride on," and Whitman is far from being a kind of inverted mystic, intoxicated not with the vision of the One but with the phantasmagoria of the Many. He is much more the poet of resolute action, of cheerful effort, of unremitting struggle. It is true that his late and cloudy Hegelianism led him sometimes to speak as if moral progress were the work of a transcendental Idea effectuating itself in history without the need of human collaboration: "the law over all, and law of laws," he wrote in *Democratic Vistas*, "is the law of successions; that of the superior law, in time, gradually supplanting and overwhelming the inferior one." This is the mere mysticism of progress, perhaps: sanguine as it is, it is too idealistic in phrasing to put much onus on the human will. But it is no more characteristic of the essential Whitman, of Whitman the prophet-poet, than it was of the hard-working mechanics and shopkeepers of Brooklyn, of the "movers" in their Conestoga wagons, or of the young men of the rank and file who fought the battles of the Secession War and whom Whitman found so Homeric in their heroism. What *was* characteristic of him, as of

257

them, was a vehement spirit of defiance to obstacles and difficulties, of rebounding from weak discouragement, of militancy and conquest. "My call is the call of battle," he wrote, "I nourish active rebellion"; and these words express the true and central moral tone of *Leaves of Grass*.

He had his own capacity, as any man of exceptional sensibility has, for suffering and doubt; and for more than one reason, as I have said, he had real enough moods of fatigue and gloom. He confessed to them only two or three times, but he went so far as to say, in a paragraph in *Specimen Days*, that he too had felt the modern tendency to turn everything to "pathos, ennui, morbidity, dissatisfaction, death." He added at once, however, that he knew very well how little all that was in harmony with the sane life of nature and how expressive merely of "one's own distorted, sick or silly soul." If he had been another sort of poet, Whitman would at any cost have revealed his own soul completely, however distorted or sick it might have been; if he had been another sort of man, he might have despaired of achieving balance or well-being in so troubled and terrible a world. In such a case, he might have been another of the great modern poets of torment and defeat. He was not that kind of man, and he did not choose to be that kind of poet. For all his flaunt of egotism, he intended to celebrate only so much of his own personality as seemed to him to represent the healthy, forward-moving life of his time; as an individual, he was determined to conquer all tendencies in himself that were not in tune with that life. If two or three times in his book Whitman allowed the minor strain to assert itself, in the most striking of these passages he did so solely to discredit it: in the poem called "Ah, Poverties, Wincings, and Sulky Re-

258

treats," he invokes his "poverties," his "foes," his "degradations," his "smother'd ennuis," only to challenge their power over him:

> *Ah think not you finally triumph, my real self has yet*
> *   to come forth,*
> *It shall yet march forth o'ermastering, till all lies be-*
> *   neath me,*
> *It shall yet stand up the soldier of ultimate victory.*

All his weak mysticisms, all his doubts of nature, all his cult of death to the contrary, the Whitman who wrote these lines is the quintessential Whitman, the real "ancestor" of our own generation and of the future.

III

The motives in Whitman we have been speaking of—his realism, his hearty sense of time and change, his masculine affirmations—go very far toward explaining the persistent vitality of *Leaves of Grass,* but of course it is still more on broadly political grounds—it is because he undertook to compose the chants of what he called the Democracy of the New World—that Whitman imposes himself now on the socialist intelligence and makes his appeal to the socialist imagination. What we must ask is how strongly he imposes or will continue to impose himself and how powerful is the appeal he makes. We have seen how, as abstract theory, his democratic convictions had their source in the liberalism of the Jeffersonians and the "equal rights" of the Jacksonian masses; we have seen how close Whitman was, in every personal and practical way, to the functioning of that electoral and representative democ-

racy of the shopkeepers and the farmers in the days before
the War; how, even during the Gilded Age, he remained,
just as office-holder or voter, on amiable terms with the
democracy of Grant and Garfield. Is he then, as a poet,
no more than the delegated skald of the fighting and feast-
ing Jacksonians? Is *Leaves of Grass* no more than the lay of
the voters and the tax-payers in their nineteenth-century
American republic? Are Whitman and his book submerged,
below historic waves, along with the progressive but one-
sided and precarious democracy of their actual day?

Not unless, in general, men have no capacity as readers,
as imaginative beings, to go beyond biography and chro-
nology, and to refresh themselves with what is enduringly
usable in the writers of the past. The question is hardly
worth discussing whether they can do this: if they could
not, Whitman would suffer no more—indeed, even then,
less—than a whole group of writers with whom it is natural
to compare him. He would suffer no more from his closeness to Jacksonianism than Shelley suffers from his closeness to the English radicalism of a hundred years and more
ago, or than Heine from his closeness to German republicanism, or than Hugo from being so much the voice of
French liberalism under the Second Empire. Comparably,
at least, with *Prometheus Unbound* and *Deutschland* and
Les Châtiments, Leaves of Grass is hallmarked in one vital
respect by its time and its class; and like them it has already a certain remoteness from our own world. It suggests
those other poems whenever it dramatizes democracy for
us as emancipation simply from "kings" and "priests," as
a snapping of the fetters of feudalism; it suggests them too
so far as it represents democracy mainly in terms of freedom, of liberty, of independence—in short, of idealistic

individualism and the nationalism of the older revolutions. On these levels Whitman is another of the poets who derive from the great declarations—of Independence, of the Rights of Man; like them, on the plane of political convictions, he demands of socialists a process of translation into a more tangible, richer, and truer idiom. Democracy as liberalism, as republicanism—and that is a large part of Whitman's democracy—is a stage that both the political intelligence and the creative imagination have transcended; so far, like Shelley, Heine, and Hugo, Whitman appeals to the imaginative faculty rather as memory than as prophecy. This is only to say, however, that like them he was one of the great eloquent voices of a progressive chapter in human experience, and that like them he will survive as the poet of freedoms that can always be given their deeper connotations.

There is much, however, in *Leaves of Grass* that goes very far beyond this, and it can be formally and inadequately indicated by saying that, more than any of the European poets, Whitman was the prophet not only of democracy as liberty but of democracy as equality. If by this one meant only that Equality was for him an abstract slogan, the expression of a grandiose political ideal, one would say relatively little for the present and future vitality of *Leaves of Grass*. One means much more than that, and it makes all the difference. One means everything that Whitman implied when he said to himself: "I advance from the people in their own spirit." Unlike the great European republicans, in short, Whitman is not to be described as having arrived, after whatever uncertainties and divagations, at a position in the forefront of popular movements; he is not to be seen as having "espoused" or "embraced" the cause of the people; not to be thought of as a daring and generous tribune or advocate. For him it was a much simpler and more natural affair than that. He was himself quite literally one of the people: his identification with them was primitive, spontaneous, and complete; the question could never have arisen for him of identifying himself with any other cause than theirs. As a result the thought of equality is for him not a rational or programmatic one mainly: it is personal, naïve, concrete, and intimate. How personal and how concrete it is becomes evident when one reflects how little, for Whitman, democracy is a question of Humanity, of Man, of the Masses, even of the People, and how largely a question of "Workmen and Workwomen," of "mechanics busy at their benches with tools," of "young fellows working on farms and old fellows working on farms," of "the boatman singing what belongs to him in his boat." Not a question, that is, of any orotund generality so much as of palpable men and women.

The equality Whitman stands for is not the incredible Equality of the *philosophes*—the Equality that both sense and science give the lie to—it is the vital equality of common work and common living in a society from which arbitrary distinctions and the privileges of caste and fortune have been banished. The practical sentiment of such equality was one for which Whitman's environment and his genius together gave him a special and profound capacity. It was what enabled him to be something more than the orator or the lyrist of democracy; to be, beyond this, its dramatist, its biographer, its image-maker. In *Leaves of Grass* democratic equality is celebrated not only as an ideal or a vision; the ideal is made dramatic, made

262

plastic, by finding for it an expressive imagery. What is most characteristic of the book is not exhortations or apocalyptic dreams, but strong images of a democratic and equal life—of "ordinary" men and women working, building, making things, growing things, sailing ships, fighting battles, eating and drinking, singing, marching. The effect of this imagery is to evoke an emotion that is hardly summoned up by any other poet of the century, a humanistic emotion that Whitman quite consciously felt it to be the part of a democratic literature to foster. "As Democracy and Science in the Modern [World]," he once wrote in a notebook, "have an entire lack of what in Greece & Rome was furnished by reverence for the Gods . . . or, under the feudal ages by loyalty, deference, caste, now unknown— *the future must substitute it by a new feeling* a profound & tender enthusiasm for the people, & especially for the poorer & less favored & educated masses."

Toward the development of such a feeling *Leaves of Grass* has contributed powerfully and almost uniquely— and in a way that lifts it unchallengeably above the special circumstances of Whitman's own milieu. The language of this short note of his, however, hardly suggests what is most characteristic of Whitman's democracy: his words here have too many of the overtones of romantic humanitarianism. Compassion for the unfortunate, pity for the *misérables,* were emotions far more natural to Mrs. Gaskell or Victor Hugo or Dostoievski than to Walt Whitman; and what his work does is far less to encourage commiseration for suffering humanity—it does that scarcely at all—than to arouse and make articulate and give a conscious drive to "the great pride of man in himself." "Whoever degrades another degrades me," he wrote in one of his moments of profoundest insight; and what equality mainly signified to Whitman was not something sacrificial or mystic or conducive to humility—any more than something emptily rational—but the equal consciousness on the part of all men of the dignity, the distinction, the irreducible *value* of individual being, of each man's individual being, whoever he might be. Whitman strove to quicken this consciousness from his first page to his last; "you whoever you are" is the phrase of his that recurs most insistently through his verse:

> *The sum of all known reverence I add up in you*
> *whoever you are.*

Does any other writer strike quite these notes of radically personal equality, of unforced respect for human personality, of quick spontaneous resentment at its degradation from outside? Does any other writer so successfully sublimate what might have been merely an intelligent conviction into a pervasive, a completely realized attitude?

If Whitman did so, it was not because his idealism somehow blinded him to all the realities of human character. There was a great fund of homely canniness in him, and it enabled him to make allowance in his own way for the imperfections of the race. His humanism rested, after all, on no ingenuous illusions. He took his account of "the wolf, the snake, the hog" that were "not wanting," as he said, in himself; and he reckoned very consciously with the "perverse maleficence" of which, as he also said, general humanity is full. It was no hopelessly visionary democrat who described "the crude, defective streaks in all the strata of the common people," or who candidly confronted "this *bad*—this nineteen-twentieths of us all." If anything,

264

he exaggerated all this: certainly it was not because he complacently ignored it that he could say, "I never have any doubts of the future when I look at the common man." He knew well enough what remained to be achieved in the "long journey" of the race from the wildness and dullness of the rock-shelters and the bush to a disciplined and clarified humanity. He simply insisted that that achievement would be and could only be the work of the people as a whole, not of favored classes or individuals. In the creative resources of the people he had endless confidence, though he knew how uncommon that confidence was. Even in America, he said, he knew nothing more rare than "a fit scientific estimate and reverent appreciation of the People—of their measureless wealth of latent power and capacity, their vast, artistic contrasts of lights and shades —with, in America, their entire reliability in emergencies, and a certain breadth of historic grandeur, of peace or war."

"Historic grandeur"!—is it such a phrase as the merely sentimental leveller would strike out? No more surely than the phrase, "gigantic manliness," which Whitman must at some time have come across in the writings of Thomas Paine; and if Whitman demanded a society of equals, it was anything but a society of the equally paltry or mediocre. "I have imagined," he once said to Dr. Bucke, "a life which should be that of the average man in average circumstances, and still grand, heroic." The author of *Democratic Vistas* did not pretend to believe that such a life had been achieved in these states—where, in "its social aspects, and in really grand religious, moral, literary, and esthetic results," he held democracy to be "an almost complete failure"—but late as well as early he regarded as a

fact and not merely as a dream what he called "the noble
character of mechanics and farmers." It is one of Whitman's chief services to the modern and democratic sensibility that he helped to dissociate such proud words as
"noble" from their old affiliations with caste and to re-
associate them with the rank and file. He could do so because his feelings themselves were so wholly re-associated:
for him it was as natural to see personal distinction, essential human grandeur, in an old farmer or a young fireman
as it was for Homer to see these things in a tribal chieftain
or for Shakespeare to see them in an English peer.

In this connection Hamlin Garland records a conversation with Whitman that is peculiarly rich in meaning.
Garland himself, he tells us, had been speaking enthusiastically of the fiction of Cable, Harris, and other "local
color" writers of the time, and describing them as the forerunners of a powerful native literature. Whitman, however, demurred at this judgment, and remarked that he
disliked the habit such writers had of exploiting whatever
was eccentric or abnormal—"*outré*"—in the characters of
the common people they described. For himself, he said,
he had been far more constantly struck, in his going and
coming among the Civil War camps, for example, by the
"decorum"—"a word I like to use"—of the common soldier,
his "good manners," his "quiet heroism"; and these, he
was convinced, were typical qualities of the American
farmer and mechanic—qualities of which "local color"
made much too little. "At any rate," he said, "I want to utter
my protest against such work and to demand that the
really heroic character of the common American be depicted in novel or drama." He had already depicted it in
verse: he had that particular warrant for demanding that

it be depicted elsewhere. In any case the contrast in feeling and insight between Whitman and Bret Harte or John Hay or Bronson Howard is immense and decisive.

To argue, moreover, that when he spoke of the "common American" Whitman was consciously or unconsciously limiting himself to the "plain man" of the middle classes is to ignore the spirit and even the letter of both his utterance and his life. It is quite true, as we have abundantly seen, that Whitman the journalist, Whitman the party-worker, Whitman the voter, rarely went much beyond the political ideology or the political practice of the American middle classes in his generation: simply as "views," his ideas about many political and social matters were no doubt those of Lincoln, of Horace Greeley, of Peter Cooper. Could anything, however, be more mechanical than to let this be the last word for Walt Whitman the person and the poet? It was not his views, it was the intuitive sympathies of his nature that led Whitman as a man to enter into vital relations with a wider range of human beings than any other American writer has done— than Melville, even, or Mark Twain; and it is not the friend of bus-drivers, of "jour" printers, of ferry-boat pilots, of common soldiers, who can be disposed of as a mere versifier of Jacksonianism. Whatever may have been true of his practical intelligence, Whitman's humane imagination, his creative sensibility, were quite as proletarian as they were bourgeois: the man who wrote *Leaves of Grass, Specimen Days,* and *Democratic Vistas,* really transcended as an artist the limitations of his class.

He did so, moreover, consciously and intentionally. "Without yielding an inch," he wrote late in life, as we have seen, "the working-man and working-woman were to be in my pages from first to last." However we may describe or qualify their presence there, the claim he made is in spirit and essence a valid one. It is reënforced, at least in the biographical sense, by the conversational expressions of his old age, and one has no sense of contemplating an about-face, a contradiction in feeling, a willful effort at expansion, when one finds Whitman remarking to Traubel that he puts his faith in "the crowd of everyday men," "the superb masses," "the workers"; or that America is not for special types but for "the great mass of people—the vast, surging, hopeful, army of workers"; or that "the crowd of the grave workingmen of our world" are "the hope, the sole hope, the sufficient hope, of our democracy." The Whitman who said these things was essentially the same person as the Whitman who, in 1856, had addressed a campaign broadside to "the great masses of mechanics," and had pointed to "labouring persons," "ploughmen," "machinists," and "workmen in factories" as "the real America." The man who could feel in this manner was a more radical democrat than any of our other writers.

On still another level the poet Whitman rose to a richer comprehension of democracy than the prosaic Whitman ever attained. If in his "politics" he remained for the most part an old-fashioned individualist, in his freer thought—and in his work—he moved well beyond the simpler formulas of individualism. To a young friend he once remarked with a twinkle in his eye: "Be individualistic, be individualistic, be not too damned individualistic." It was the humorous expression of a feeling he had entertained long and seriously. Unlike some of his teachers in the school of self-reliance, Whitman had had a sense, almost

268

from the beginning, of the menace to democracy that lurked in that heady doctrine. For all his own announced determination to "effuse egotism"—for all his insistence on the message, "Produce great Persons, the rest follows" —Whitman had never succumbed to the Emersonian and certainly not to the Carlylesque idolatry of heroes. His individualism, taken in its whole setting, its real spirit, is anything but a weapon for the superman, the "leader," the member of a "natural élite." Against any such undemocratic humbug he was biased almost by nature and certainly by all that was congenial to him in his environment. How typical is a sentiment he once expressed as editor of the *Times!* "We cannot help regarding hero worship as a great evil," he there wrote, "whatever the characteristics and position of the hero himself."

It was a feeling that, if anything, grew upon Whitman as time went on. He had no taste, for example, for the biographical interpretation of history. Such books as Foster Kirk's *Charles the Bold* or Carlyle's *Cromwell* and *Frederick,* he said to Traubel, seemed to him insidious, poisonous; and he added: "I am very impatient of stories [histories?] which imply the concentration of all historical meanings in single eminent persons." On another day that impatience came to the surface again as the two of them talked about the leaders of the Civil War, including Lincoln. "We must not give too much importance to personalism," said Whitman, even in that fond connection—"it is easy to overcharge it—man moves as man, in all the great achievements—man in the great mass." So it is, he was convinced, and so it ought to be: he himself wished, he said, to be taken as a witness not for "saviors," "exceptional men," but for "the average man," "the whole."

269

How fairly he spoke for the book he had actually written!
—for surely in no comparable volume does the illustrious
individual, the named eminence, even the great rebel or
the great tribune count for so little, and the anonymous
average man for so much. The Civil War was perhaps
the first war to be celebrated by its poet in terms almost
exclusively of the rank and file, and how completely, even
in the tribute to Lincoln, is that one leader identified
with a great natural scene and a whole population! The
poet's very reluctance to call the dead president by name
is itself significant.

The individualism he had chanted had been voiced
so exultantly, so defiantly, and sometimes so stridently,
partly because it released so effectively his own intense
self-consciousness and self-delight, partly because it was
in harmony with all the egotistic, self-reliant, separatist
forces in his America. There were contrary needs in Whitman's own nature, nevertheless, and contrary impulses in
the life of his countrymen. The Utopian communities of
which he superficially made so little, were symptomatic of
a drive toward fellowship, toward collectivism, toward a
constructive social and moral unity, which was no less
genuine, no less true to the inner history of American
life, for not being the dominant and "successful" drive.
It corresponded in a certain sense to Whitman's own urgent, his passionate need—despite his love of independence
—for sympathy and friendship, for the physical presence
of crowds, for intimate and affectionate association with
his fellows, for the vital sense of participation in a common life. "Egotism" and "charity" struck Edward Carpenter as being the opposite poles of Whitman's really complex nature; and even if the second of these words is not

quite the right one, it is certainly true that Whitman was closer to the Utopians and the socialists in temper, in tendency, in imaginative sympathy, than he ever was in conscious agreement or in practice.

If not at the very beginning, still very early—and steadily as time went on—he felt that the vehement individualism of his first poems demanded to be counterbalanced by some other motive, some other value, if his book was not to remain lop-sided and untrue. It is the reason why the poems of comradeship, the "Calamus" poems, appeared so conspicuously in the edition of 1860, and why the theme they express began to seem to Whitman the second of his three primary themes—the others being individualism and religion. He said this most plainly, as it happens, in a preface which he wrote toward the end of the War for a possible English edition of *Leaves of Grass*. The idea of the sovereignty of the individual, he observed, "isolates, for reasons, each separate man and woman in the world;—while the idea of Love fuses and combines the whole. Out of the fusing of these twain, opposite as they are, I seek to make a homogeneous Song." And, from 1867 on, his book was to open with the poem whose first two lines finally read:

> One's-self I sing, a simple separate person,
> Yet utter the word Democratic, the word En-Masse.

Surely it is not meaningless that "the word Democratic" should be associated here rather with the idea of union than with the idea of separateness. At any rate, though Whitman was to insist to the end on the idea of individuality more emphatically than on its antithesis, he was more than once to reveal how acutely he was conscious

271

of the falsity of a monolithic individualism. He revealed it, for example, in the much-pondered pages of *Democratic Vistas*. "Not that half only, individualism, which isolates," he wrote in those pages. "There is another half, which is adhesiveness or love, that fuses, ties and aggregates, making the races comrades, and fraternizing all." And a little later: "The liberalist of to-day has this advantage over antique or mediaeval times, that his doctrine seeks not only to individualize but to universalize. The great word Solidarity has arisen." Here, as a matter of fact, Whitman was speaking not only of union and separatism in general but of the problem of nationalism and internationalism; yet his language has a larger application, and so it did when he talked on one occasion with Traubel about the same political issue. Whitman had been remarking that there was a sense in which he wished to be patriotic and a sense in which he wished to be cosmopolitan. "That," suggested Traubel, "is the same old question —adjusting the individual to the mass." Whitman repeated his sentence. "Yes," he continued, "the big problem—the only problem: the sum of them all."

How he had dealt with the problem in his book—how, at least, he had dealt with it most directly—is familiar enough. He had resolved to be "the poet of comrades" as well as of selfhood, and in the "Calamus" poems he had given bold utterance to that "manly attachment," that "intense and loving comradeship," that "adhesive love," that "beautiful and sane affection of man for man," which he maintained to be as strong and normal an emotion in men as love between the sexes, and the free development of which he promised would "make the continent indissoluble," would "solve the problems of freedom yet," would "weld together" and "anneal" the United States of the future into a "Living Union." It was in highly personal language that he sang this emotion, and the images he found for it are sometimes singular ones—images of two boys "together clinging," of "dauntless and rude" men touching "face to face lightly," of parting friends embracing each other ardently. Pictures such as these have an inevitable oddity in "Anglo-Saxon" literature, and it may as a result be a question how seriously the political purport of these poems can be regarded by men in general: there can be no question how seriously Whitman meant it to be regarded. "The special meaning of the *Calamus* cluster of LEAVES OF GRASS," he wrote in one of his prefaces, "mainly resides in its Political significance." Indeed he believed that, essentially, no other bond than this bond of sentiment and emotion would effectually unify the society of the future.

For a long time this gospel of comradeship was accepted at its face value by Whitman's disciples: later it was drastically challenged. It was challenged by the German writer, Eduard Bertz, who had begun as an enthusiastic Whitmanite; it was challenged by the English physician, W. C. Rivers; and more recently Mr. Mark Van Doren has pointed out that what Whitman half-consciously meant by "manly attachment" was not simply a normal brotherly feeling among men but homosexual love: it was the unwitting expression of his own abnormal sexuality, and as such has no serious meaning—certainly no serious political meaning—for healthy men and women. His "democratic dogmas," since they base themselves on this eccentric and unwholesome emotion—this "wateriest of foundations for democracy"—are wholly without meaning, wholly invalid,

273

for the men of to-day and of the future. "No society can be made out of him," says Mr. Van Doren of Whitman. "We could not be like him if we would. He has revealed himself to us, and that is all."

It is a painful judgment to radical democrats who do take Whitman seriously on these political grounds, but it is a judgment that cannot be dismissed light-mindedly. For one thing the fact of Whitman's homosexuality is one that cannot be denied by any informed and candid reader of the "Calamus" poems, of his published letters, and of accounts by unbiased acquaintances: after a certain point the fact stares one unanswerably in the face. The man Whitman was at least as unmistakably homosexual as any of the great Greek or Renaissance writers and artists. It is true that he must have been, in a difficult sense of that word, "unconscious" of all that was implied by the tendency of his nature, but the tendency was powerfully there, and some of his poems are the astonishingly direct expression of it. They have a serious interest on this account, but so far as they are this primarily, they represent an experience that quite certainly neither can nor ought to be important and decisive for the mass of mankind. Whatever is specific and biographical in them will have less and less meaning, not more and more, in a healthy and integrated society. They indicate, moreover, that Whitman's political outlook was distorted in at least one way by his emotional organization: it did certainly lead him to hope for too much from the cohesive force of spontaneous affection, and to make much too light—in a care-free, transcendental way—of the "institutions" which he said he was neither for nor against. It encouraged him, along with his idealism, to feel that he could afford to be

ignorant of the practical details of any political program.
A more normal man and poet, however transcendental,
would have been less contemptuous than he was even of
"an agreement on paper."

Does all this mean, however, that Whitman's whole
prophecy as a democratic poet—and especially as the poet
of "universal democratic comradeship"—is invalidated by
having its psychological basis in a sexual aberration?
Not, surely, unless the personal origin of political, of
ethical, of philosophic ideas in general is to be taken as
the test of their validity. It is hardly customary, and it
would certainly be uncritical, to dispose of the ideas in
the *Republic* because there is a homosexual strain in
Plato, and homosexuality is only one of the eccentricities
or pathologies that may give a particular bias to a writer's
work. The sense of impotence, the feeling of inferiority,
an abnormal horror of the physiological, the delusion of
persecution—these are others; and the history of literature
is eloquent of what splendid fruits may be grown in such
bitter and unlikely soil. Not its obscure and private origins
but its general and public bearing is the test of a great
creative conception, and from this point of view what
really interests us in Whitman is not that he was a homosexual, but that, unlike the vast majority of inverts, even
of those creatively gifted, he chose to translate and sublimate his strange, anomalous emotional experience into
a political, a constructive, a democratic program. In doing
so, he made himself the voice of something far larger and
more comprehensive than his own private sensibility, and
this in a manner that is not at all necessarily invalidated
by the facts of that sensibility.

Not necessarily, but still conceivably. It is quite pos-

275

sible that, even if we ignored the personal, eccentric basis of Whitman's democratic comradeship, and concentrated on the poetic "teaching" itself, we should feel that this teaching had been somehow colored and warped by the poet's personality in a way that kept it from being available to men in general as it ought to be. If we do not feel this of *Leaves of Grass* as a whole, of *Specimen Days*, of *Democratic Vistas*—and thousands of readers have failed to feel it—it must be because a strong and even pathological idiosyncrasy does not have all the consequences either in life or in art that Mr. Van Doren attributes to it. What else, indeed, do experience and reflection and special knowledge constantly suggest to us? The line that can be drawn between the normal and the abnormal, though a real one, is at best an uncertain and somewhat arbitrary line, drawn rather for practical convenience than for the sake of absolute distinctions, and it is one of the profoundest lessons of modern mental science that the extremest abnormalities are only exaggerations, distortions, unhealthy over-growths of the most normal traits and tendencies. If this were not true, it would be hopelessly inexplicable why neurotics or psychotics of genius should again and again have succeeded in uttering the powerful, undefined, inarticulate impulses of normal men and women. The men of the French Revolution were untouched and undisturbed by Rousseau's paranoia: they were inflamed, they were electrified, by his political ideas; and so it has repeatedly been in human history.

There are the harmless germs of paranoia in all healthy human beings, or Rousseau might well have been a wholly ineffectual prophet; and a similar thing must be said of Whitman's idiosyncrasy. There is, so to say, a harmless,

wholesome, sane "homosexuality" that pervades normal
humanity as the mostly powerless bacilli of tuberculosis
appear in the healthiest of lungs: if it were not so, we
could hardly account for the abnormal emergence of the
tendency in whole peoples and its dominance in particular cultures. The normal imagination is bound to feel
that, whenever this occurs to peoples or to individuals,
something has gone tragically awry with the free, full, and
balanced development of social life and human personality. If Whitman's book were likely to become part of any
such general aberration, we might well feel about it as
many ancients doubtless felt about Anacreon or Strato.
It is a somewhat fantastic fear to suppose that this will
happen, and meanwhile what is far more real and important about *Leaves of Grass* is the power and beauty with
which it gives utterance to the warm fraternal emotions
that are not only latent but active and efficient among average men. There was a core of abnormality in Whitman's
emotional life, but it was no more the whole of his nature
than Rousseau's delusion of persecution was the whole of
his: it shaded off, in every direction, through endless
nuances of tenderness, of affectionate sympathy, of benevolence, of good-natured companionableness, to its wide
circumference of diffused and fruitful social feeling. Exceptional as he was, Whitman was no mere invert, no
mere "case": he remained to the end, in almost every real
and visible sense, a sweet and sane human being—a human
being who had proved himself capable of easy and genial
friendship with hundreds of ordinary people. Is it then
unaccountable if—just as Rousseau's delusion of persecution could become the effective symbol of many genuine
persecutions—so Whitman's very specially circumstanced

"love of comrades" should become the symbol for an incomparably more general and historic drive toward a true fraternity?

There is not only nothing unaccountable in this, but it is the kind of thing that has happened again and again in the history of poetry and of social life. A poem has no simple, objective existence, independent of the desires and the needs of the individuals or the groups who receive it: it is a plastic thing, responsive within certain limits to far more conditions than the restricted ones that called it forth, and it would not be incredible if even the most personal poems in "Calamus" should come to be cherished, as Shakespeare's sonnets have been, by thousands of normal men and women. In fact, they have already begun to be so; but it is now time to say that, after all, *Leaves of Grass* as a gospel poem of genuine fraternity is far from standing or falling on the pieces in the "Calamus" group alone. It is not in these poems, in any case, that Whitman's principle of comradeship is most significantly, most validly, expressed; it would be preposterous to speak as if the communal strain in *Leaves of Grass* were exhausted by pieces like "Scented Herbage of My Breast" and "To a Western Boy." On the contrary, that strain is diffused through the book so widely and so subtly that it cannot be isolated and separated from the rest except by an artificial process of analysis. It gave voice, as I have said, to a deep-seated necessity in Whitman's nature and this had been reënforced by his own kind of intuitive reflection. There is no accident in the continual recurrence through *Leaves of Grass* and the prose writings of such words as "ensemble," "en-masse," "rapport," "sympathy," and "solidarity": Whitman was determined, from an early stage, that the

278

realities behind such words should find their due place in his book side by side with the realities of independent selfhood. More perhaps than even he realized, *Leaves of Grass* is a book of friendship, of neighborliness, of union, of companionship.

Compare it with the whole utterance of any other American poet and the difference between them will at once throw all this into high relief. Think only of the grave, countrified solitude of Bryant, of Emerson's meditative aloofness—Emerson who had himself enjoined the poet to "sit aloof"—of the ghoul-haunted loneliness of Poe, of Emily Dickinson's shutting of her door on society— think of these and then of the jovially peopled pages of Whitman's book, and say whether any other American poet has risen to the conception of a free and wholesome communality as Whitman rose to it. How relatively small a role the uncomfortable ambiguities of "manly love" really play in that conception! Its presence is felt from time to time elsewhere than in the "Calamus" poems, but along with how many other motives of simple, strong, and unambiguous fraternity! Not even the hastiest reader can fail to see how the book abounds in the imagery of participation, how robust it is in its evocations of common work, of common play, of common struggles, of common aspirations. In the very earliest of all these poems, the note of civic and moral cohesion is struck sharply and resoundingly:

> *This is the city and I am one of the citizens,*
> *Whatever interests the rest interests me. . . .*

It is only the explicit statement of what is implied in page after page of *Leaves of Grass*—in all those pages in

279

which Whitman requires his readers to picture him, sometimes literally, sometimes imaginatively, working side by
side with house-builders hoisting their beams, with clam-
diggers on the flats when the tide is out, with the jour
printer blur-eyed at his case; or to picture him laughing
and competing with others at bees, huskings, house-rais-
ings, enjoying picnics or games of baseball, drinking and
shouting at "he-festivals," claiming kisses as his reward at
apple-peelings; or "scattering" himself among men and
women as he travels along the open road after the "great
Companions"; or parading through city streets with new
recruits, marching in hard-prest ranks along an unknown
road in the darkness, or sharing in spirit the sufferings of
wounded men while he tends them as a wound-dresser in
the hospitals. Here—and not mainly in the erotic pieces—
is Whitman the poet of fraternity most usably to be found.

He is really to be found in such passages because, far
from being merely literary and schematic, they correspond
to the friendly and sociable actualities of his nature and
his experience. There was a perfectly real Whitman who
was a solitary, a wilding, a "stranger," as Mr. Van Doren
puts it: there is a solitary or a stranger in every man, especially in every man of genius, and more especially still in
every man afflicted with some marked abnormality. But
it depends on the man whether or not he will yield his
whole personality to whatever is eccentric or anti-social
in it, and the obvious truth about Walt Whitman is that
he stubbornly refused to do this: "I take part," he said of
himself in a certain connection—and in plain fact he had
"taken part" in the ordinary life of his fellows far more
fully than most of the aloof, nonjuring writers of his generation. Set beside Thoreau the youth who spoke at Demo-

cratic rallies, served on county committees, and acted as a
Free Soil delegate; set beside Poe the young editor who
once spent an uproarious day with sixty other good citizens
at a clam-bake at Coney Island; set beside Hawthorne the
man who sometimes drove buses for his friends the Broadway drivers when they were laid up in bed, or beside
Emerson the man who played "twenty questions" with
common soldiers, or beside the aged Melville the old poet
who made friends with railway brakemen and Camden
attorneys and Philadelphia business-men—set beside any of
those other writers the Whitman who had "taken part" in
all these ways and many more, and the full, deep, humane,
available quality of his social feeling will appear again in
its true light. "We could not be like him if we would,"
says Mr. Van Doren: so much the worse for us if we cannot be like Whitman the citizen, the neighbor, the friend.

He did well, as it turns out, to insist on the political significance of the "Calamus" poems, though he should have
extended this particular claim more inclusively to the
book as a whole. Wrong as he was about the futility of
"agreements on paper"—dangerous as the idealism was
that led him to make light of "institutions"—Whitman was
on firm ground when he spoke out for the vital feelings
that must enrich and sublimate all merely political ref-
ormations if they are not to remain formal and barren.
Political leaders, practical builders, may do a basic, indispensable work in the achievement of a unified society, but
their work will be precarious and transitory if it is not
given life by new myths, new symbols, new emotions. The
achievement in the past of political and social liberties was
made possible not only by politicians but by poets: if freedom had not become so luminous an emblem as the poets

made it, it would never have become so solid a practical reality. The case will be the same with the fraternal union at which practical men are now aiming as they once aimed at independence. Neither the lurking egotism of the natural man nor the fevered individualism of our recent heritage will ever be rooted out of civilized life, as feudal servility was once rooted out, by agreements on paper alone: only the growth of a new quality in human relationships will accomplish that end, and for this new quality—this inclusive sense of racial union that, for all its long background in human experience, remains still to be realized securely—new symbols will have to be found.

It is their sense of this necessity that leads contemporary writers like André Malraux and Thomas Mann to use such phrases as "virile fraternity" and "a patriotism of humanity"—slogans, both of them, for that strong and warm emotion of fellow-feeling that will have to bind together the world society of the future. In the slow cultivation and diffusion of such an emotion no contributory strain will be wasted and none can be ignored without folly. We must cling to what we inherit both from ordinary social experience and from the insights of great artists before we can hope to move on beyond what has already been accomplished. Out of our nineteenth-century past, out of our American past, we inherit nothing potentially more fruitful than the vision Walt Whitman had of an all-embracing human solidarity—a solidarity lifted above the level of rational conviction and political convenience to the level of sensibility, of social practice, of culture in its largest sense. In the same way in which he found living images for the abstraction Equality, Whitman found living images for the abstraction Fraternity: perhaps not all of them are available for normal men and women, but granted that this is an open question, the images that *are* available preponderate overwhelmingly in *Leaves of Grass,* and we should be selling our birthright for a mess of feeble skepticisms if we failed to preserve, and to adapt to our own purposes, the Whitmanesque slogans of "adhesiveness," of "manly attachment," of "comradeship." A literature of sane and serious fraternity can still take its cue from Whitman.

It can do so particularly because he himself so consciously saw what such a literature might mean in the final realization not only of national union but of a democratic internationalism. The purpose behind all the rest in *Leaves of Grass,* he wrote late in life for the preface to a possible Russian translation of the book, is "such hearty comradeship" as he had been describing, "for individuals to begin with, and for all the nations of the earth as a result." That had hardly been the single guiding purpose of the book from the beginning, and the claim has an *ex post facto* air that one learns to expect of the elderly Whitman. Nevertheless, in spite of its over-emphatic simplicity, it is a claim that Whitman had a better right to make than any of the other poets of his time. For all his passionate nationalism, if not on account of it, he had early risen to the conception of a free and popular internationalism in which the integrity of national cultures would not be lost but in which the destructive conflicts among nations would be submerged and stilled. The germs of this conception he had doubtless inherited from the liberal cosmopolitanism of the Enlightenment—from the cosmopolitanism of Volney and Thomas Paine ("My attachment is to all the world, and not to a particular part"). In its earliest embodiment—

283

in the "Poem of Salutation" which he printed in 1856 and
later called "Salut au Monde!"—Whitman's internationalism has a good deal of the rational, philosophic catholicity
of the eighteenth-century liberals:

> I see male and female everywhere,
> I see the serene brotherhood of philosophs,
> I see the constructiveness of my race,
> I see the results of the perseverance and industry of
>   my race,
> I see ranks, colors, barbarisms, civilizations, I go
>   among them, I mix indiscriminately,
> And I salute all the inhabitants of the earth.

Yet it is no mere enlightened cosmopolitanism that ani-
mates the "Poem of Salutation": it is something more personal, more substantial, more dramatic than that—something indicated by the zest with which Whitman conjures
up the presences not only of "peoples" and "races" but
concretely of "the sharp-eyed Samoiede and the Finn,"
"the seal-seeker in his boat poising his lance," the "sturdy
Austrian," the "working-man of the Rhine, the Elbe, or
the Weser," the "working-woman too." There is a simple
and palpable humanity in this internationalism which one
does not expect of the *philosophes*.

There was to be a rebellious urgency in it, too, which
had much less the color of an elder humanitarianism than
of the radical democracy of Whitman's own time and later.
In the year in which the "Poem of Salutation" appeared
there began to assert itself, in the extraordinary last paragraph of his broadside, *The Eighteenth Presidency*, the
approach of an internationalism that would have its base
among the enfranchised and liberated masses of the whole
world. The somewhat jingoistic patriot of the Mexican

War days was passing over into the planetary-minded Whitman of the later stage. It is not only in America, he observes in his broadside, that the time is full of portent. "Freedom against slavery is not issuing here alone, but is issuing everywhere." A new and more august drama than any hitherto is about to be enacted upon the stage of the world, and those who have played leading roles in the earlier acts must now prepare to take their departure or be forced to take it. "Frontiers and boundaries are less and less able to divide men." The inhabitants of the earth are being linked up as groups in one family, not only by the cohesive modern inventions, but by a new and more and more universal demand for justice and equality. "What historic denouements are these we are approaching? On all sides tyrants tremble, crowns are unsteady, the human race restive, on the watch for some better era, some divine war." So Whitman felt in the mid-fifties: ten years later the thought was still so present to him that he incorporated some of the phrases of this prose passage in a new poem, "Years of the Modern":

> Years of the modern! years of the unperform'd!
> Your horizon rises, I see it parting away for more
> august dramas,
> I see not America only, not only Liberty's nation but
> other nations preparing,
> I see tremendous entrances and exits, new combina-
> tions, the solidarity of races . . .

That last phrase, as it happens, had not occurred in the broadside, but it struck a note that had become more congenial to Whitman in the meantime, as other lines in the poem suggest:

Are all nations communing? is there going to be but
one heart to the globe?
Is humanity forming en-masse?

The Civil War was barely over when Whitman published this poem: in the next few years he was to be more
and more obsessed with the problem of developing a spirit
of true union among the re-united states—a union not
merely political or utilitarian but "spiritual and heroic."
"The lack of a common skeleton, knitting all close, continually haunts me," he wrote in *Democratic Vistas*, and
in poems of these and the following years he came back
more than once to the theme of an American unity that
was perhaps not yet attained but was certainly ideal and
indispensable:

> *Thou Union holding all, fusing, absorbing, tolerating*
> *all . . .*

> *Thou! mounting higher, diving deeper than we knew,*
> *thou transcendental Union! . . .*
> *Equable, natural, mystical Union thou . . .*

It was no longer, however, merely of a national union that
Whitman now spoke and sang: more and more it was of
a great world union of free peoples which he saw emerging, in the not very distant future, from the marchings and
counter-marchings of those portentous years. In 1868 the
completion of the Suez Canal and the Union Pacific Railroad seemed to him symbolic not only of the transcendental
reconciling of man and nature which he chanted in "Passage to India," but—what he hailed in the same poem—of
the final spanning, linking up, and welding together of all
lands and races in a "rondure of the world at last accom-

plish'd." Two or three years later he came back to this achievement, along with that of American union, in the "Song of the Exposition":

> *Thou, also thou, a World,*
> *With all thy wide geographies, manifold, different,*
> *   distant,*
> *Rounded by thee in one—one common orbic language,*
> *One common indivisible destiny for All.*

In the year of the American national centennial Whitman declared that the great idea behind the exposition at Philadelphia was "the glory of Labor, and the bringing together not only representatives of all the trades and products, but, fraternally, of all the Workmen of all the Nations of the World." Even if this was far from being the real purpose of the men who planned the centennial, it was much that an American poet should imagine it to be, after a hundred years of independence. The great idea of international fraternity, at any rate, had become so dear to Whitman that, at about this time, he began to insist on its implied presence everywhere in *Leaves of Grass*. In that same year of the centennial he composed at Camden a personal address "to the foreign reader" of his book, which was to remain one of his unused prefaces; in it, however, he announced that he had come to see the peculiar glory of the United States not in its political, military, or economic greatness but more and more "in a vaster, saner, more splendid COMRADESHIP, typifying the People everywhere, uniting closer and closer not only The American States, but all Nations, and all Humanity." Is not that, he demanded of his brother poets in all countries, a Union worth chanting, worth struggling for? Certainly, he felt, it could be achieved essentially only by poets, only by men of creative insight and power who would vitalize and humanize the work of the statesmen by finding the right songs and symbols for it. To that end Whitman proposed, even at this late date, to "inaugurate" from America "new formulas, international poems."

He himself, weakened by illness and old age, was not to succeed in composing such prophetic pieces, but how deeply he came to wish that, even as it stood, his book might seem a foretaste of what the new literature would be—this we can gather from a preface he wrote ten years later for an English edition of *Specimen Days*. "Let me fondly hope," he there wrote, "that . . . in the volume, as below any page of mine, anywhere, ever remains, for seen or unseen basis-phrase, GOOD-WILL BETWEEN THE COMMON PEOPLE OF ALL NATIONS." He said this as solemnly as he was capable of speaking: it was probably the profoundest sentiment of his later years. A year or so after he had written it, indeed, he told Horace Traubel that that line or two in an English preface was what he liked better than anything else in all the hundreds of pages he had printed. Perhaps he felt that it pointed more sharply than anything else in his published work toward the universally comprehensive solidarity which was the obsession of his old age. Certainly the word "solidarity" itself had become his favorite shibboleth. "I like much to see that word," he said to Traubel as he sat stirring the fire one cold December day—"solidarity, intercalation: not Philadelphia alone, Camden alone, even New York alone, but all together, all nations—the globe: intercalation, fusion, no one left out." Then, after a little talk about the use of the word by men like Comte, Hugo, and Tolstoy, he came back to the word itself and what lay behind it, protesting his affection for it "for broadest reasons," and declaring at last, as if he could hardly repeat it too often or in too vast a connection: "Solidarity is the future."

It is surely the strain on which he would have been happiest to have any discussion of his life and work concluded. In no literal or rounded sense had Whitman been, in *Leaves of Grass,* the poet of an international social democracy: on the contrary, he had been in those senses and others the poet of the exuberant, middle-class, nationalistic democracy of nineteenth-century America, and indeed he had given utterance to some motives in that older American culture that were fruitless or mischievous. He had given utterance, however, to far more in it that was profoundly progressive, profoundly humanistic: to all *that* he was measurably closer, in his characteristic genius, than any other of our important writers and than all but a handful of writers anywhere. Whatever his limitations as a person or poet, his nature was more sensitive, his sensibility more subtly responsive than those of other writers to all that was freest, boldest, most popular, most companionable in the contradictory life of his age: he had a magnificent plastic power, simply as an artist, in rendering it all with extraordinary life and originality in verse. What is weakly transcendental or too simply egoistic or waywardly personal in Whitman's book will rapidly be—or is already —discarded and forgotten. Enough and more than enough remains to fortify the writers and the men of our time in their struggles against a dark barbarian reaction, and to interest and animate the peoples of a near future in their work of building a just society. To such men it is and will be clearer and clearer that, from our recent past, we inherit no fuller or braver anticipatory statement than *Leaves of Grass* of a democratic and fraternal humanism.

CHRONOLOGY

CHRONOLOGY

1819 Whitman born at West Hills near Huntington, Long Island, May 31.

1823 Whitman family removes to Brooklyn.

1829 Walt taken by his father to hear Elias Hicks preach.

1831–33 Works as printer's-devil on the *Long Island Patriot* and the *Long Island Star*.

1833–36 Uncertain years; probably works as a printer, etc., in Brooklyn and New York. Family returns to the country to live.

1836–39 Teaches in country schools on Long Island.

1839 Establishes and edits the *Long Islander* at Huntington.

1839–41 Teaches school in various villages and works as a type-setter on the *Long Island Democrat* at Jamaica. Is active in local Democratic politics. "Sun-Down Papers."

1841–45 Works at various journalistic positions (on the *Aurora*, the *Tattler*, etc.) in New York. Contributes tales, sketches, etc., to the *Democratic Review, New World, Columbian Magazine,* and other periodicals.

1842 *Franklin Evans.*

1845–46 Works on the Brooklyn *Evening Star*. Family returns to Brooklyn.

1846–47 Edits the Brooklyn *Daily Eagle*.

1848 Leaves the *Eagle* in January. Works for a few weeks on the *Daily Crescent* in New Orleans. Is active, on his return to Brooklyn, in the Free Soil movement.

1848–49 Edits the Brooklyn *Freeman,* a Free Soil paper.

1850 Contributes "Song for Certain Congressmen" and other pieces to the New York *Evening Post* and *Tribune.*

1851 Speaks on "Art and Artists" at the Brooklyn Art Union.

1850–55 Engages irregularly in newspaper work and in house-building with his father.

1855 First edition of *Leaves of Grass.* Death of his father in July.

1855–56 Contributes "New York Dissected" articles and others to *Life Illustrated.*

1856 Second edition of *Leaves of Grass.* Writes but does not publish *The Eighteenth Presidency.*

1857–59 Edits the Brooklyn *Daily Times.*

1860 Third edition of *Leaves of Grass.* Goes to Boston to supervise its publication by Thayer & Eldridge. Sanborn's trial.

1862 Contributes articles entitled "City Photographs" to the New York *Leader.* In December goes to Virginia to look for George Whitman, reported wounded at Fredericksburg.

1863–65 In Washington. Becomes a visitor and volunteer nurse in the army hospitals. Contributes articles on the hospitals, etc., to the *Eagle* and the New York *Times.* Works in the office of an army paymaster.

1865 *Drum-Taps.* Obtains a clerkship in the Indian Bureau but is shortly dismissed as an indecent writer by James Harlan, the Secretary of the Interior. Obtains another clerkship in the Attorney General's office.

1865–73 Remains in Washington except for brief visits to Brooklyn.

1867 Fourth edition of *Leaves of Grass.*

1871 Fifth edition of *Leaves of Grass. Democratic Vistas* (based partly on articles in the *Galaxy* in 1867 and '68). Publishes *Passage to India* (with a few other poems) as a pamphlet or "annex." Writes "After All, Not to Create Only" (later called "Song of the Exposition") for the Fortieth Annual Exhibition of the American Institute in New York.

1872 Sixth edition of *Leaves of Grass.* Reads "As a Strong Bird on Pinions Free" (later called "Thou Mother with Thy Equal Brood") as a commencement-poem at Dartmouth College. Publishes it (with a few other poems) as a pamphlet.

1873 Has a paralytic stroke and moves to Camden, N. J., to live with George Whitman and his family. Death of his mother in May.

1874 Writes the "Song of the Universal" for Tufts College commencement.

1876 Seventh edition of *Leaves of Grass.*

1877 Edward Carpenter's first visit.

1879 Travels through the Middle West and the Mountain States.

1880 Visits Dr. Bucke at London, Ontario, and travels elsewhere in Canada.

1881 Eighth edition of *Leaves of Grass* published by Osgood in Boston. Visits Boston and Concord.

1882 Osgood edition withdrawn on threat of prosecution by the District Attorney. *Specimen Days and Collect.*

1883 Elbert Hubbard's visit.

1884 Moves to 328 Mickle Street, Camden, where he spends the remainder of his life. Carpenter's second visit.

1888 *November Boughs.*

1888–89 Ninth edition of *Leaves of Grass*.

1890–91 Visits by Dr. John Johnston and J. W. Wallace of Lancashire.

1891 *Good-Bye My Fancy*.

1892 Tenth edition of *Leaves of Grass*. Whitman dies on March 26.

BIBLIOGRAPHY

BIBLIOGRAPHY

The following is a list of the works to which most frequent reference has been made in these notes, with (in parentheses) the brief titles by which they have been cited for convenience.

CARPENTER, EDWARD. *Days with Walt Whitman*. London, 1906. (Carpenter.)

Complete Writings of Walt Whitman. Vols. I–X. New York, 1902. *(Complete Writings.)*

FURNESS, CLIFTON JOSEPH. *Walt Whitman's Workshop*. Cambridge, 1928. (Furness.)

HOLLOWAY, EMORY. *The Uncollected Poetry and Prose of Walt Whitman*. Vols. I and II. Garden City, 1921. *(Uncollected.)*

HOLLOWAY, EMORY, AND SCHWARZ, VERNOLIAN. *I Sit and Look Out*. New York, 1932. (Holloway and Schwarz.)

RODGERS, CLEVELAND, AND BLACK, JOHN. *The Gathering of the Forces*. Vols. I and II. New York, 1920. (Rodgers and Black.)

TRAUBEL, HORACE, *et al. In Re Walt Whitman*. Philadelphia, 1893. *(In Re.)*

TRAUBEL, HORACE. *With Walt Whitman in Camden*. Vols. I–III. New York, 1906–1914. (Traubel.)

WHITMAN, WALT. *Leaves of Grass*. 1855–1892. *(L. of G.)*

WHITMAN, WALT. *Leaves of Grass. Inclusive Edition*. New York, 1924. *(Inclusive.)*

WHITMAN, WALT. *Complete Prose Works*. Boston, 1907. *(Prose.)*

All students of Whitman are indebted to the editors of *The Uncollected Poetry and Prose, I Sit and Look Out,* and *The Gathering of the Forces* for having made available Whitman's newspaper writings as editor of the Brooklyn *Daily Eagle* and the Brooklyn *Daily Times*. I have used these books very freely, as the following notes will indicate, but in the trail of their editors I have also consulted the files of the *Eagle* and the *Times* myself, and have from time to time referred to them in these notes when new material was in question.

CHAPTER I

Reginald A. Beckett's article on "Whitman as a Socialist Poet" appeared in *To-day, A Monthly Magazine of Scientific Socialism* for July, 1888. W.'s comment on the article may be found in Traubel (II, 4). Judgments of W. in this connection are quoted from Sherman, Stuart P., *Americans* (New York, 1922), 176-177; Canby, H. S., *Classic Americans* (New York, 1931), 327; Dell, Floyd, "Walt Whitman as an Anti-Socialist," *New Review* (June 15, 1915); Calverton, V. F., *The Liberation of American Literature* (New York, 1932), 296. I have also quoted from the preface to *November Boughs*, "A Backward Glance o'er Travel'd Roads" (*Inclusive*, 535), and from the poems, "To a Historian" and "Thoughts."

CHAPTER II

I. W.'s speech in the Park was reported in the New York *Evening Post* on July 30, 1841; a summary of the speech, quoted from the *New Era* by W. himself in the *Eagle*, may also be found in Rodgers and Black (II, 5). To illustrate W.'s opinions of political leaders I have quoted Rodgers and Black (I, 8, 80, 92, 219; II, 178-179, 181-184, 192-194, 196) and Traubel (III, 30, 139, 174-175, 229). W. summed up his political principles in an editorial on "The Principles We Fight For," reprinted in Furness (225-226). His partisan loyalties come out in several passages in Rodgers and Black (I, 7; II, 31, 33, 40, 42, 61-65, 77-83) and *Uncollected* (I, 175). For his early and later attitudes toward the Mexican War see Rodgers and Black (I, 240-266) and "Attitude of Foreign Governments during the War" in *Specimen Days* (*Prose*, 58). The Oregon

Question is treated in Rodgers and Black (I, 271) and Holloway, Emory, "More Light on Whitman" (*American Mercury,*
Feb., 1924). An article on "Whitman in 1840" by J. J. Rubin
(*American Literature,* May, 1937) throws an interesting light
on W.'s activities during the Log Cabin campaign.

II. W.'s contradictory feelings about agitation and conflict
appear in such poems as "To a Foil'd European Revolution-
aire," "Myself and Mine," and "Adieu to a Soldier"; in the
"Letter to Ralph Waldo Emerson" (*L. of G.,* 1856), 357; in
Furness (81), and in Traubel (II, 21). For his racial chau-
vinism I have quoted Barrus, Clara, *Whitman and Burroughs,
Comrades* (Boston, 1931), 335; Johnston, J., and Wallace,
J. W., *Visits to Walt Whitman* (London, 1917), 159; and
Complete Writings (VIII, 226). Hostile judgments of the
Abolitionists appear in *Uncollected* (II, 9, Note 3), Rodgers
and Black (I, 192), and Holloway and Schwarz (87). For W.'s
conflicting views about John Brown see Kennedy, W. S.,
Reminiscences of Walt Whitman (London, 1896), 49; Glicksberg, Charles I., *Walt Whitman and the Civil War* (Philadelphia, 1933), 161; Sanborn, F. B., *Life of Henry Thoreau*
(Boston, 1917), 310; Traubel, Horace, "Whitman on His Contemporaries" (*American Mercury,* July, 1924), and Traubel
(II, 486; III, 206). On the rights and wrongs of the slavery
issue I have quoted *Uncollected* (II, 8-10, 183-184), Rodgers
and Black (I, 187-191, 192, 219), Holloway and Schwarz (86-
90), Furness (74), Traubel (III, 5), and the Preface to the
1855 edition of *L. of G.* (*Inclusive,* 491). The verses about
Negroes appear in "Song of Myself," "Salut au Monde!" and
Pictures: an Unpublished Poem of Walt Whitman, edited by
Emory Holloway (New York, 1927). For W.'s reminiscences
of the Abolitionists see "One or Two Index Items," *Specimen
Days* (*Prose,* 196), "Father Taylor (and Oratory)," *November
Boughs* (*Prose,* 385-387), and "Old Actors, Singers, Shows, &c.,
in New York," *Good-Bye My Fancy* (*Prose,* 514-519). The bearing of slavery upon free labor is summed up in editorials in
Rodgers and Black (I, 205-206, 208-214). On the Constitution
and on Free Soil see Furness (105) and Rodgers and Black (I,
194). The Brooklyn Free Soil meeting was reported in the New

York *Evening Post* for Aug. 7, 1848 (see also *Uncollected*, I, xxxv, Note 3).

III. W.'s reasons for his drift away from politics may be found in Traubel (I, 6). His having voted for Hale in 1852 is established by the facsimile of a manuscript sheet printed in the catalogue of the Schwarz Whitman Collection published by the Anderson Galleries (New York, 1936), 67. On the corruption of the Democratic Party and on Pierce and Buchanan see "Origins of Attempted Secession," *Specimen Days (Prose,* 251-255), Furness (100), and the letter to Emerson in the 1856 edition of *L. of G.* (352). W.'s disillusion with political parties is expressed in Furness (104-105). The "Dough-Face Song," "Blood Money," and "Wounded in the House of Friends" (or "The House of Friends") may be found in *Prose* (334, 372-373) and in *Uncollected* (I, 25-27). For remarks on the Fugitive Slave Law and the Kansas-Nebraska Act see Furness (78, 80-81, 96, 109) and Holloway and Schwarz (92). The Homestead Bill is mentioned in the Brooklyn *Daily Times* for May 21, 1858. W.'s strong sentiments on the subject of the Union appear in such passages as Rodgers and Black (I, 229-230, 235-238), Furness (99), and "Death of President Lincoln," *Specimen Days (Prose,* 61-62). For his vacillations on the eve of the War see Holloway and Schwarz (98).

W.'s remarks on the outbreak of the War and on its importance to him are quoted from "Opening of the Secession War," *Specimen Days (Prose,* 15-16), "Three Years Summ'd Up" (*Ibid.,* 71-72), the Preface to the 1876 edition of *L. of G.* (*Inclusive,* 517, Note), and Traubel (I, 13). On the ruling class of the Confederacy and on the Copperheads see Rodgers and Black (I, 203-208), *Complete Writings* (VII, 244, 247), and Traubel (III, 101, 544, 546). W.'s attitude toward the War itself, the Draft Riots, etc., comes out in "America's Bulk Average," *Good-Bye My Fancy (Prose,* 523-524), in the poems, "Beat! Beat! Drums!" and "Song of the Banner at Daybreak," in *Complete Writings* (VII, 175-176, 183), and in a letter (No. 281) to his brother, Jeff Whitman, in the collection of the Walt Whitman Foundation in Camden. His work in the hospitals is described in, among many passages, "My Preparations for Visits" and "Summer of 1864," *Specimen Days* (*Prose,* 32, 45-46). For the prosperity of the North during the War see Stephenson, Nathaniel W., *Abraham Lincoln and the Union* (New Haven, 1918), 223.

IV. Andrew Johnson, Reconstruction, and General Grant are referred to in various ways in the Preface to the 1876 edition of *L. of G.* (*Inclusive,* 521), Glicksberg, *op. cit.* (101), Burroughs, John, *Notes on Walt Whitman as Poet and Person* (New York, 1867), 126; Conway, M. D., *Autobiography, Memories, and Experiences* (Boston, 1904) (see facsimile letter opposite p. 218, Vol. I), and the poems, "What Best I See in Thee" and "Death of General Grant." For W.'s impressions and judgments of Hayes, Garfield, and Cleveland see "President Hayes's Speeches," *Specimen Days* (*Prose,* 147), *Complete Writings* (VII, 226; VIII, 14-15), Traubel (I, 80, 324; III, 20), the poem, "The Sobbing of the Bells," and the New York *Herald* for Jan. 26, 1888. Howells's remark on Hayes and the coal strike may be found in his *Sketch of the Life and Character of Rutherford B. Hayes* (New York, 1876), 185. On the political corruption of the Gilded Age see *Democratic Vistas* (*Prose,* 198, 204), *Uncollected* (II, 58), and the poems, "Nay, Tell Me Not To-day the Publish'd Shame," "From Far Dakota's Cañons," and "Wandering at Morn." For W.'s later attitudes toward the two parties I have quoted *Democratic Vistas* (*Prose,* 227), and Traubel (I, 14, 101, 406; II, 84, 317, 399). I have also quoted the *Letters of Charles Eliot Norton,* edited by Sara Norton and M. A. DeWolfe Howe (Boston, 1913), I, 505, and *The Education of Henry Adams* (Boston, 1918), 262, 271, 272.

CHAPTER III

I. My account of W.'s attitudes toward the morals of industry and frugality is based on the Brooklyn *Daily Eagle* for Dec. 22, 1847, the Brooklyn *Daily Times* for Nov. 24, 1857, and Nov. 2, 1858, Furness (259), Rodgers and Black (I, 158), and Traubel (II, 535). His remarks on business and money-making appear in *Democratic Vistas* (*Prose,* 205; 215, Note),

"A Word about Tennyson," *November Boughs* (*Prose*, 403), Kennedy, W. S., *Walt Whitman's Diary in Canada* (Boston, 1904), 72-73, Furness, C. J., "Walt Whitman's Politics" (*American Mercury*, April, 1929), Kennedy's *Reminiscences* (8), Carpenter (38), and the poem, "Outlines for a Tomb." On the prosperity of America in the forties see Rodgers and Black (I, 18, 27; II, 59-61). W.'s reactions to the panic of 1857 and to the recovery from it come out in the Brooklyn *Daily Times* for July 29, Aug. 26, Sept. 29, Dec. 4, 1857, and in Holloway and Schwarz (146-147). On the prosperity of the post-War period see, in *Specimen Days*, "The First Spring Day on Chestnut Street," "Two City Areas, Certain Hours," "Lawrence and Topeka, Kansas," "Denver Impressions," "America's Characteristic Landscape," "St. Louis Memoranda," and "The Boston of To-day" (*Prose*, 121, 126, 133, 139, 143, 147, 172), the poems, "Song of the Exposition" and "The Prairie States"; *Complete Writings* (VIII, 37, 43), and Furness (193). W.'s most characteristically petty bourgeois ideals come out in *Democratic Vistas* (*Prose*, 215), "Our Real Culmination," *Specimen Days* (*Ibid.*, 332), Holloway and Schwarz (145), Carpenter (39), and Traubel (III, 315). Elbert Hubbard described his visit to W. in *Little Journeys to the Homes of American Authors* (New York, 1896), 176-190. I have also quoted from *Triumphant Democracy*, by Andrew Carnegie (New York, 1886), 471, Emerson's essay on "Wealth," Thoreau's letter to Harrison Blake of Nov. 16, 1857, and Keats's letter to George and Georgiana Keats of Oct. 13-15, 1818.

II. The quotations from the "Sun-Down Papers" are from *Uncollected* (I, 37, 38, 44-46, 47). For W.'s real attitude toward business success and money see the Preface to the 1855 edition of *L. of G.* (*Inclusive*, 502), *Complete Writings* (VIII, 11), *In Re* (35), Furness (245), Rodgers and Black (II, 130-136), and Holloway, Emory, and Adimari, Ralph, *New York Dissected* (New York, 1936), 120-121. On the superiority of the artist to the man of affairs see *Uncollected* (I, 237, 241-247). The notebook passage on the mania of ownership is quoted from *Idem.* (II, 67), and the line about poverty from the poem, "Great Are the Myths" (rejected). For George Sand see notes on Chapter IV, II.

III. W.'s sentiments on the subject of low wages are expressed in the Brooklyn *Daily Eagle* for March 26, April 3, Sept. 10, and Oct. 8, 1846; *Uncollected* (I, 137), and Rodgers and Black (I, 148-151, 156-157). His sentiments on hours of labor and conditions of work appear in the *Eagle* for Oct. 15, Oct. 26, and Nov. 7, 1846, and April 6, May 1, June 11, and Sept. 22, 1847; in Rodgers and Black (I, 157-158), and *Complete Writings* (VIII, 263-264). For W.'s critical attitude toward industrialism see the Brooklyn *Daily Eagle* for June 25, 1847, and Rodgers and Black (II, 69, 70-71, 231). His strain of social radicalism comes out in the "Song of Myself" (*Inclusive*, 65), *Complete Writings* (III, 261-262), Holloway and Schwarz (82-83), and the article on "Walt Whitman's Politics" (already cited) in the *American Mercury*. The tale from the *Herald of Freedom* (for the issue of Oct. 2, 1846), entitled "The Redeemed Homestead," was the second of a series of "Letters from Lowell" by a writer who signed himself "Wamesit"; it was reprinted in the *Eagle* for Oct. 15, 1846. I have also quoted from Brisbane's paper, the *Phalanx* (Oct. 5, 1843), and Godwin, Parke, *Democracy Constructive and Pacific* (New York, 1844), 17.

IV. W.'s account of the Grand Review, in a letter to his mother, may be found in Holloway, Emory, "Some New Whitman Letters" (*American Mercury*, Feb., 1929). His remarks on the social and economic corruption of the Gilded Age may be found in *Democratic Vistas* (*Prose*, 203-204), and those on the labor question, strikes, unemployment, etc., in "The Tramp and Strike Questions," *Specimen Days* (*Prose*, 324-325), *Democratic Vistas* (*Ibid.*, 247), and *Complete Writings* (VIII, 132, 136; IX, 188). The "Songs of Insurrection" appear on pp. 363-369 of the 1872 and 1876 editions of *L. of G.*; the unused introductory note to them may be found in Furness (229). W.'s latest feelings and opinions on social questions may be pieced together from such passages as Johnston and Wallace, *op. cit.* (150), Traubel (I, 42, 113, 193, 363; II, 187-188, 282;

III, 69, 344), and Traubel, Horace, "With Walt Whitman in Camden" (*Forum,* Aug., 1915). Since Traubel's authenticity as a reporter has been and is still likely to be called in question, it may be worth while to cite an observation by another friend of W.'s later years, Mr. Harrison S. Morris (*Walt Whitman,* Cambridge, 1929): "Horace has caught the very accent of Walt's voice in these intimate records of the daily intercourse between them. . . I can detect the phrase and the modulation of Walt's slow, hesitating and sonorous speech on every page of Traubel's valuable records" (p. 96). John Sherman's remark is quoted from Nevins, Allan, *The Emergence of Modern America* (New York, 1927), 32, and Howells's, from Howells, Mildred, *Life in Letters of William Dean Howells* (Garden City, 1928), I, 429.

CHAPTER IV

I. The passage on exact science and the poet is quoted from the Preface to the 1855 edition of *L. of G.* (*Inclusive,* 497). For the lectures at the Brooklyn Institute and the use of ether in a minor operation see the *Eagle* for March 5 and 7 and Nov. 16, 1846; Jan. 8, Oct. 14, and Nov. 26, 1847, and Jan. 6, 1848. On the value of popular scientific lectures see Holloway and Schwarz (52). W.'s appeal for an observatory in Brooklyn is reprinted in Rodgers and Black (II, 146-149). How W. acquired scientific information from his acquaintances may be gathered from *Complete Writings* (IX, 54, 129, 136-137) and "Scenes on Ferry and River," *Specimen Days* (*Prose,* 118). On Henry Whitall see "Whitman's Knowledge of Astronomy," by Clarence Dugdale (*University of Texas Studies in English,* No. 16, July 8, 1936). Some notion of W.'s reading in scientific literature (in book form) may be gathered from the *Eagle* for June 28, 1847 (the review of Liebig), and *Uncollected* (I, 126, Note 2). The newspaper and magazine clippings I have referred to are listed in Part V of "Notes and Fragments," *Complete Writings* (X, 63-97). On the papers read at the Albany meeting of the A. A. A. S. see *Proceedings of the American Association for the Advancement of Science.*

Tenth Meeting, Held at Albany, New York, August, 1856 (Cambridge, 1857).

W.'s veneration for Paine appears in the notes "In Memory of Thomas Paine," *Specimen Days* (*Prose*, 89-91) and in Traubel (II, 206; III, 191). For the influence on him of Volney and Frances Wright see Traubel (II, 204-205, 445, 500; III, 513). To illustrate the views of these writers I have quoted from Volney's *The Ruins* (Albany, 1822) and Frances Wright's *A Few Days in Athens* (Boston, 1869). See also *Frances Wright*, by W. R. Waterman (New York, 1924), 178. W.'s enthusiasm for the scientific spirit and the achievements of science appears in "A Backward Glance" (*Inclusive*, 528), Carpenter (44), and Traubel (II, 562-563; III, 98). For his sense of the bearing of these things on poetry see the Preface to *As a Strong Bird on Pinions Free* (*Inclusive*, 508), the Preface to the 1876 edition of *L. of G.* (*Ibid.*, 520), and "A Backward Glance" (*Ibid.*, 525). The line altered in the "Song of Myself" may be found in *Inclusive* (52, 571). Dr. Abbott's Museum is described in Holloway and Adimari, *op. cit.* (27-40). The quotations from *The Age of Reason* may be found in the Patriot's Edition of Paine's works (New York, 1925), VIII (50, 284).

II. To illustrate the religious views of American scientists I have quoted from Dana, E. S., *et al.*, *A Century of Science in America* (New Haven, 1918), 31-32; Jordan, David Starr, *Leading American Men of Science* (New York, 1910), 229; Dana, James Dwight, *Manual of Geology, 4th Ed.* (New York, 1895), 1036; *Dictionary of American Biography* (XIII, 185); Fiske, John, *Life of Edward Livingston Youmans* (New York, 1894), 501. For W.'s acquaintance with Youmans see Traubel (I, 101). His connections with and feelings about the Quakers appear in "Elias Hicks, Notes (Such as They Are)," *November Boughs* (*Prose*, 457-474), and in Traubel (II, 19, 143; III, 109). The quotations from Hicks are from the *Journal of the Life and Labors of Elias Hicks* (New York, 1832), 70, 122. For W.'s opinions of Burns, Bryant, Cooper, and Scott see "Robert Burns as Poet and Person," *November Boughs* (*Prose*, 395-402), "A Backward Glance" (*Inclusive*, 529), *Uncollected* (I, 163), and Traubel (I, 96; II, 533; III, 550). For Goethe,

Rousseau, and Schlegel see *Uncollected* (I, 135, 139-141) and *Complete Writings* (IX, 80).

W.'s enthusiasm for George Sand may be gathered from Traubel (III, 35, 422-423), Gilchrist, Grace, "Chats with Walt Whitman" (*Temple Bar*, Feb., 1898), and Morris, Harrison S., *op. cit.* (94). The quotations from *Consuelo* and *The Countess of Rudolstadt* are from the Shaw translations in the first four volumes of the *Harbinger*. Dwight's prefatory remarks may be found in the *Harbinger* for June 14, 1845. Esther Shephard's *Walt Whitman's Pose* (New York, 1938) deals inadequately with George Sand's influence, and is too largely based on the unwarranted assumption that W., who spoke many times and wrote more than once of the Frenchwoman, attempted to *conceal* his debt to her.

W.'s interest in Coleridge and Carlyle appears in "Death of Thomas Carlyle," *Specimen Days* (*Prose*, 160-163), *Uncollected* (I, 129-131), and Traubel (II, 366). His attitude toward Channing, Margaret Fuller, and Parker may be learned from "Book-Classes—America's Literature," *Specimen Days* (*Prose*, 332), *Uncollected* (I, 130, 132), Traubel (I, 257; III, 175), and Zunder, T. A., "Walt Whitman and Nathaniel Hawthorne" (*Modern Language Notes*, May, 1932). On W. and Thoreau see Traubel (I, 212, 231; III, 375, 405). My account of W. and Emerson is based on "Emerson's Books, (The Shadows of Them)," *Specimen Days* (*Prose*, 314-317), "Old Actors, Singers, Shows, &c., in New York," *Good-Bye My Fancy* (*Ibid.*, 514-519), Rodgers and Black (II, 270-271), *Complete Writings* (IX, 159), *Pictures* (already cited), Traubel (II, 69), "Emerson's Essays," by a Disciple (*Democratic Review*, June, 1845), Kennedy's *Reminiscences* (76), Trowbridge, J. T., *My Own Story* (Boston, 1903), 367.

My conclusion that W.'s knowledge of Hegel and other German philosophers was at least partly acquired during or after the Civil War is based on a manuscript scrap in the Whitman collection at the Library of Congress (Division of Manuscripts); a reference in this to the article on Schelling in Vol. XIV of the *New American Cyclopaedia*, which was not published until 1862, establishes a date that has a certain significance. Other references in this ms. note are to articles on Fichte and Kant in Vols. IX and XII of the seventh edition of the *Britannica*. W.'s having owned a copy of Hedge's *Prose Writers of Germany* is indicated by a list of books (at the Mickle Street House, Camden) containing W.'s autograph. The *Atlantic* article on Leibniz is mentioned in the Brooklyn *Daily Times* for May 21, 1858. W.'s interest in the German systems appears in "Carlyle from American Points of View," *Specimen Days (Prose*, 163-170), *Democratic Vistas (Ibid.*, 245), and *Complete Writings* (IX, 166-186). His claim to be their poetical representative is quoted from Furness (236).

III. The account of W.'s anti-clericalism is based on such sources as the letter to Emerson in the 1856 edition of *L. of G.* (352), "By Blue Ontario's Shore," *Democratic Vistas (Prose*, 204), Furness (41), *In Re* (38), Traubel (III, 497-498), Traubel, Horace, "With Walt Whitman in Camden" (*Forum*, Aug., 1915), and Traubel, Horace, "Walt Whitman, Schoolmaster" (*Walt Whitman Fellowship Papers*, No. 14, Philadelphia, 1895). On supernaturalism see the Preface to the 1855 edition of *L. of G.* (*Inclusive*, 497) and "Song of Myself" (*Ibid.*, 64). On his views of God and the soul see "Starting from Paumanok," "Song of Myself," "Song of the Open Road," "Song of the Rolling Earth," "By Blue Ontario's Shore," and "Song of Prudence"; the variorum readings in *Inclusive* (607, 641), *Complete Writings* (IX, 5), Furness (43-44), and Traubel (III, 317). W.'s pluralism, his love of change, etc., are expressed in "Eidólons," "Song of Myself," "Song of the Open Road," "Myself and Mine," and "Our Old Feuillage." For his attitude toward evolution and Darwin see "Song of Myself" (*Inclusive*, 50, 69), "O Star of France," "Great Are the Myths"; Traubel (III, 94). His feeling for machines comes out in "The Return of the Heroes," "Passage to India," and "To a Locomotive in Winter"; in "Our Eminent Visitors," *November Boughs (Prose*, 377-380), the letter to Emerson in the 1856 edition of *L. of G.* (355), Traubel (III, 365), and Rodgers and Black (II, 210, 227).

IV. The note for poems on the different sciences is quoted from *Complete Writings* (X, 20-21). In the "Song of Myself"

(Inclusive, 43), the "Song of the Universal," and the Preface to the 1876 edition of *L. of G. (Ibid.,* 520) W. expresses his sense of the limitations of science. Conflicting attitudes toward Darwinism come out in "Carlyle from American Points of View," *Specimen Days (Prose,* 169), "Darwinism—(Then Furthermore)" *(Ibid.,* 321), and Traubel (II, 423; III, 70). For W.'s irrationalism see "Birds—and a Caution," *Specimen Days (Prose,* 175), *In Re* (325), Traubel (I, 156), and the poems, "Song of Myself" *(Inclusive,* 49, 75), "Song of the Open Road," and "Song of the Broad Axe." The influence of Transcendentalism on W.'s conception of style may be put together from the Preface to the 1855 edition of *L. of G. (Ibid.,* 495, 496), the Preface to the 1876 edition *(Ibid.,* 521), "What Lurks behind Shakespeare's Historical Plays," *November Boughs (Prose,* 390-392), *Complete Writings* (IX, 32-33, 34-35, 37), and Carpenter (43).

For the religious purpose of *L. of G.* see "Starting from Paumanok" and the Preface to *As a Strong Bird on Pinions Free (Inclusive,* 510). W.'s increasingly theistic and spiritualistic outlook may be traced in such poems as "Eidólons," "Starting from Paumanok," "Song of Myself," "Scented Herbage of My Breast," "Passage to India," and "Thou Mother with Thy Equal Brood." The change in his feeling for nature is marked by passages in "Me Imperturbe," "Starting from Paumanok," "Passage to India," and "Yet, Yet, Ye Downcast Hours," and his growing preoccupation with death and immortality, in "A Song of Joys," "Out of the Cradle Endlessly Rocking," "When Lilacs Last in the Dooryard Bloom'd," "To Think of Time," and "The Untold Want."

CHAPTER V

I. In the *Eagle* for Jan. 8 and Aug. 13, 1847, and in Rodgers and Black (I, 54; II, 68, 229) W. voices his sentiments on the extension of governmental power. Owen's World's Convention, the Greeley-Raymond debate, and the Wisconsin Phalanx are mentioned severally in the *Eagle* for June 6, 1846, and for June 12 and Aug. 19, 1847. W. himself described Brisbane on

Broadway in an article for *Life Illustrated* reprinted in Holloway and Adimari, *op. cit.* (129), and Brisbane's wife, Redelia Brisbane, speaks of W.'s gift of *Passage to India* in her *Albert Brisbane: A Mental Biography* (Boston, 1893), 15. The discussions at O'Connor's are mentioned by Eldridge in Barrus, Clara, *op. cit.* (335). W.'s remarks on Owen and the communities are drawn from the *Eagle* for June 6 and 23, 1846, and June 11, 1847, and from *Uncollected* (I, 229). He confessed his inability to "study" in "Old Poets," *Good-Bye My Fancy* (*Prose*, 484-488). The Atlantic Docks strike is discussed pro and con in the *Eagle* for March 26, April 15, 18, 20, 22, 23, and 24, May 11, and July 15, 1846. The conversation with Morse is recorded in "My Summer with Walt Whitman, 1887" (*In Re*, 367-391). At the end of this section I have quoted from Traubel (I, 200, 215, 221; III, 422, 481). On American Fourierism see, among many sources, Brisbane, Albert, *The Social Destiny of Man* (Philadelphia, 1840) and Noyes, John Humphrey, *History of American Socialisms* (Philadelphia, 1870).

II. In discussing W.'s realism I have quoted from such poems as the "Song of Myself" (*Inclusive*, 42, 64), "Spontaneous Me," and "A Song of Joys." For his voluntarism and affirmativeness see *Democratic Vistas* (*Prose*, 213) and the poems, "Song of the Open Road," "To You," "Thou Orb Aloft Full-Dazzling," and "Ah, Poverties, Wincings, and Sulky Retreats." W.'s confession of a tendency toward morbidity may be found in "February Days," *Specimen Days* (*Prose*, 102).

III. To illustrate the essential nature of W.'s equalitarianism I have quoted Holloway, Emory, "Notes from a Whitman Student's Scrapbook" (*American Scholar*, May, 1933) and the poems, "To a Historian," "I Hear America Singing," "Starting from Paumanok," "Song of Myself" (*Inclusive*, 44), and "A Song for Occupations." For his sense of human limitations see *Democratic Vistas* (*Prose*, 211), "Old Poets," *Good-Bye My Fancy* (*Ibid.*, 484-488), and "Crossing Brooklyn Ferry." Other aspects of W.'s populism appear in *Democratic Vistas* (*Prose*, 209-210), Bucke, Richard Maurice, *Walt Whitman*

311

(Philadelphia, 1883), 51, Garland, Hamlin, *Roadside Meetings* (New York, 1930), 135-137, and Traubel (191). For his proletarianism see "A Backward Glance" (*Inclusive*, 533), Furness (95, 112), and Traubel (II, 35, 187; III, 418).

W.'s impatience with extreme individualism, hero-worship, etc., appears in Holloway and Schwarz (84) and Traubel (I, 230; II, 424; III, 122, 206-207). For his insistence on the antithetical forces, I have quoted *Democratic Vistas* (*Prose*, 213-214), Carpenter (58-59), Traubel (I, 230; III, 132), Furness (128), and the poems, "One's-Self I Sing" and "Song of Myself" (*Inclusive*, 57, 65). On "manly attachment" see the Preface to the 1876 edition of *L. of G.* (*Inclusive*, 516-518, Note), *Democratic Vistas* (*Prose*, 239; 240, Note), and the poems, "In Paths Untrodden," "For You O Democracy," "We Two Boys Together Clinging," "What Think You I Take My Pen in Hand?" and "Over the Carnage Rose Prophetic a Voice." Criticism of W.'s gospel of comradeship may be found in Bertz, Eduard, *"Walt Whitman, ein Charakterbild"* (*Jahrbuch für sexuelle Zwischenstufen*, 1905), Rivers, W. C., *Walt Whitman's Anomaly* (London, 1913), and Van Doren, Mark, "Walt Whitman, Stranger" (*American Mercury*, July, 1935).

The following poems and passages have been drawn upon in the discussion of W.'s internationalism: "Salut au Monde!" "Song of the Exposition," "Passage to India," "Thou Mother with Thy Equal Brood," "Years of the Modern"; the Preface to the 1876 edition of *L. of G.* (*Inclusive*, 517-518), *Democratic Vistas* (*Prose*, 203), "Two Letters," II, *Specimen Days* (*Ibid.*, 311-312), "Preface to the Reader in the British Islands," *November Boughs* (*Ibid.*, 432), Furness (112-113, 163-164), and Traubel (III, 360-361, 367).

INDEX

INDEX

315

317

INDEX

Miller, Joaquin, 5-6
Mitchell, O. M., 156-7
Montgomery, John B., 26
Morgan, Lewis Henry, 171
Morris, William, 248
Morse, Sidney, 99, 243-4, 247
Morton, Dr. W. T. G., 154

Napoleon, 196
National Labor Union, 138
"Nay, Tell Me Not To-day the Publish'd Shame," 77-8
Newcomb, Dr., 156
New Orleans *Daily Crescent*, 238
Newton, Sir Isaac, 218
New York *Courier and Enquirer*, 236
New York *Evening Post*, 10-11, 50, 114
New York *Herald*, 75
New York *Sun*, 98, 217
New York *Tribune* 26, 50-1, 186, 234, 236
Nietzsche, 207
North American Phalanx, 237
Norton, Andrews, 185
Norton, Caroline E. S., 113
Norton, Charles Eliot, 68
Noyes, John Humphrey, 240

O'Connor, William Douglas, 237
Olmstead, Denison, 158, 215
Oregon Question, 25
"Outlines for a Tomb," 91
Owen, Robert, 233, 236, 238
Owen, Robert Dale, 163

Paine, Thomas, 162-4, 166, 170, 172, 174, 197-8, 240, 265, 283
Parker, Theodore, 24, 29, 30, 41, 49, 88, 186-7, 216
Parsons, Albert, 101
"Passage to India," 225-6, 237, 286-7
Peabody, George, 91, 110, 150
Peirce, Benjamin, 160
Phillips, John, 102
Phillips, Wendell, 33, 39, 43
"Pictures," 37, 189
Pierce, Franklin, 47-8, 51, 54, 71
Pierson, Elias, 157
Plato, 275

318

Poe, Edgar Allan, 18, 31, 225, 279, 281
Polk, James K., 19, 22-6, 43-4, 82-3
Popular Science Monthly, 169
Powderly, Terence V., 101
Priestley, Joseph, 157-8, 181
Pushkin, 205

Quakers, 41, 145, 172-5

Raymond, Henry J., 236
Rhys, Ernest, 248
Ripley, George, 185, 192, 234-5, 240
Rivers, W. C., 273
"Roaming in Thought," 256
Rousseau, 177, 276-7
Ruskin, John, 113, 212
Rynders, Isaiah, 38

"Salut au Monde!" 32, 284
Sanborn, F. B., 30, 40-1
Sand, George, 113, 178-81, 184, 197
Santa Anna, 27
"Scented Herbage of My Breast," 278
Schelling, 182, 191-5, 206
Schiller, 113
Schlegel, Friedrich, 112, 177-8
Schoolcraft, Henry Rowe, 160
Schopenhauer, 227
Scott, Sir Walter, 177, 188
Scott, Winfield S., 24
Seward, William H., 59
Seymour, Charles C. B., 86, 111
Shakespeare, William, 222, 266, 278
Shaw, Francis George, 178
Shelley, Percy Bysshe, 4, 72, 162, 197, 260-1
Sherman, John, 134-5
Sherman, Stuart P., 4
Sherman, William Tecumseh, 134
"The Ship Starting," 256
Silliman, Benjamin, 154, 157, 171
Sloat, John D., 26
Smiles, Samuel, 86
Smith, Adam, 91
Smithsonian Institution, 154, 169
"The Sobbing of the Bells," 74
Social Reform Unity, 237
"Song for Certain Congressmen," 50
"Song of Myself," 27, 38, 116, 130-1, 157, 195, 223